THE
CAMPER VAN BIBLE

THE CAMPER VAN BIBLE

LIVE, EAT, SLEEP, (REPEAT)

SECOND
EDITION

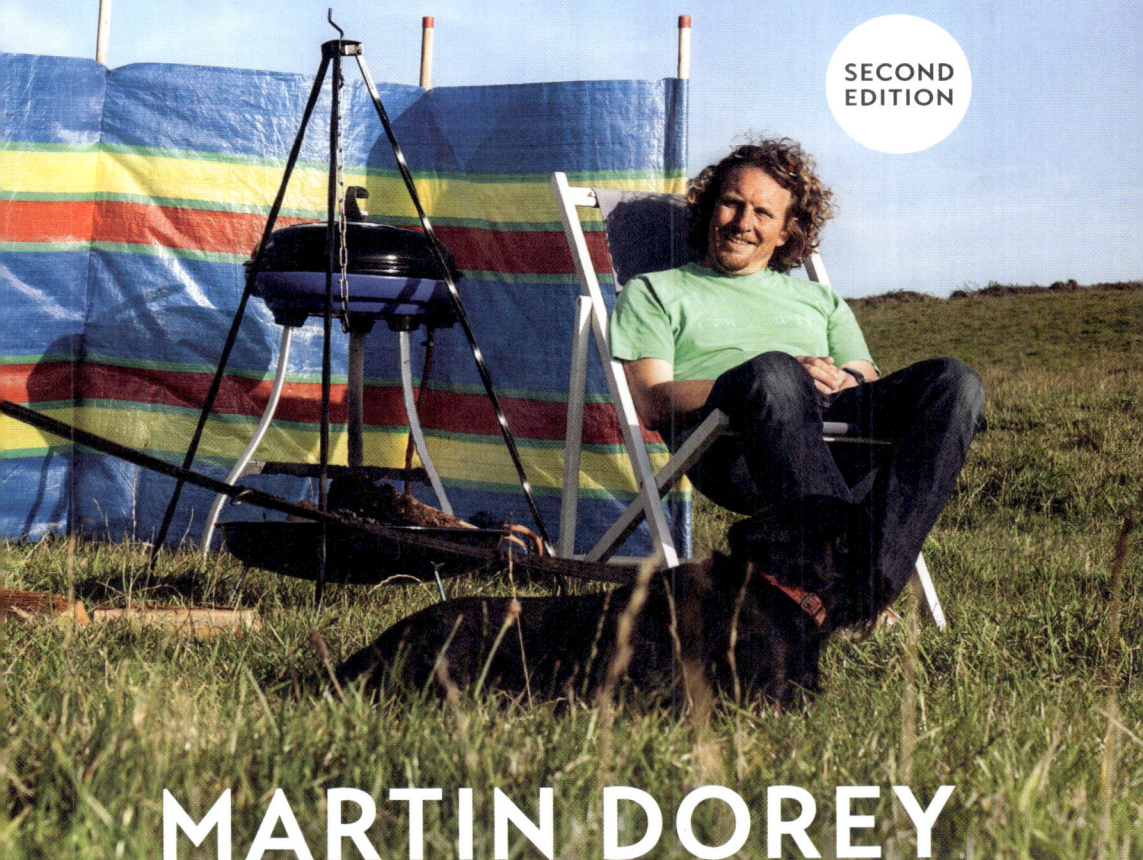

MARTIN DOREY

CONWAY

LONDON · OXFORD · NEW YORK · NEW DELHI · SYDNEY

CONWAY
Bloomsbury Publishing Plc
50 Bedford Square, London,
WC1B 3DP, UK
29 Earlsfort Terrace, Dublin 2, Ireland

BLOOMSBURY, CONWAY and the
Conway logo are trademarks of
Bloomsbury Publishing Plc

First published in Great Britain 2016
This edition published 2023

A catalogue record for this book is
available from the British Library

Library of Congress Cataloguing-in-
Publication data has been applied for

ISBN: PB: 978-1-8448-6600-7;
ePub: 978-1-8448-6598-7;
ePDF 978-1-8448-6597-0

10 9 8 7 6 5 4 3 2 1

Typeset in IBM Plex Serif
Designed by Austin Taylor
Printed and bound in India
by Replika Press Pvt. Ltd.

To find out more about our authors
and books visit www.bloomsbury.com
and sign up for our newsletters

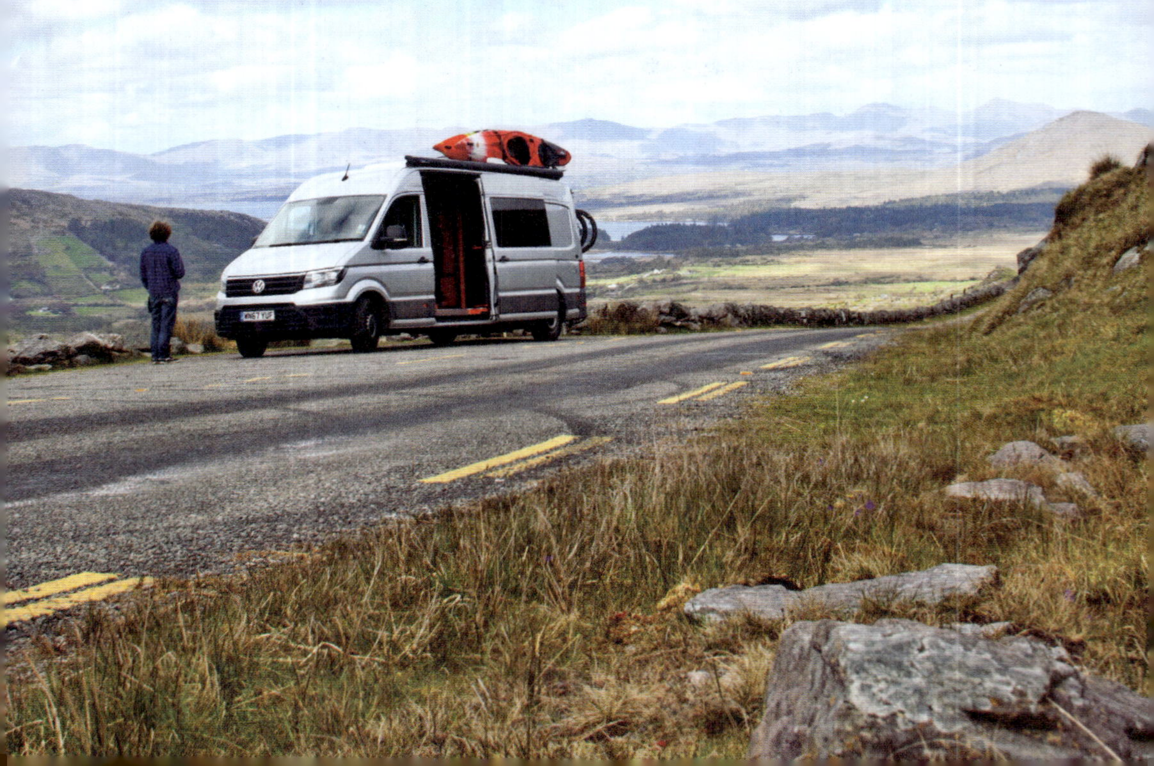

CONTENTS

LIVE 24

EAT 160

SLEEP 242

REPEAT 332

For the van dwellers and moho travellers
who love this lonely, liveable planet of ours, and
who are prepared to fight to keep it that way.

A NEW BEGINNING

Thanks for finding this book.

Since it was first published in 2016 there have been some interesting and significant changes to the way we view camper vans and motorhomes. During the Covid-19 pandemic they became the ultimate escape bubble, enabling us to holiday in perfect isolation. Unsurprisingly, sales went through the roof.

Some camper vans have also been given something of an eco-makeover in recent years, with the first electric versions of much-loved base vehicles trickling out, so making our favourite way of taking it easy potentially more planet-friendly than ever. If only we could afford them; we may be able to cook on induction hobs and install lithium-ion batteries to reduce our needs for propane gas or LPG, but we are still some way from being able to become fully electric at a price that's affordable. It's coming, but just not yet. In time, too, a network of charging points at campsites will emerge, ready for this new, all-electric wonderland. Let's hope we don't become too giddy too quickly, and remember to source 100 per cent of that power from renewables.

Until then, and afterwards, too, we need to remain mindful of the impact we make on this planet and reduce it drastically – at all costs. So this new edition contains tips on how to reduce your carbon footprint, ideas for more planet-friendly camping and ways of contributing to the places you go so they remain living, breathing and relevant after you leave. This is more important and more urgent than ever.

Technology moves fast, and I have tried to include as many of the innovations impacting campers and motorhomes as I can in this new edition. Since the last book, the rules on home conversions have changed, too, as have the rules for travelling to some cities, and so you'll find updates on both.

That said, as I also stated in the first edition of *The Camper Van Bible*, if you own a camper or motorhome, dream of owning a camper or motorhome, or are in the process of trying to own a camper or motorhome, then this book is for you. And if you love camping, waking up to lovely views, watching the stars at night and sharing good times with friends, then it's definitely for you, too. And even if you enjoy a little more than the basic luxuries on your travels, dare I say it, this book is even meant for you.

The motor caravan – and by that I mean motorhome (moho), A-Class or camper van – is more than just a bed on wheels. It's a universal symbol for the open road, free-spiritedness, love, peace and harmony. It is about getting out, off the couch and living life. It's about taking you to the places you love the most, the places you haven't seen before or the places you yearn to see one more time before work, life and the mortgage drag you back again.

In a post-Covid world, your motorhome is also an isolation pod – a self-contained, safe space that enables you to travel in times when travel has become ever more difficult and precarious.

Of course, your moho is also just a vehicle, with an engine and a steering wheel. But, if you already own one, I'll bet it's got a name. Am I right? And if I am, what does it tell you about the way you feel about it and what it does for you?

It's more than just a vehicle. I rest my case.

ENVIRONMENTALLY CONSCIOUS CAMPING

THE MESSAGE

If there is a message I'd like you to take away from reading this book, it is this: leave it nicer. What I mean by this is that we should leave anywhere we stay – a campsite, wild spot, the planet – nicer than it was when we arrived. You could also say that this is a metaphor for the way we live in general.

Given what we now know about the planet and the climate crisis, it has become ever more important and urgent to tread lightly and to clean up after ourselves. This can be as simple as picking up litter, right up to camping plastic-free or changing the way we tour and park up, or even changing the vehicles we drive or the fuel we use to cook.

Whatever it is we choose to do, it all counts. Everything you do towards a cleaner, more sustainable future has a positive effect, just as it has a very bad effect if you leave a pitch filthy or chuck litter out of the window.

ENJOYING THE NATURAL WORLD

One thing that sometimes gets forgotten – particularly for those who leave the remains of their picnics on beaches or who release their black waste into roadside gullies – is that the whole point of camping and motorhoming is to enjoy the natural world. So it makes sense to help preserve it, conserve it and even help to repair it so you may continue to enjoy it and others may too, after you have gone.

I find it very distressing when we forget that we are part of the environment and depend on it for everything. It isn't there to be exploited, overcome, dominated or used up. It's there to support us, as if it were our own fluttering, life-loving heart.

This section is about that. It's about trying to work out how to camp and live, in the way we love, without doing too much damage to the environment. And in some cases, helping to repair it.

THE GREENEST KIND OF HOLIDAY?

Motorhoming and caravanning and camping in general have long been recognised as greener ways to holiday. They might not be as green as cycling, walking or taking the train, but, when you compare a weekend on a local campsite with flying thousands of miles to lie in the sun, they look very good indeed, especially if you're in a vehicle with a modern engine, driving carefully and parked up on site.

However, driving is still driving and of course it has an impact. Especially when you consider the sheer numbers of us doing it. Whether it's CO_2 from using fossil fuels, our tyres leaving nano plastics on the road or fumes being released in towns and villages, driving has an impact and we shouldn't forget it.

So, if you, like me, are trying to reconcile driving hundreds of miles with the climate crisis, it might be time to take a few extra measures to reduce your impact.

Reducing your carbon footprint

Even though our vans and motorhomes, on the whole, are powered by fossil fuels, it is possible to reduce their impact, even when touring. This means using the van less and relying on your own steam to get you around. Instead of pitching up in a different campsite each night, try staying for a few days and exploring by bike or on foot. And when you do drive, and only if you have to, do it slowly and gently. You'll cut

Quick tips

- Consider exploring closer to home.
- Stay in the same place more than one night.
- Drive more efficiently.
- Cycle or walk to the shops or for days out.
- If you don't yet own a van, go by train and pick up a rental when you get there.

your fuel bills – and with fuel costs – and fossil fuel companies' profits soaring – that's more relevant than ever. Think about it like this: every time you drive carefully you are denying an oil executive another day at his villa in Barbados. Surely that's motivation enough?

Restoring nature and offsetting your trip

As a principle I don't agree with offsetting, especially if we believe it allows us to act with impunity. If you plant a tree, for example, it doesn't mean it's OK to drive an extra 100 miles, just because you planted a tree. The idea is that you reduce your carbon footprint (rather than just offset it), *as well as* compensating the planet for the harm you have done.

If you contribute to tree planting schemes, get involved in conservation or help with a litter pick, you are doing something really positive while you are away. You could count up your miles on each trip and use a calculator to work out how many trees to plant and then pay to plant double. It's not expensive, in the grand scheme of things, and will be a positive contribution.

Calculate your carbon footprint here: **www.carbonfootprint.com**
Contribute to the National Forest here: **www.nationalforest.org**
Help to support the Woodland Trust here: **www.woodlandtrust.org.uk**

Making the right decisions

There are tough decisions ahead for all of us and the sooner we realise it, the easier it'll be. For me, it'll be worth it because I want my kids to enjoy the same freedoms and beauty I enjoyed when I was their age. It's a simple as that.

Pitch up carefully

This is the key. And it applies to all kinds of pitches. Whether you're pitching up on a beach in the Outer Hebrides or settling down for a night on a campsite in the south of France, the choices you make can have a lasting effect on the environment.

STAY ON SITES WITH GREEN CREDENTIALS

If we are to take our leisure time seriously then we need to see it last. Supporting campsites that win awards, have incredible green policies, ban plastics or even use long drop or inventive toilet facilities is a must. When they are successful, others will follow. Don't make the bad guys rich.

The David Bellamy Conservation Award is a badge that is awarded to the best sites and touring parks for their outstanding work for the environment. To gain the accreditation, parks must manage their land as a haven for wildlife, reduce their use of energy, water and other resources, reduce, reuse and recycle the waste they produce, and support their local communities.

EDUCATE YOURSELF ABOUT THE PLACES YOU GO

I use parking up on a beach in the Outer Hebrides as an example of why it's important to understand a little about where you're going, because parking up on a beach in the Outer Hebrides is an idea that many aspire to. I've done it myself. And yet the Outer Hebrides is home to one of the rarest habitats in the world – the machair – which hosts insectivorous plants, rare orchids and all kinds of fabulous blooms.

And yet campers drive on it, eager to live the dream but oblivious to the fact that they're killing the dream at the same time. So, if you can, find out about where you are going. Be careful where you stray from the path and do it in such a way that you won't damage anything there.

ENCOURAGE OTHERS TO DO BETTER

If you stay on sites where bad practice is rife, talk to the owners about it. If they don't listen, don't go there again. You could even consider writing reviews asking them to make positive changes.

Support those with green credentials

Some organisations in our world are doing better than others. Some are making genuine efforts to change, act responsibly and help our planet recover. They include campsites, clubs, magazines, tourist attractions and the adventure sector, which includes outdoor clothing brands and activity providers. You can check out **www.ecoattractions .com** and **www.greentourismguide.co.uk** for great green days out.

Stop blaming everyone else

A lot of people argue that there are too many people in the world, or that developing countries are causing air pollution or are responsible for the plastic in the ocean. It may be true (to some extent,) but it's

important to remember that we in the West also pollute, have by far the biggest carbon footprints and still have a responsibility. It doesn't mean you can do nothing because China is building new power plants. If you do nothing, nothing happens. Everything we do matters, and the sooner we quit blaming everyone else for the mess and start dealing with our own, the quicker things will get done.

LEAVE IT BETTER: PICK UP LITTER

Picking up litter is an amazing thing; it can make you angry, sad and despairing but it can also make you feel very, very good. Picking up litter can be a catalyst for bigger changes and is a really good way of saying to those who might judge you that you care about the planet and are a responsible camper. Tidying somewhere up and seeing the result is instant and refreshing. I love it.

So, please, when you arrive and before you leave, do a sweep of your pitch (wherever it is) and tidy up. If you leave somewhere and there is a mess (even if it isn't yours) we will all get the blame for it. And the consequences of this are that there will be fewer and fewer places where we are welcome. Height barriers will go up, rocks will appear on lay-bys and the dreaded 'No Camper Vans' signs will breed like rabbits.

FORGET THE SINGLE-USE PLASTICS

Everything comes in plastic these days. Salad, bananas, cucumbers, water, hummus ... it's, frankly, ridiculous the amount of packaging our supermarkets and food stores force on us, even when we don't need it. It's almost as if bananas, cucumbers and apples didn't have a protective outer casing on them anyway!

So if you can, please forget the single-use plastics. They don't biodegrade, they turn toxic in water and they break down into microplastics that will, in time, hurt us all. When you think about it, it doesn't make any sense to use a piece of plastic to carry your food home only to then discard it. Unless, of course, you consider your personal convenience to be more important that the environment. I know that it's not easy being green sometimes, but there are choices we can make in the way we buy our food that can have a positive effect on the places we visit, so helping to make them better, too.

GO BPA-FREE

BPA is a chemical used in the manufacture of plastics. It has been linked with all kinds of medical issues because it leaches from plastic when used over time or when heated. Some of these issues include

TAKING YOUR FIRST PLASTIC-FREE STEPS

- Buy loose fruit and veg where possible. Go to the deli counter with used and washed takeaway containers to buy ham, meat and fish.
- Cook from scratch when you can (see pages 196–241 for lots of easy camping recipes).
- Take your own mug for takeaway coffees.
- Carry a water bottle and get a refill. Bottled water is 500 times more expensive and 92 per cent of it has traces of plastic in it. Plus, Europe's tap water is the best in the world (it's only marketing by bottled-water companies tells you it's not).
- Carry a reusable shopping bag whenever you visit a supermarket. Consider also using reusable vegetable bags for loose fruit and veg.
- Refuse plastic at takeaways and in restaurants (we're talking straws) and, if necessary, carry a spork or fork that you can wash and reuse.
- Try out a waste-free shop for your staples like flour, pasta, rice, cornflakes, nuts and herbs.

increasing the risk of certain cancers, reduced fertility, diabetes and birth defects. Lots of manufacturers produce products that are BPA-free, making it easier than ever to do better.

BUY LOCAL WHEN YOU CAN

Buying local food, from local producers, markets and shops makes so much sense. If it's been grown locally by local producers it's putting money straight into the local economy. You'll also get super fresh produce that hasn't been flown halfway around the world or grown in countries where food and labour standards might be lower than ours. You might discover something unusual or very special when you buy local. Plus, you might meet some nice people, too. And it's a darn sight better than a soulless supermarket experience.

LESS WASTE: MORE RECYCLING

Recycling isn't the answer to our packaging problems, but it's a start. So it's important to do it. If only to show others how it's done. Any campsite worth staying at will have recycling facilities. Please use them and get into the habit of separating your waste. Of course, it isn't always easy, as recycling varies from one county and country to another, but a little research helps.

Recycle as much as you can and if it can't be recycled, do without it.

YOUR GREEN CAMPING KIT LIST

- Refillable water bottle for days out, hikes and while driving – water is free and better for you than pop. Plus, 92 per cent of bottled water has plastic in it.
- Reusable coffee cup – no need for takeaway cups.
- Beeswax wraps for food storage – these can be reused time and time again.
- Folding litter picker for the cab of the van – tidy up that pitch!
- Washable cotton bags-for-life – several for shopping, one for litter picking.
- Coconut husk scourers (can be composted) – traditional scourers and sponges contain plastic that goes straight down the sink.
- Wooden scrubbers and nail brushes – no plastic!
- Bamboo toothbrushes – just put them in the compost when they are dead!
- Plastic-free loo paper – no plastic wrapping!
- Reusable vegetable bags – great for weighing and transporting veg.
- Lightweight titanium (or bamboo) knives, forks, spoons and straws.
- Toothpaste powder or tablets – saves waste.
- Solid shampoo and conditioner bars – saves waste and easier to deal with on sites.
- Safety razors and solid shaving soap.

THE TETRA PAK PROBLEM

Tetra Paks provide us with a conundrum. While they are recyclable and can save space in the fridge (because they are square and fit neatly together or on their side), only about 11 per cent of the material used in their construction is recoverable. This is because they're a composite of tin foil, plastic and paper, which cannot be easily separated. Also, few local authorities in the UK will accept them for recycling. Best avoided.

HELP YOUR SITE — CREATE LESS WASTE

Campsites have to pay for the waste they (you) produce because they have to pay business rates. So the less waste you produce, the less they pay, and the less there is to be collected and taken away. It's very simple!

COOK WITH REUSABLES

If you cook on gas, try to choose cookers with gas cylinders that can be refilled. It's a simple thing but can save a lot of unnecessary waste. Portable gas cookers might seem like a good idea (and they cook nicely, with a good flame), but they're very wasteful and expensive.

Help regenerate

Once we've cleared up the mess we've made, the next thing to do is to start regenerating what we've lost. When I travel in my van, I 'offset' my travels by contributing to planting trees. I've done this for the last two books I have written and will do it for this book, too. It doesn't cost a huge amount (about £50 to plant trees to offset 10,000 miles of driving), but it helps to compensate the planet for the loss I cause.

While offsetting helps to negate the impact of your travels, you might want to actually get your hands dirty and get involved with conservation by volunteering some elbow grease and time.

- The Conservation Volunteers is a charity devoted to exactly that. They can help you to find volunteer work near you, or near somewhere you are going on a trip. See **www.tcv.org.uk/getinvolved**.
- The National Trust is Europe's biggest conservation charity. Volunteer with them by logging on to **www.nationaltrust.org.uk/volunteer**.

Thanks for listening.

WHAT TO EXPECT FROM THIS BOOK

For once it's OK to judge the book by its cover. *The Camper Van Bible* is, as the title would suggest, a book all about camper vans. It's also a book about all camper vans. And motorhomes, too. That means it includes information about A-Class motorhomes, coachbuilt motorhomes, self-build camper vans, converted larger vans and everything in between.

While many might think of a camper van as a classic VW Split-Screen, other makes are most definitely available and there is no wrong answer to the question of 'what makes a camper van', unless you are the UK Driver and Vehicle Licensing Agency (DVLA). Take a look at the next page for a definition of what makes a camper van or 'motor caravan'.

Owning a classic camper van might be a dream for many but it isn't the be-all and end-all. In my camper van-owning career I have owned a classic, three not-so-classic classics (that have since become classics), a VW California and a VW Crafter. I recently spent time pondering how

to convert a 1976 Citroen 2CV AK 400 into a passable camper. It didn't work. My current camper is a Fiat Ducato – the base vehicle for the majority of motorhomes in Europe – and it will be my last diesel vehicle. The next one I own will be electric.

So please don't think this book is just for people who like classic VWs. Far from it. If you can live, eat and sleep in it then it's for you. Inside, you'll find lots of useful and practical information and advice about all kinds of camper vans. We'll talk about buying a camper, choosing layouts, types of facilities you will encounter and what to expect from them, as well as some of the tricks of the trade and rules of the road.

This book isn't about how to convert a base vehicle to a camper van – there are plenty of brilliant books to help you do that already. However, if you are planning a conversion there may be information in here that will help. Take a look, in particular, at the pages on payloads and the DVLA. While putting butler's sinks and real wood worktops in a van might be cute and cool, they add to the weight of the vehicle, potentially making it dangerously and illegally overweight when you drive it away. The information on speed limits on pages 376–378 may also help you to stay legal while driving on dual carriageways at speed. I have also put together a glossary of terms you might come across while camping or reading this book, so, if you feel the need, you can talk camper van around the campfire to your heart's content.

I'd like to think that some of the pictures you'll find between the covers will make you reach for the phone or your tablet, or even to the person sitting next to you, to start making arrangements for your next (or first) camping trip to somewhere absolutely amazing.

If you do feel inspired to hit the road then don't forget to take this book with you. You might need it along the way. It might well save your life, your marriage, a little bit of face or time, or possibly even a small fortune. At the very least I promise it'll get you out of a foodie fix if you run out of ideas, with a bunch of no-nonsense, back-to-basics, (mostly) vegetarian recipes that anyone could make and enjoy.

Ready? Let's do it.

LIVE

LIVING THE DREAM

I've heard this phrase used a lot. Sometimes it sounds trite, like a soundbite or throwaway that's lost its meaning through overuse. Sometimes it's used sarcastically when things go wrong or for little, insignificant wins. At other times, when said with sincerity, I think I understand what it is supposed to express. We use it to describe our perfect, best-case, once-imagined scenario. It becomes totemic for the thing we most desire out of life. Living the dream is having the thing you have most longed for or had hoped would happen. I can't speak for everyone but I have a pretty good idea what those things might be. My idea of living the dream is living without responsibility, in comfort

and safety with those I love, doing the things that move me the most. At times, your van will deliver that to your door.

I am the first to admit that life on four wheels isn't always a breeze. You still need to find somewhere to stay, something to eat and, if you like company, someone to share it with. Those things don't always come easily and without cost, especially if you set your sights impossibly high.

Sometimes you have to manage your own expectations, be pragmatic and take it on the chin if it doesn't work out. Life isn't perfect and neither is travelling in a van or motorhome. Things can and will go wrong (although I hope this book will help when they do).

But – and it's a big, fat, juicy but – spending time in a van strips life down to its most basic elements, which means you have less to worry about (hopefully), less to deal with and less to get stressed over, even if it's just for the weekend. And that's what makes you feel free. Your van also gives you the gift of transience so you can move on if things don't work out. It is a powerful mix.

You might not be able to go exactly where you'd like – the law prevents us – but you can move on if you feel the need to get away from inclement weather, noisy neighbours, people, civilisation or places that remind you of hard times. You can put the van in gear and drive. For the time you are away all you need is food, water and fuel, and the physical and mental ability to do what you want – and enjoy it.

A lot of people I have met over the years consider their van or motorhome to be their safe space. For them it is a retreat and sanctuary. It is the first place they think of when things get tough in the real world and they need comfort. I understand this completely. Running away from it all might not actively solve problems back in the grown-up world of mortgages, rent, heating bills and council tax, but it can help to clear your head for a bit.

For others, being able to travel in a camper van or motorhome makes travel possible in the first place. Having anxiety or complex physical needs can make conventional travel very difficult – and sometimes impossible. But having everything on hand in an escape pod on wheels, even down to medical devices hoists and medicines, means these people can experience things that they might not be able to otherwise. That's true freedom, even if it's just a few nights away on a local campsite.

Travelling by camper van can give people who are on their own the confidence to travel, too. That safe space becomes all the more so when you feel vulnerable. It enables you to be brave and to face the world, knowing that you can retreat if you need to. You can be alone, if that's what you want, and can do things on your own terms. Being sociable – chatting to other people on a campsite, eating in a restaurant or going to a bar – then becomes your choice. That's powerful stuff for those who find themselves in difficult personal circumstances.

In recent years, camper vans and motorhomes have also enabled people to live more simply, with fewer overheads and pressures, either because they want to or because they have no choice. Some people have taken to living an itinerant existence because they cannot afford to live in any other way or because they have a job that allows them to work from anywhere. I know of those who lived in a van because they couldn't afford to rent a house in their home town. Others have become 'digital nomads', freed from conventional living by onboard internet and the work-from-home culture. That's a dynamic shift, and the nomad lifestyle is becoming more and more possible for more and more people.

Others have taken to the highways to become influencers and online celebrities. Whatever you think of them, you have to admire the kind of chutzpah it takes to go for it. That's living the dream, as long as it isn't hurting anyone or selling your soul. There's a fine line sometimes.

And that, for me is the crux of it. As long as you tread lightly and are being true to yourself, living the dream can be anything you want it to be. It doesn't have to be some kind of far-off aspiration or cosplay for the camera. It can be as simple as freeing yourself from the sofa, meeting up with old friends, riding your bike, taking a few days off to explore a river by stand-up paddleboard (SUP), or it can be as seismic as packing up and leaving an unhappy place or seeing the outside world when you have been trapped by your circumstances.

When it comes down to it, living the dream is really just living.

And if it involves living simply, parking somewhere fantastic without damaging the environment, eating good food, feeling the wind in your hair or the sand between your toes, being in company you love or being on your own, getting away from the grit and grind of everyday life or just having a day or two to hare down a hill on your bike, so be it.

Small things bring great happiness.

Live a little, and with love.

WHAT IS A CAMPER VAN?

The camper van is many things. It's a place to eat, sleep and live as much as it is a vehicle to take you places. It could be a daily driver or a once-a-year escape vehicle. If you run the marketing department of a vaguely surfy clothing brand it will provide you with an easy metaphor for freedom and good times. If you own one it will be a part of the family, no doubt, and we'll find out all about that later.

But let's define what it is, according to 'official sources' and UK law.

A **camper van** (or campervan) 'is a van equipped with beds and

cooking equipment so that you can live, cook and sleep in it'. It is also defined as a 'self-propelled vehicle that provides both transport and sleeping accommodation'.

A **motor caravan** (which encompasses both motorhomes and camper vans), according to the UK Driver and Vehicle Licensing Agency (DVLA), is a very specific type of vehicle. For a camper van to be registered as a motor caravan on its V5 log book, it must meet the following criteria:

- It must have a door that provides access to the living accommodation.
- It must have a bed with a minimum length of 1,800mm or 6ft. It can be converted from seats but must be permanently fixed within the body of the vehicle.
- It must have a seating and dining area permanently attached to the vehicle. The table may be detachable but must have some permanent means of attachment to the vehicle.
- It must have a permanently fixed means of storage.
- It must have a permanently fixed cooking facility.
- It must have at least two windows on the side of the accommodation and be identifiable to other road users as a camper van or motorhome.

That settles it then. Well, not really. I know many camper vans that would meet few of the above criteria. Their owners still classify them as camper vans, but UK law does not.

A potted history of the camper van

There has been much written about the history of the camper van. It often begins with Hitler's 'people's car' and ends in 2014, with the final Type 2 VW transporters rolling off the production line in Brazil. But there is more to it than that.

The Volkswagen (VW) has become so ubiquitous that it's almost completely eclipsed the memory of those other campers that went before it or that have driven beside it (and continue to do so). Yet there were, and still are, other makes available. The reason the VW has endured is due to its amazing popularity, which is down, in part, to VW's strategy to create a global network of dealerships. This has made parts available all over the world since the 1960s and is a major advantage over other 'domestic' vehicles when it comes to overlanding. The support has always been there.

Of course, the VWs were always simply made, well-built and easy to work on, and this has contributed to their success, there is no doubt. After all, how many other makes of vintage camper van did you see rolling by the last time you took to the highway last bank holiday? Not many, I'll wager.

These days, though, things are different. While VW continues to dominate the market for smaller van conversions, converters are now turning to other vehicles because of VW's cost and

reputation. Lots of manufacturers are now building good vans, while Nissan has produced the e-NV200, which has been converted successfully into a micro camper. Other electric versions will follow. The rise of the Ducato (Relay or Boxer) cannot be ignored either. And there's more about that in a bit. Meanwhile...

BACK TO THE BEGINNING

And it starts, as with everything, with a basic need for people to sleep and live on the move. Whole mythologies have been built upon it. Indeed, nations have been built on the notion of a generation hitching up their wagons and taking to the land on a great lifetime's adventure. Think of gypsy caravans, showmen's wagons and shepherd's huts. Think of the prairies, too, with all the hope and optimism of setting off in a covered wagon to look for the Promised Land. Sound familiar?

However, for our intents and purposes we're going to side-step the horse-drawn caravan or wagon (because that's another book entirely) and concentrate on the self-powered home on wheels. How did it happen?

Phillip Aldridge

'She isn't just our van, she's part of the family!'

Our camper van is a 1979 Devon Moonraker called Bluebell. We refer to her as our first house! We purchased her with what was our first house deposit and have never looked back, carrying out a full restoration since we took her home in 2013. Owning her has meant that we have learnt so much about camper vans and camper van travel. It has also opened doors for us to new social circles, friends, involvement with clubs and, most importantly, given us the opportunity to spend even more quality time with our families! Owning Bluebell has meant that we can get away from our stressful everyday working lives to a place we call home. But at the same time, she has enabled us to travel all over the UK and beyond, to places we would never have normally visited but now could not imagine never visiting. We have spent single-night trips, weekends, weeks and longer away in our camper van. She isn't just our van, she's part of the family!

In the early part of the 20th century, camping and touring by car became popular in the USA and the UK, with 'motorised vagabonds' taking to the road in large numbers. So really, it was inevitable that someone would forget their tent and kip in the car at some point. We've all done it. Thereafter it's only a little leap to making it more comfortable, perhaps with a few modifications, a cooker and a washbasin. Or maybe an old shed, plonked directly on the chassis.

THE EARLIEST RV?

Big companies weren't slow to cash in on this new movement of people seeking solace in green spaces. One of the very earliest 'production' self-powered camper vans, which earned its place in the camper van hall of fame as 'the earliest RV', was the Pierce-Arrow Touring Landau. It was a luxury camper with all mod cons, including a rear seat that folded into a bed, a sink 'behind the chauffeur' and a chamber pot. It also had a telephone connection between the passengers and chauffeur so, as you can imagine, wasn't massively democratic or cheap. The Landau was unveiled by Pierce-Arrow in 1910 at Madison Square Gardens in New York City. Production continued until 1913.

ON THE ROAD DOWN UNDER

Meanwhile, in Australia, what is accepted as the country's first motorhome was built by GC 'Pop' Kaesler, an engineer from Nuriootpa. He decided he wanted to go walkabout, so in 1929 he built his 'Home

The Kaesler

from Home' on the chassis of a 1924 Dodge Four motor truck. In the following years, his family enjoyed the comfort of a 12 x 6ft interior with wireless, stove, beds, tables and wardrobes on trips across South Australia, Queensland, New South Wales and Victoria. It was bought by the mayor of Goolwa later in 1929 and languished there until it was restored in 2000. It now resides at the National Trust's Goolwa Museum, having enjoyed a further restoration in 2008.

THE TILLY — THE FIRST KOMBIS

In the UK, it began in much the same way as it had in the USA, with a company called Martin-Walter, coachbuilders that were based in Folkestone, Kent. The company's first forays into converting vehicles brought the 'Utilicon', an all-purpose vehicle made in 1935. The Utilicon could be used as a working van during the week and then a family seven-seater at the weekend. Is the story beginning to sound familiar now? The Utilicon was used extensively in the Second World War by all government departments in the UK, and many thousands were made.

After the war, Martin-Walter turned its attention to creating a 'bedroom on wheels' with a prototype Dormobile that was exhibited at the Commercial Motor Show in 1952. This was after seeing traders throwing cushions in their daily work vans to take the family away for

The Plattenwagen

the weekend. The Dormobile was an immediate success. It seated seven for driving and converted to twin beds at night. The Dormobile caravan, with elevating fibreglass roof, was introduced in 1957. The first Dormobiles were based on the Bedford CA van, with other conversions following on behind, including our beloved VW Type 2. For a while there in the 1960s, Dormobile was the generic term for a 'camper van' (although don't let the Dormobile Owners Club hear you call it such). The Bedford CA, which is rare these days, was Vauxhall's response to the need for a small and agile delivery van that VW had tackled so well with the Type 2 Transporter.

THE VW STORY

And I think that brings us neatly to the story of the Volkswagen, which begins a little earlier than 1952, with a man called Adolf Hitler and a 'people's car', the much-loved and lovable Beetle. While production of the Type 1 Volkswagen never really happened under Hitler, it was resurrected by a legend in the VW world: a Major Ivan Hirst, a British Army officer who was tasked with the job of overseeing the original factory in Wolfsburg, Germany after the war. He is the man responsible for resurrecting the Type 1 and bringing the factory back into working order (and in doing so, perhaps playing a major part in Germany's post-war economic miracle).

The next stage comes with the 'Plattenwagen', a vehicle Hirst designed to carry heavy parts around the factory. It was based on the Kubelwagen, a vehicle produced in the factory during the war. Enter Ben Pon, another VW legend, a car dealer from the Netherlands who was looking to import the Beetle for sale in his showrooms. Having seen the Plattenwagen – and understanding the need for a light, load-carrying vehicle – Ben Pon was inspired to draw the now famous sketch of the Type 2. Long story short, VW took on the idea and launched it at the Geneva International Motor Show in November 1949, with the first Transporter panel vans rolling off the production line in March 1950.

There is a lot more to it than that but that's the crux of the story. However, we have yet to convert our T2 into a van that we can live in. That would have to wait until 1951, when, so the story goes, a British officer took his new VW to a coachbuilding company called Westfalia. He asked them to make him a camping interior, which could be easily removed and wouldn't look out of place in his house. The result was the Camping Box, Westfalia's first VW conversion. The company saw the potential and went into production with it almost immediately. In 1958, the company was recognised by VW as the makers of the VW Westfalia Camper Van. It was the first to have official VW approval. In time, Westfalia offered all kinds of conversions with awnings and accessories.

The first Type 2s are generally known as 'Splittys' because of their split windscreen. They were superseded in 1968 by the Type 2 'Bay Window' camper. This was refined until 1979, when it was replaced by the air-cooled Type 3 (Type 25). This became water-cooled in 1981, with the last air-cooled VW being produced in Germany in 1982. A 4 x 4 version, the Syncro, was introduced in 1985. The T25 was replaced by the T4, a front engine version in 1990. In 2003 this was replaced by the T5, which was replaced by the T6 in late 2015.*

---

*If you want to know more about the history of VW then seek out the books of Dave Eccles. His knowledge is encyclopaedic. Mike Harding's *The VW Camper Van: A Biography* is also well worth a read for the way he has placed the VW in a social and historical context.

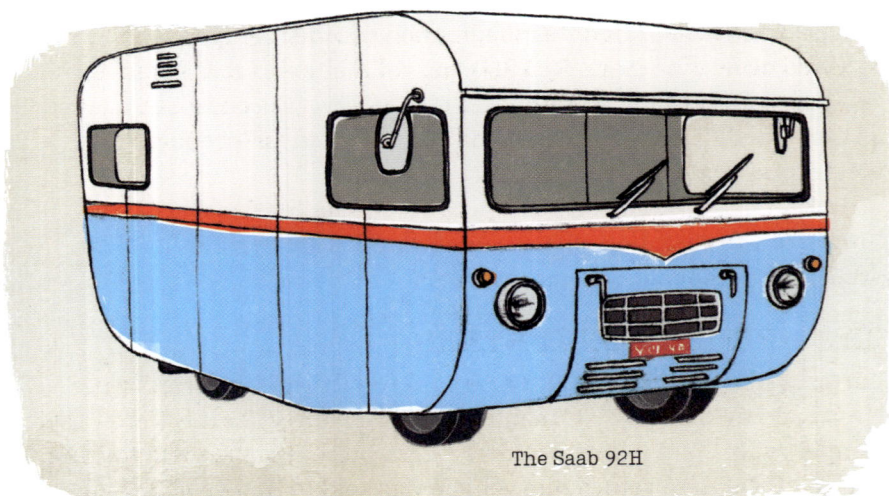

The Saab 92H

Westfalia conversions are the most sought-after of all the conversions available on the market and continued to be produced until 2004, when the company was taken over by Mercedes-Benz. After that, VW decided to produce its own coachbuilt camper van for the very first time, based on the T5 Transporter. This was the California. Of all the campers on the market, it is one of the best designed and best built.

THE SWEDISH CONNECTION

We take a little aside now to look at an intriguing vehicle, the Saab 92H, one of the world's first A-Class motorhomes. It was created in Sweden by Torsten Johannesson, a man who figured you could marry a car and a caravan and make something that you could drive and camp in. Basically, it's a caravan that drives itself! Unfortunately, the vehicle failed its inspection and was abandoned, and then consigned to a slow death rotting away in a forest.

Torsten then began work on the second generation, which was based on a Saab 95. Saab refused to recognise the project and it came to a halt. Several decades later, the 95 was found in a forest clearing, after which it was discovered there were two of these vehicles. They were both fully restored. They are truly remarkable vehicles and worth a google.

THE FATHER OF MODERN MOTORHOMING

Now, let's go back to the US of A, where we pick up with a gentleman by the name of Raymond Frank, the man who is credited with giving the 'motorhome' its moniker. In 1958, Frank built his first motorhome on a Dodge chassis, so that he could see a bit of the States. As with all good

things, the idea captured the imagination of other campers and Frank received orders for more. By 1960, he had made and sold seven, so he decided to start Frank Motorhomes Inc. In 1961, the company changed its name to Dodge Motorhomes and so the first mass-produced motorhomes were launched.

In keeping with the trend for producing smaller, van-based conversions, Frank turned its attention to smaller vehicles in 1968, producing campers in smaller vehicles.

THE BRITISH CONVERTERS

But of course, on this side of the pond, a number of converters were already doing that. In 1959, a chap called Calverley Trevelyan built a camper for his family from a Morris J2, so he could take them touring in France. On their return, the vehicle was sold to Henlys of Bristol, who almost immediately ordered five more, and then another 12. Soon after, the company Auto-Sleepers was created. It has survived crashes and fires and now makes some of the best – if the not the best – motorhomes and camper conversions in the UK market. It was also the first company to be given official approval as converters of the Volkswagen T4.

Meanwhile, other companies were also getting in on the act. The other big names in the VW conversion racket in the UK are Devon and Danbury. Devon Conversions is 'probably' the oldest converter in the UK. Its founder, Jack White, like many converters, started out converting a Type 2 Transporter for his own use and then found there was demand for more. The company was formed in 1956 in Sidmouth and soon became one of VW's small number of approved converters. Its Moonraker model is one of the most sought-after VW conversions in the UK, with a full-length side elevating roof that offers a huge amount of double bed space 'upstairs'.

Brazilian Type 2 import

1970S GROOVE, MODERN WHEELS

Danbury Motorcaravans was formed by Joy and George Dawson in 1967, also converting the VW Type 2 Transporter. It was an official VW converter, but lost the status in 1971, only to regain it in 1978. The company went out of business in the 1980s but the name was resurrected by Jason Jones and his brothers, who began importing VW Beetles from Brazil in 1997 and then Type 2 vans in 1998. They re-registered the name Danbury Motorcaravans in 2002. Danbury was the sole importer of Brazilian Type 2 VW campers until production ceased in 2014, after which it imported used vans. The company also invented the innovative and space-gaining T5 Doubleback, a strange hybrid camper with a pull-out rear section. For a while, Danbury were instrumental in bringing the 1970s groove back to campervanning – but without the hassle of actually having to drive a Type 2 from the 1970s.

Danbury was sold to Pilote in 2017 and since then the focus has been on converting moderns vans, including Fiat Ducatos.

THE RISE OF THE DUCATO

In 1981, Fiat launched the Ducato chassis as part of a joint venture between the company, Citroën and Peugeot, and US-based manufacturer RAM. While intended for the light van market, it was also destined for the camper van and motorhome market. The third generation Ducato was introduced in 2006. Since its launch it has

been a huge hit with camper van converters because of its versatility. Today, around two-thirds of all motorhomes and camper vans in Europe are based on a Ducato chassis, either as a converted van or from a cutaway cab that is used for A-Class or coachbuilt motorhomes. In 2019, the Ducato won the 'best motorhome Base of the Year' for the 12th time in a row.

Why are they so popular for converters? One major advantage of the Ducato over other vans is that they are 1,870mm wide (a little over 6ft), which means that they can take a transverse (sideways) bed. Similar vans, like the Mercedes Sprinter or Volkswagen Crafter, are a few inches narrower. Also, the Ducato van is a box shape and doesn't get narrower towards the roof, unlike the Crafter or Sprinter, which means bunks are feasible and cabinets demand less shaping.

The transverse bed is important as it saves up to 610mm (2ft) or more and allows converters to fit more into a shorter van, enabling the possibility of creating a camper van with motorhome facilities out of a medium wheelbase van.

TODAY'S CAMPERS AND MOTORHOMES

These days, anything goes when it comes to the motorhome and camper van market, with everything available from a huge number of big European manufacturers and plenty of independent converters doing their own thing and trying to offer something different in terms of layout and facilities. That said, the big van and coachbuilt market is dominated by the Ducato, with the Sprinter and the Crafter coming in joint second. After that ... well, there aren't that many more big base vehicles available.

When it comes to smaller campers, the VW is still king with its T6, although lots of converters are offering different base vehicles all the time to counter the fact that VW are usually more costly than anything else available on the market. VW's reputation hasn't always fared well, either. Ford is now offering a funkier transit, while Renault and Vauxhall are offering plausible base vehicles. The Vauxhall Vivaro has recently been converted into an e-Camper by Wellhouse Leisure.

Micro campers are popular, too. Advantages include that they drive and park like cars. But the drawback is obvious: space is limited. The smaller the conversion, the more space-saving cleverness gets in the way of simplicity.

The Volkswagen (at the time of writing, we're on the T6) is, of course, a very popular choice for converting to a smaller camper van, while its new-shape Crafter, which came out in 2017, is gaining in popularity, like the new Mercedes Sprinter.

As a nod to the motorhome market, Volkswagen brought out its big van version of the massively popular California in 2018, the Grand California, which is based on the new Crafter, with the Grand California XXL following in 2019. In 2020 and 2021, the order books for the grand California were brimming over, partly due to the pandemic and partly to the popularity of the camper van as a mode of safe holidaying.

INTO THE FUTURE

We're going electric, whether we like it or not. Either that or we're back in tents.

The only trouble is that the electric van market is way behind the electric car market. UK converter Hillside Leisure released the first electric camper van in 2014. It was based on a small electric vehicle, the Nissan e-NV200. It's neat and tidy, but definitely in the 'micro' category due to its size. It has a range of 147 miles on one charge and can get 80 per cent charge in just 45 minutes.

Recently, Nissan has developed the Volita, a high-topped version of the e-NV200, which increases load area by about 90 per cent and will surely lead to a camper van at some point...

ElektroFahrzeuge Stuttgart in Germany produced the world's first electric motorhome, the Iridium, in 2019, but it was withdrawn due to a lack of interest (the manufacturers told me), which is disappointing. Its range was 249 miles (astounding) but its price tag was £175,000 (doubly astounding).

At the time of writing, all major manufacturers are on the verge of launching electric versions of their vans. However, at an eyewatering cost (the Renault Trafic is £57,000), it doesn't seem terribly democratic for the general camper van market. Costs will have to come down, charging will have to be faster and more accessible (the Caravan and Motorhome Club are looking at this in detail in their future plans), and the range better before people fully adopt the technology.

The electric Ducato is in production, but boasts a range of just 150 miles on a single charge, which is one of the issues with e-vehicles, particularly when it comes to touring. Currently, this vehicle (like many other equivalent electric vans) is much better suited to city-based delivery vehicles that will avoid higher emissions charges and road taxes by being electric.

VW is busy hyping the ID. Buzz, an electric concept vehicle that looks like a Split-Screen van from yesteryear and was launched at the end of 2022. A camper version will be available at some point.

The VW Type 6.1 ABT e-Transporter is new on the market, although there are no plans for a California version of it.

VW partners have developed an updated Split-Screen in an electric version. It looks awesome but costs the earth. Time will tell, but the

barriers to be overcome at the moment are cost and range. Until one comes down and the other goes up, it's going to be a difficult sell.

Personally, I hope that manufacturers, and/or governments, bring down the costs related to running electric vehicles, making electric campers a reality. I don't want to stop motorhoming in the future but, as the climate emergency deepens, it seems we will need to make greater changes than ever to save our dying planet.

THE ELEPHANT ON ELECTRIC AVENUE

One thing that we all seem to be able to gloss over when it comes to electric vehicles is where the power comes from. By this I mean how the power is generated. Driving an electric car might be good for reducing taxes and zero emissions, but it means nothing climate-wise unless the electricity you use to charge it comes from renewables. For us, that means choosing utilities companies that are green for home charging, or installing solar panels on our roofs, while on-the-road charging will require more planning and research.

So, while driving an electric camper might feel like it's saving the planet, you may still have to charge on the forecourt of a fossil fuel company, will still leave microplastics from your tyres on the road and in the culverts at the side of it after rain, and will still be a 3-tonne weapon driving in our cities.

The solution? Drive less and shorter distances. Appreciate your own country more. Stay on sites for longer. Use your feet, a bike or public transport to go on day trips (and get fitter). Be more considerate. Avoid cities. These are just some things to ponder as we hurtle towards climate disaster...

WHY A CAMPER VAN?

This is a good question to kick off with. No doubt you've already arrived at this decision. But let's look a little closer.

On one level, it's a relatively simple question to answer. I think. It's because a camper van makes getting out into the world more convenient. But there is, of course, more to it than simple convenience.

What is it that brings us back, time and time again, to a little tin (or extruded plastic) box on wheels? Are we caught up in the whirlwind of hype? Have we been seduced by a promise of freedom? Have we fallen at the altar of iconoclasm? Are we misty eyed at romantic thoughts of living a simpler, more fulfilling life?

For me, owning a van means getting outside and being able to take my life with me. Well, the parts of my life I need with me. I like to be able to take the kitchen, diner, lounge and bedroom with me. The camper van is castle and keep, a home from home, a shelter and a sanctuary. A place to call your own.

When I started sleeping in camper vans it was because I wanted to wake up next to the surf. This was in North Wales, and the place my friends and I camped was a site overlooking a beautiful

reef where, under the right conditions, clean and crisp waves would thunder in towards the shore. The waves were always better around two hours after the tide, so we wanted to be there when the moment came, no matter what time of the day it was. We wanted to turn out of bed into our wetsuits and then, at the end of the day, we wanted to put out the driftwood fire and turn in again. And we wanted to do this all year round, come rain or shine. The camper van made it all possible.

We tried tents and cars and sleeping under the stars but it just never quite cut it. Tents can't be moved that quickly, can't be pitched anywhere and are often cramped, cold and leaky. Caravans are similar in that they have to be placed on caravan sites, rather than the place you really want to be.

On some days, the surf wouldn't show. That meant we had to drive somewhere else to find our slice of golden sunset and cerulean. Once there, we were home again, cocooned in warmth and comfort, no matter how far from our real home.

Camping, then as now, is one of the cheapest ways to holiday. And if you can camp wild, it's free. So, the camper van offers a cheaper alternative to conventional holidays.

What about the freedom? Is that just a myth?

The camper van's long association with counterculture means that it has become a symbol of freedom, the open road, free choice and a life without barriers. So, whether you like it or not, you take that baggage with you every time you step into one. It's not a bad bag to carry. Even if you don't have the freedom to go wherever you want or do whatever you want to do, you can still enjoy the association that it brings. Even if it isn't real freedom, it certainly feels like it.

The potential is always there… If only you didn't have to [insert what holds you back here], you could jam it into first gear, set a course for the location of your dreams and drive off into the sunset.

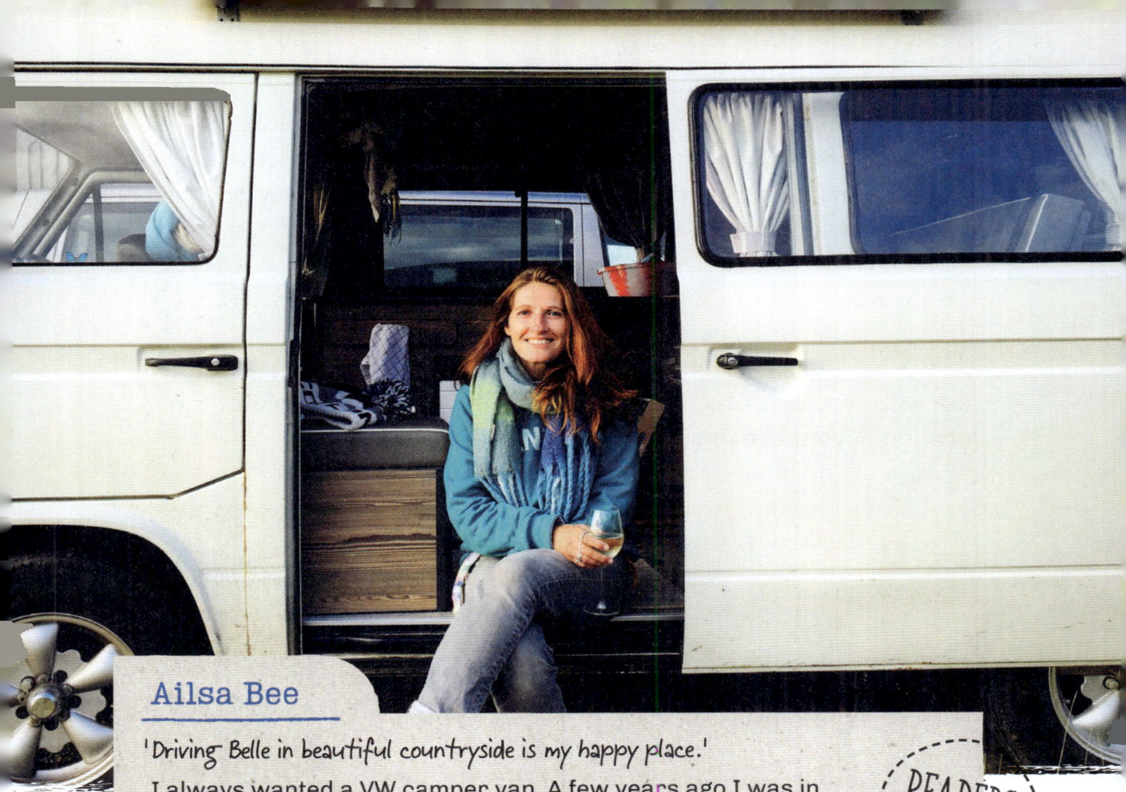

Ailsa Bee

'Driving Belle in beautiful countryside is my happy place.'

READERS' DRIVES

I always wanted a VW camper van. A few years ago I was in an unhappy relationship with two small children and we had no money to even dream about it. I thought there would be no way it would ever happen. And then, the universe conspired. The relationship ended, the house was sold and I found myself alone with a bit of money. First thing I did was get searching for my perfect van. I decided a high top T25 was a perfect solution for my need for practical, balanced with my wish for old and characterful. All those I found were beautiful on the outside but so tired on the inside. Then I found Belle – beautiful inside and out. I had to have her!

Belle is the best purchase I've ever made. Me and my girls, our old dog and more recently our new pup, have had such adventures in her. We've been to the very south of France and the very top of Scotland. Driving Belle in beautiful countryside is my happy place. To my children and I she is freedom, adventure, the exciting unknown. I long for a more alternative life and Belle gives me a taste for it. When the girls spread their wings I think I'll be off round the world, never to live in a house again!

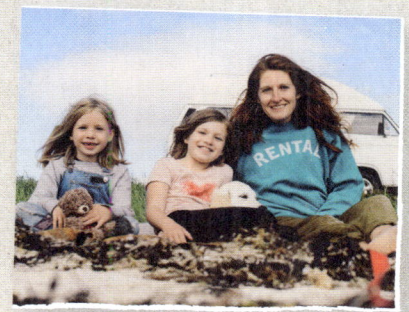

What's yours called?

All camper vans and motorhomes should have names. It's the law. Lots of people give their vans names like Mopsy or Daisy and anthropomorphise them as if they were posh 1950s children. Others find names naturally as they travel. One way to go about it is to name your van after the first place you break down – just avoid going anywhere crap when you take it out for the first time! And avoid Tesco like the plague, now and forever.

A few years ago I did a very unscientific poll among my van-loving friends to find out what they called the vans and where they found their inspiration. The results are below:

AFTER A DEARLY DEPARTED

'We called her Margaret, after my mum. The number plate features the letters GAL, which was my dad's lifelong pet name for her. As soon as we saw the number plate we knew she would be ours.'

INCLUDE 'VAN' IN THE NAME

My favourite? Victor Van Doom, 'because it breaks down quicker than one of Katie Price's relationships.' Also, Frank-en-van, Nelson Van Dela, Dick Van Dyke etc.

'Mine is Vanny DeVito. Coz you know, he's a van and he's a Vito.'

LET THE KIDS DECIDE!

How about Beep Beep (because the horn got stuck on)?

'Ours is Pam because my then two-year-old fell in love with her, but his speech wasn't the best and he used to call her Pamper Pam.'

MUSIC-INSPIRED NAMES

Van Morrison, Ludwig (Camper Van Beethoven), Lola ('cos she looks like a girl but underneath is all man), Billie (Holiday) and Betty ('cos the engine went BAM-a-lam).

'My camper is called Hendrix 'cos he whizzes around in a purple haze.'

LET THE GOOD TIMES ROLL

The Happy Bus, Summer, Wanda, El Nido (Spanish – The Nest) and Florence (Go with the Flo).

'She's called Betty because she's my personal rehab.'

TELL IT HOW IT IS

Rusty, Rosy, Piglet or Dotty might tell you how it looks, but how does it feel to ride in it? Iceberg or Frosty might tell you something about the experience of ownership!

'Ella, 'cos she costs an 'ellava lot of money.'

IT'S ALL ABOUT WHERE YOU TAKE IT!

Skippy (Australia), Syd (Sydney), Harlyn (Cornwall), Widdy (Widemouth Bay) and Russel (Russel Bay, NZ) and the very fabulous Roxy Hourtin De Gironde.

'Chester ... because on our first big camping expedition to Anglesey he blew an oil pressure switch just outside Chester. We limped home but still got to camp at a beautiful site, just 2 miles from home and had one of the best weekends away ever.'

What a camper means to me

In the first edition of this book I wrote about how buying a van marked the end of a very difficult time in my family's life. My daughter, Maggie, was being treated for leukaemia in Bristol and my second daughter, Charlie, had just been born. Running away in a van meant escaping and survival against the odds. It still does, but times move on.

Maggie and Charlie are young women living their own lives now. They love to travel, camp and explore. That's vindication for me that we did something right when they were growing up. They have forgiven me for stuffing them into a Type 2 Volkswagen for 12 weeks when they were still at primary school, and were gutted when I sold it.

Nowadays I travel in the van for work (I count my blessings daily) and have had the privilege of travelling in Scotland, Ireland, France, Spain and Portugal to write books about these places. I have also travelled through 16 countries – including Finland, Denmark and Sweden – to become a member of the Blue Nosed Caravan Club (I have a certificate, too) by reaching the Arctic Circle in a motorhome with my friends at Bailey and the Caravan and Motorhome Club. I'm still thrilled that I was invited on such an incredible adventure. I wouldn't have done that if I'd spent my life on aeroplanes or sitting at home.

The van gives me the gift of being able to immerse myself in new places and to explore the world, or even my local area, in a unique way. It is still relatively cheap to live in and still gives me the joy of simplicity. That's something I appreciate more than ever. We use the van to go to festivals, for weekends away and for fun, as well as for work (if you can call it that). Thankfully, we still feel the excitement of driving to a ferry, setting up on a great campsite or sitting on the step by the slider for a cuppa and slice of something sweet.

I travel with Lizzy these days. She's a botanist, wild swimmer and lifelong camper, and that helps me to get even more out of my time in the van. Together, we are braver, stronger and happier. Her knowledge helps me to better understand the landscapes we pass through, while her love helps me to manage my everyday existence. And the van makes it all possible. I am forever grateful.

Our future plans are centred on the van, too, if we can find a way of doing it better. That means using our feet and bikes more, staying put for longer and making a huge effort to live without making a mess. It's a tough call, but we are ready.

Bring it on.

The perfect escape pod

THE ONLY WAY TO HOLIDAY

In the original *Camper Van Bible* I wrote about how camper vans, and particularly classic VW camper vans, have become the icons of cool – a shorthand for freedom, the open road, love and friendship. We love them because they remind us of simpler times. In the past, they were also ubiquitous. Between 1950 and 1967 around 1.47 million Type 2 Split-Screen VWs were made. After that, VW produced almost 3.3 million Bay Window Type 2 vans, which ranks them among the most popular vehicles of all time. Perhaps these numbers tell us all we need to know – because there were so many Volkswagen vans on the road, many of us have memories of them from childhood. They were also used as bread vans in Ireland, fire trucks in Germany, ambulances in Australia and just about everything just about everywhere else. Parts were available almost anywhere, too, thanks to VW's extensive global dealer network, and this helped to cement them as the traveller's choice for overlanding.

We also love them because so many of them still survive today. Compared with modern-day vehicles, old-style campers look like they have personalities and soul, turning heads wherever they go. They have become objects of desire, the coolest tip of the iceberg when it comes to outdoor living.

But as times change, so do tastes. Why have character when you could have reliability, economy, speed and space? The Ducato can fit a transverse bed in the back, so making oodles more living space. The Crafter is like driving a Golf. The e-NV200 runs full electric. The Ford Terrier gives the T6 a really good run for its money and costs a lot less.

THE RISE OF #VANLIFE

In recent times it's become terribly hip to live in a van. It's a concept born largely out of a lack of space and spiralling housing costs. And it's perfectly reasonable, too: why would you buy a house to live in debt when a van will do?

What was once necessity has in some circles now become a lifestyle choice. Hundreds have taken to the road in their campers to start new careers as social media influencers and digital nomads, presenting those of us stuck in the 9 to 5 with envious imagery of a life less ordinary. If you can work from anywhere, want to save money and have somewhere to park night after night, it's easy to understand the draw.

But it's also far too easy to scroll through social media and feel that the #vanlife lifestyle is beyond your reach. Just remember that it's not all real. For every idyllic camper van shot on the shores of Lake Como there are many more of us simply getting on with it, facing the weather, fetching milk from the shop, slipping on cowpats and enjoying every moment of it. Vanlife is what you make it.

And vanlife is not a verb.

THE POST-COVID HOLIDAY

During the Covid pandemic, the travel industry faced disaster after disaster. But the camper van and motorhome industry escaped this fate. With stories of record sales and a backlog of orders, the camper van came into its own during lockdown.

You might say it finally grew up.

In a world where air travel – and even travel in Europe – became impossibly risky and difficult, suddenly a motorhome holiday (some call it a 'staycation') began to make a lot of sense. Families who might have jetted off to southern Spain in other, less remarkable times for their holidays suddenly found themselves looking closer to home.

In 2020, campsites opened up before any other kind of accommodation, although many insisted that you needed to be self-contained to be able to stay (as such, sales of Porta Potties went through the roof; people were even offering them on eBay for more than the RRP!) If you had a camper or a motorhome – or could snatch a week's hire – you were good to go. Your own isolation pod was sitting on the driveway, waiting for you to take it off into the sunset.

And that's the point. You *are* good to go. Whether you get there by ferry, Eurostar or by staying at home to explore your own country, you can head off in a safe, self-contained home from home on wheels.

There has never been a better time to drive a camper.

The camping experience

We've been in love with recreational camping for well over a hundred years. Thanks to the father of the Scout Movement, Robert Baden-Powell (*Scouting for Boys*, 1908, is still the world's second best-selling book of all time) and the father of modern camping Thomas Hiram Holding (*The Camper's Handbook*, 1908, is widely acknowledged to be the starting place of the recreational camping movement), the idea of sleeping under canvas for its own sake has become a part of our psyche. 1908 was a good year for being outside.

The Camping and Caravanning Club (as it is now known) began life as the Bicycle Touring Club when it was formed by Holding in 1878. In 1909, Captain Robert Falcon Scott became the president, until his death, in Antarctica, in 1911. In 1919, Sir Robert Baden-Powell, who was by then famous the world over for starting the Scout Movement, became president.

Why tell you this? Because it's important to know where our love for the great outdoors comes from – and just how much it is a part of our culture. That three such highly regarded and remarkable individuals should have been at the helm of the movement is testimony enough that camping is important to us.

I remain ever grateful to the Scout Movement for inspiring my grandfather to camp in the 1920s and to become a Scout leader in later years. His knowledge and guidance saw me through some rough weather, while his obsession with lightweight camping haunts me still. However, I am also extremely grateful to those who put camping on wheels in the name of the greater good (and greater comfort) at around the same time.

Why?

Because camper vans are better than tents.

Why a camper van is (sometimes) better than a tent

I have camped all my life. I've seen it all, and have experience enough to make up my mind about the way I like to camp – and I choose a camper van (although these days I also carry a tent – more on that later).

My personal love of campers comes down to portability, which might seem odd considering tents are the ultimate pop-up homes. But bear with me. The fact remains that a camper van is a home that can be driven. That means you don't always have to make major alterations to move it. If you've got it right then you should be able to drive your camper away from your camping spot without having to do too much. Yes, so you might have to de-pop a pop top roof, pull the bed down and pack away a few clothes, but at least you don't have to dismantle it entirely to make a swift getaway.

What are the other reasons I prefer a camper over a tent?

- Vans offer a level of protection a tent never could. They don't blow down in the night. They don't flap and flail and keep you awake. Rarely will you wake to the sound of ripping nylon or humming guy ropes – the sounds that tell you disaster is close at hand.
- They can be driven, meaning that when the weather gets really bad, there is the threat of a flood, or snow, wind and rain, you can always move on.
- Vans allow you to sleep in a real bed, off the ground, which makes it more comfortable and a lot warmer.

Why a tent is (sometimes) better than a camper van

These days, I carry a tent in my van just in case I need it. There are times when you can only wild camp in a tent and others when the excitement of tented camping cannot be matched. Hiking into inaccessible places sometimes requires a tent, as does cycling long bike routes. There is no reason why you can't do a bit of both. Leave the van at a campsite and take to the hills or the bike trail for a night. Why not? That way, you get to save a bit of fuel and wake up away from it all – properly – where vehicles cannot go. You'll have an experience like no other. And tomorrow you get to go back to a real bed!

BUYING A CAMPER VAN OR MOTORHOME

You have your heart set on a camper van or motorhome. Fantastic. I look forward to meeting up with you on the road. But first, before you buy, there are a lot of questions you need to ask yourself. I've listed them in detail in the following pages so that you'll know what to look for and what kind of recommendations can be made.

Big decision coming up, right? Buying a 'leisure vehicle' is a big commitment, both in time and money. Will you get to use it often enough? Will it keep its value? Will you be able to drive it every day? Before you commit, there are some important decisions to be made:

- Are you replacing a car? Does it therefore need to be a daily driver?
- How many people do you need to sleep?
- Will you use it in the winter?
- How long will you go away in it for?
- What sort of places will you take it?
- Is reliability important?
- How much have you got to spend?

New versus old

Do you go for new or old? Good question. A lot of it depends on budget. But when I say new versus old, I don't mean 'modern' versus 'classic'. I mean *new* as in *brand new* and *old* as in *preloved*.

BUYING BRAND NEW

Brand new camper vans, or a van that is being converted for you, are wonderful, but they can cost upwards of £30k. And when I say upwards I mean *skywards*. It shouldn't be a surprise that some new A-Class motorhomes can easily fall into the £100k bracket, although there is a lot on the market between £40k and £70k.

If you have the money, you'll have a lot of fun choosing all the bits and pieces, add-ons, gadgets and widgets. It's a bit like ordering a new car but with two or three more times the number of options. You want memory foam, a heater and an underslung tank? How about the winter pack or the driver's pack? There's a lot to take in, and we'll talk more about all these things later.

The point is, there is no such thing as a standard camper or motorhome, even one that's off the peg. For example, the choices when buying a motorhome from a dealer may be as simple as buying an add-on 'pack', or far more complicated. Some even come with

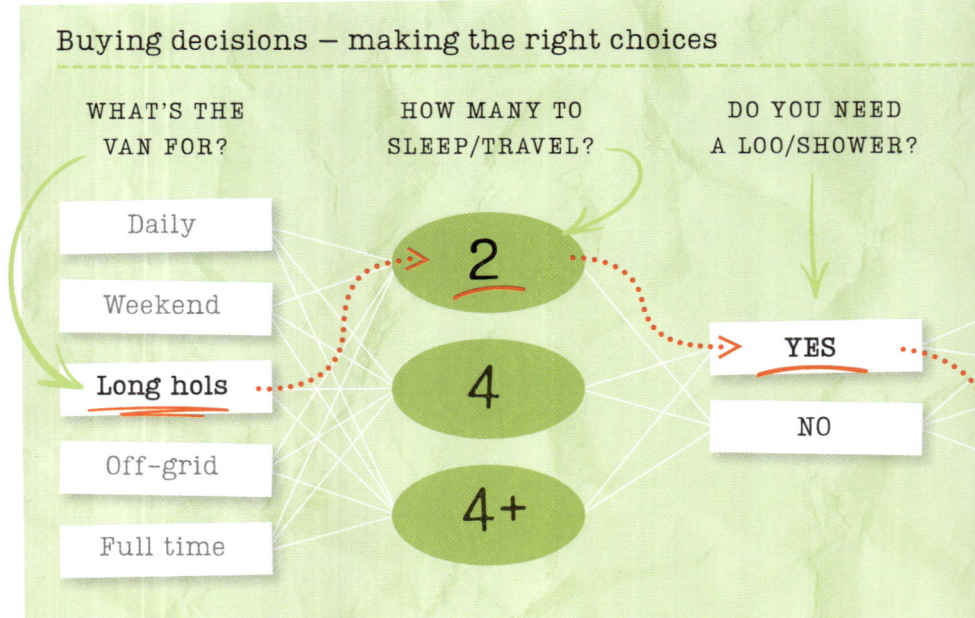

Buying decisions — making the right choices

WHAT'S THE VAN FOR?	HOW MANY TO SLEEP/TRAVEL?	DO YOU NEED A LOO/SHOWER?
Daily	2	YES
Weekend	4	NO
Long hols	4+	
Off-grid		
Full time		

'compulsory options', which means you pay above the base price for something you have no choice about. There's a lesson in there for sure – keep your eyes wide open.

Even going to a converter and choosing one of their models will lead you down all kinds of roads of possibility, as you'll have to choose a base vehicle and all the bits and pieces it comes with before you even get to your camping set-up.

Visit a dealer

While I'm not advocating for wasting anyone's time, I do think it's a good plan to visit a big motorhome or camper van dealership to see what's available, what things cost and what you can get for your money, even if you're thinking of buying second hand.

If you can also get a factory tour at the same time then you'll get a good insight into the way campers are put together, the work that goes into converting new (or old) campers and the possibilities when it comes to choosing layouts, accessories and your individual specifications. You'll also be able to ask them about realistic lead times for new vehicles (they can be long). Seeing the different marques and brands available on the market up close will give you a really good idea of which brands offer quality and which can often be lacking in build quality.

BUDGET?

£0–10K

£10–40K

£30–70K

Self-build

Small van

Medium van

Large van

e-van

Moho

A-class

- **Check with the manufacturer for lead times.** This is especially important after the Covid-19 pandemic and Brexit, as supply has been severely disrupted. Some manufacturers have six-month-to-a-year lead times, partly due to stock and supply issues. Others, like converters, have issues because they are so busy and demand is so high. Decide how long you are prepared to wait and start looking at vans that can be delivered within your time frame.

- **Decide what's important to you,** especially when it comes to buying motorhomes. Do you need storage space for chairs, bikes, toys etc., and therefore do you need a garage? Or would you prefer to have more living space?

- UK-designed motorhomes and vans tend to have **more living space** due to the good old British weather. Designers and manufacturers in Europe tend to assume you'll be spending a lot of time outdoors, which is reflected in less living space.

- **Do you like making the bed?** Fixed beds sound like a great plan – you have a ready-made bed, waiting to go! But they often mean a massive compromise on living space. If living space is important, maybe consider that it's not so bad to make the bed each night. Or go for a drop-down bed, which can save a lot of space.

- **Smaller, more niche brands** often provide good service and superior quality when it comes to the little things, like fittings and fixtures. However, you may find them more expensive if they are hand-building to your spec.

- Cheaper motorhomes may come as standard with lower-powered or lower-spec base vehicles. **Check the base vehicle** is what you want and need and that it is enough for the motorhome.

- Base vehicles can come with all kinds of **extras that you will inevitably pay for**, just like with a new car. Do you need parking sensors (useful, yes)? Do you need alloys (less useful, no)?

- Check your **Mass In Running Order** (MIRO, or recreational vehicle weight) and payload (the maximum weight you can load on to your vehicle). Some motorhomes have very little payload when the water tank is full, meaning you can't take much stuff and remain legal.

- **Check that the water tanks** are big enough for your needs. Do you want to shower or go off-grid for days at a time? You might need a big capacity.

- Check how your **water tank contributes to the payload.** Some manufacturers recommend travelling on a 20 per cent full tank of water, which increases the payload, but may put you overweight when you drive with a full tank.
- Check you can drive the camper with **your licence.**
- **Look at the build quality.** If you are limited in terms of budget, choose brands with better reputations and buy their cheaper models rather than being seduced by cheaper brands' more expensive models, with all the frills and add-ons. Good build quality means longevity.
- **Check what's included** in the basic price. Engine upgrades, winter packs (insulating the water tanks), driver packs (alloys, armrests) and media packs (satnav, iPhone and phone connectivity) are add-ons that will push the price up considerably.
- In the motorhome market there may seem to be little difference in price variation, since they all cost between £45k and around £70k. The real difference, though, is in the little things, like warranty, add-ons, equipment supplied and the base vehicle. **Be thorough in your purchasing** and make sure you are getting everything you need.
- If you're travelling with kids and babies, **make sure the seats have ISOFIX** or are crash and pull tested.
- **Consider how many people** will need to travel with you. Is there the same number of berths as travel seats? Could the kids sleep in a tent?
- Don't assume that the base vehicle will have everything you need as standard. **Check what the base price includes.**
- **Space-saving ideas** like electronic drop-down beds can make a van versatile by allowing the garage to be bigger or smaller, but can also result in a loss of locker space for your clothes and effects.
- **The more gadgetry on board,** the more there is to go wrong.
- If you like to cook, **make sure the kitchen is big enough.** Lots of vans compromise on the kitchen appliances and food prep space.
- Small things like the number of **electrical sockets and USB ports** might not bug you when you buy, but once you are negotiating with the family over who gets to charge what and when, they suddenly become very important...

CONVERTING FROM A BASE VEHICLE

There are plenty of companies who can source used vans to convert or will convert new vans for you. Obviously this adds another level of complication to the buying process, as you need to choose a base vehicle that's specced right from the off.

Choosing the base vehicle can be just as important as choosing the conversion because some base models are more difficult to convert

than others, simply because of the way they are finished. Often, the more basic the better, as it provides a blank canvas. However, make sure you get what you need from your base vehicle: parking sensors, DAB, cruise control. These things may not matter to you, but they will to some. Also, check their availability; you may not be able to wait, and that may inform your final decision.

Quick tip

When searching for a base vehicle it may be worth looking at ex-demo vans from manufacturers' websites. They only show what's in stock and therefore what's available immediately. A van with less than 2,000 miles on it may well be significantly cheaper than a brand new vehicle.

KEEP YOUR EYES OPEN. STAY CALM. SET YOUR BUDGET. STICK TO IT.

BUYING PRELOVED

Don't think that buying second hand gets any easier. In fact, I'd say it gets harder. In choosing something that's right for you, be prepared to face a few conundrums and choices, from the type of bed you choose to the type and age of the base vehicle. There are always compromises to be had.

My recommendation: go to as many big dealers, motorhome retailers, VW festivals and conventions as you can. Nose about in as many vehicles as you can. Check out the layouts, seating arrangements and costs, and try to identify the vehicle that's perfect for you.

There will be one, all you have to do is find it.

WHAT IS CLASSIC?

Classic, according to HM Revenue & Customs (HMRC) is anything over 40 years old. That means anything made before 1 January 1983 (at the time of writing) is considered classic and you don't need pay tax on it. It also doesn't need an MOT.

This means all Volkswagen Type 2s (that's Bay Windows and Split-Screens) and even a few Type 3s (Type 25) are exempt. Also included in this would be early Hymermobils, most Citroën HY vans and most Commer vans. Even vans made in the 1980s may be considered 'classic', even though they don't qualify.

Buy well, buy safe

When you are buying a vehicle, the thing always to keep at the back of your mind is 'buyer beware'. That means if it dies or falls apart or doesn't live up to expectations, the only person you can blame, in most cases, is yourself.

However, the law will protect you in certain circumstances. If you buy from a dealer, then through sale of goods legislation (the Sale of Goods Act 1979) you are entitled to expect that any goods you buy are of satisfactory quality. That means they must be of a reasonable quality that a reasonable person could expect, in relation to the way the goods were described, the price and the fact that they were second hand. So, is it fit for purpose? Is it of satisfactory appearance? Is it as described? If not, then you are entitled to a full refund (within a reasonable time of the sale), but you'll need to demonstrate the goods were not of satisfactory quality at the time of sale.

When you buy privately you don't have as many rights. You can still expect the vehicle to be as described and if it is not, you can sue for compensation. But the best advice is to be fully aware of what you are buying. Check it over and check it over again. If things go dreadfully wrong, talk to the seller.

I know how fraught it can be buying an old vehicle. I also know what it feels like to drive away knowing you have just committed a huge amount of cash to something that, really, you don't know much about yet. You have to believe a little, but you also have to insure yourself against problems by being as cautious and questioning as you can.

TOP TIPS FOR VIEWING VANS

Stay Covid safe

With Covid-19 still a consideration, it may be impractical or unsafe to go and see every van you like the look of. However, these days it is perfectly reasonable to ask sellers to give you a walkthrough of the van via a video calling app (for example, FaceTime, WhatsApp, Snapchat) from the comfort of your own home. That way, you can either write it off or get even more excited once you're armed with more knowledge. Do this before committing to travel to see a van and ask the owner to show you everything. If you still think it's a goer, go and see it. When you do view in person, keep a window open, wear a mask and stand back from the seller.

Take a mechanic with you when you view

If you can, take someone with you who can give the vehicle a good going over when you view any vehicle for the first time. That means looking at it properly inside and out, underneath and on top. If you are viewing a classic or vintage camper, take a checklist and carefully examine each item in turn.

Follow your instincts

Look at the seller. Check their body language. How do they seem to you? Honest? Above board? Are they willing to let you give the vehicle a good going over? Does it feel good? If it doesn't, don't let your excitement get the better of you. Take some time to think about it.

Never assume it will be all right — assume the worst

Sometimes, 'it'll be grand' isn't enough. Trusting to luck can leave you out of pocket and with a very red face if things go wrong.

Lower your expectations and be pleasantly surprised

You might want it to be perfect, but don't expect it to be so. Lower your expectations and you may be pleasantly surprised. If you think it's going to be a crock and it isn't, you'll be pleasantly surprised.

Ask questions

Ask lots of questions about everything. Be relentless. Cover history, cost of ownership, miles per gallon (MPG) – anything and everything you can think of. Get as much info as you can from the seller. And don't be afraid to call up if you think of anything in the meantime.

Look at the log book and history

The history of a vehicle can tell you a lot about how it's been treated. If it's had lots of owners or if there are MOTs missing or bills showing what work has been done, then you'll find out more about it than the owner may be able or willing to tell you. No history doesn't always mean dodgy history, but it could be a sign of something wrong.

Test everything to check it works

Turn on the gas. Fire up the fridge. Open the cupboards. Pull out the bed. Pop the top. If things are broken or not working as they should, then you can either use it to negotiate a drop in price or as a reason not to buy. Don't ever feel pressured – if it's not right, don't buy it, no matter how pretty it is.

Be careful with the money

Don't hand over any cash until you know it's right for you, that you have the seller's details and that you have 'insurance' (and by that I mean you've actually got the keys).

Searching for your perfect camper

GO TO A BIG MOTORHOME SHOW

See how the big boys do it. There are caravan, camping and motorhome shows all over the UK and Europe. The biggest are held at the Birmingham NEC (usually February and October) and in Düsseldorf (September). Warners Group also put on shows around the UK.

Expect to see everything from micro campers and the latest in camping technology (e-vehicles and more), to huge A-Class monsters from Europe's biggest manufacturers.

GO TO A VW MEET–UP

If you're looking for anything VW, get yourself to a VW meet-up or show. There are VW shows all over the UK all summer, the biggest being Busfest held at the Three Counties Showground in Malvern, Worcestershire, and the VolksWorld Show at Sandown Park Racecourse, in Esher, Surrey. A visit to the 'Show and Shine' field (where the best vehicles are displayed) may well give you van envy, but there will undoubtedly be countless vehicles for sale. It's a good place to meet converters and suppliers of kit, too.

If you decide to go down the VW route, these shows will give you a taste of the kind of community you can join (or buy into) when you

buy a VW. They're fun events and often feel more like a festival, with parts jumbles thrown in.

RENT BEFORE YOU BUY

I think this is so important, I've dedicated an entire section to it later in the book. Some people find out very quickly that a camper van is not for them when they rent, so saving themselves thousands. Even if they find the perfect layout or van, they may still find that it's not for them in the long run. See pages 144–147 to find out more about renting camper vans.

GO TO A LARGE DEALERSHIP OR CONVERTER

Here, you'll get an opportunity to look at a lot of vans in one place. There are loads of dealerships and converters to choose from, but these are the ones I know well:

- **Marquis Motorhomes & Caravans** have dealerships in every corner of the UK, with hundreds of models to look at in each location: **www.marquisleisure.co.uk**
- **Danbury**, importers of the Brazilian Type 2 until it ceased production in 2014, has a large showroom near Bristol, UK, with hundreds of camper vans to choose from, including used models: **www.danburycampervans.co.uk**
- **VW Kampers**, on the UK's south coast, sell a vast stock of used Danbury Brazilian VW imports as well as those made in Germany, Australia and South Africa: **www.vwkampers.com**

JOIN A FACE-BOOK GROUP

There are loads of Facebook groups where vans get bought and sold every day. Even if you don't buy one from Facebook (buyer beware), you'll be able to see what other people are asking. And the comments are priceless.

SEARCH ONLINE

There are tons of places online where it is possible to browse camper vans and motorhomes for sale, as well as get sound advice. The Caravan and Motorhome Club has a good classifieds section for second-hand motorhomes and bits and pieces on its website, while eBay is a favourite, both for buyers and

the odd dodgy seller. It bears repeating: buyer beware.

SEARCH FOR A CLASSIC

The Classic Camper Club concerns itself with makes other than VW, thankfully, although it's tough to get away from them! Take a peek. You may well fall in love yet. See **www.classiccamperclub.co.uk**.

READ MAGAZINES AND BOOKS, ER, LIKE THIS ONE

Read *MMM Magazine*, *Campervan Magazine*, *VolksWorld*, *VW Camper & Bus*, and any other specialist magazine and you'll soon see what's available, mind-boggling though it may be.

ACCOST PEOPLE AND BE NOSY

I love showing people around my camper if they ask politely when I'm out and about. So if you see one you like the look of, just ask. All they can say is no. But they might show you around and it may even be up for sale...

RUST-FREE VW? CONSIDER AN IMPORT

VWs from hot countries like Australia and South Africa are often rust-free (and right-hand drive). Plenty of companies import them to restore or drive as they are. Imports from California and Mexico are good for the left-hand drive lovers. See **www.gdaykombis.co.uk**.

Mark Beresford

'Camper vans help create memories and those are our most treasured possessions.'

Twelve years ago, after a particularly wet and grim camping trip to Anglesey with our young kids, we decided we needed to 'upgrade'. With little money to spend on an expensive camper van, we ended up scouring the internet for a 'project'. Enter 'Chester', as he would come to be known, a tatty ex-taxi VW T25 with no interior, that we got for a few hundred pounds. Several weeks later and many long days and nights, he was finished, built with a mixture of second-hand parts and ingenuity.

Chester became our chariot of adventure to sunny coves, steep mountains and, more importantly, a second home for our autistic son, Joel. Autism throws up many challenges in family life, but one of the things that helped Joel was being outside with nature. The van allowed him (and all of us) to enjoy that freedom, but with the reassuring feeling of home within the van. Each trip we took with Chester went further and further, and eventually we braved 2,000-mile trips to France. Even as teenagers, Erin and Joel love the van. Indeed, Erin just returned from a three-day horse riding course where she stayed over in the van.

As with all old vans, they cost money to keep going, but Chester is one of the family now and we could never be without him. Camper vans help create memories and those are our most treasured possessions.

85

LIVE

Six things to think about when buying your camper

It can be confusing trying to get to grips with all the options and choices available to you. There are all kinds of considerations and compromises to think about. So, in this section I've tried to simplify the buying and choosing process into a series of questions that you can ask yourself. Hopefully, in answering them you'll be able to narrow down your choices. You'll need to think about your budget, your family (now and in the future), the amount of time and love you are prepared to invest in your vehicle and what kind of camping you want to do.

Oh, and how fast you want to travel.

QUESTION 1 Why do you want or need a camper van or motorhome?

QUESTION 2 What will it be used for?

QUESTION 3 What's your budget?

QUESTION 4 How many do you need to sleep/carry?

QUESTION 5 How do you camp?

QUESTION 6 What do you need up top?

1 WHY DO YOU WANT OR NEED A CAMPER VAN OR MOTORHOME?

There is no wrong or right answer to this simple question. Why do you want to own a camper van or motorhome? Whatever your answer, this will help you to define and set out your aims and dreams for the vehicle you hope to own. You define its use and the way you see it. Are you looking for something to cherish, to bring back to life, to take you on the biggest adventures of your life? Do you want a van because you think it's cool, because you are too long in the tooth to camp in discomfort or just because you want to save a few quid?

Is it to own a classic?

Yes? That's fine. But be prepared to lavish money and time on your new ride. Lots of it. You'll get looks and envious glances but you'll be driving something quirky and interesting, that's for sure.

87

LIVE

Is it to travel the world?

Great! You won't be the first and you'll be joining a long line of adventurers who have dropped everything to tour in a camper. Choose an overlander, a 4 x 4 or something super reliable and as fully equipped as possible. In all likelihood you'll need heating, water tanks, shower and loo, as well as solar and the ability to go off-grid.

Is it to get away every weekend?

The camper is the ideal weekend getaway vehicle. You may not need a loo or shower if you're going to sites and you may not even need solar or huge on-board water tanks. A day van (one with a bed and not much in the way of kitchen equipment) may do. A van with a removable kitchen pod may be useful, especially if you want to use the vehicle during the week for something else.

Is it because you want to save money on accommodation?

Yes, you can save on hotels, but when you consider the costs of purchase and ownership (especially if it's older) then you may not end up saving a lot – unless you sleep in it a lot.

Is it because you want to carry sports gear/equipment?

If you're taking part in sports such as triathlons, surfing, kayaking or even snowboarding, and you need to travel to do it, a van or motorhome can be perfect. Some big motorhomes have garages for kit like blow-up SUPS, bikes and even motorbikes, while some vans have huge cargo areas where the rear bed lifts up enough to fit in bikes and kit. Rear-mounted bike carriers can be limited on weight, especially when it comes to ebikes, and for bikes that need to be cocooned.

Kayaks are more difficult on bigger vans as you may need ladders to get them up. If you're travelling solo, you might require a specialist rack to load a kayak on your own. See **www.karitek.co.uk** for kayak and canoe mounting racks for tall vehicles. Thule (**www.thule.co.uk**) makes all kinds of racks and ladders for tall vans and motorhomes.

You still want to camp but don't want to give up your comforts?

Lots of people come to camper vans and motorhomes from tent camping, or because they like their home comforts too much to camp under canvas. You can decide what level of comfort you go for, but basically anything goes! If all you want is a dry bed you can drive around, then a camper may be enough. If you want space and all mod cons, a motorhome may be the go-to for you.

2 WHAT WILL IT BE USED FOR?

This might sound like a silly question, but it's not, simply because you need to decide whether or not you'll be using your van or motorhome exclusively for camping or as a daily driver too. If it's to be a vehicle you use to pop to the shops as well as for camping then I suggest a smaller camper van is best, simply because it makes parking in busy towns easier. Large vans, like Boxer and Ducato, are wide and can be a struggle to park. If you opt for a long wheelbase van then it will be longer than an average parking space, which makes everyday driving difficult.

It's the same with motorhomes; some are over 7ft wide and many are longer than the average car parking space.

You'll also need to consider if you're going to tour or park up on your camping trips. If you like space and tend to park up for a while, a big van is fine. If you like to tour around, a bigger vehicle may prove impractical.

Also, think about where you'll be going. If you like to tour the narrow lanes of Cornwall, your needs will be different from someone who intends to navigate the open roads of Europe. Do you need 4WD (four-wheel drive) for skiing? Will FWD (front-wheel drive) do?

On top of that, motorhomes and campers that only go on occasional outings are likely to have fewer miles on the clock, be less worn and may well have a higher resale value.

3 WHAT'S YOUR BUDGET?

Sorry, but this is the nitty-gritty. Once you set your budget you are well on your way to having some of your choices made for you. Your budget decides everything, from the age of the vehicle to the interior, condition, mileage and number of owners.

It's easy to spend a small fortune on a camper and you could do this just as easily with a modern camper as with a classic from the 1960s. It's not unusual to see a 1970s Bay Window camper on sale for £50k or a new A-Class motorhome with all the extras for £60k. Some van conversions go for more than £100k. It all depends on how far you want to go, and your answer(s) to Question 1 will help you to decide.

It's worthwhile totting up the running costs, too. Keeping an old camper on the road can be just as costly as buying it in the first place. Then again, it is possible to self-build from an older, cheaper vehicle for just a few thousand. It all depends on how much time you're willing to invest and what kind of carpentry skills you possess.

91

LIVE

HOW MUCH YOU SHOULD EXPECT TO PAY

Model	££££s
2021 VW T6 California Ocean (4 berth)	57k–76k
2021 VW Crafter Grand California 680 (2 berth)	76k–90k
2021 Danbury Surf (4 berth) pop top, no kitchen	46k–66k
VW Bay Window Type 2	5k–40k+
A-class motorhome (second hand)	10k–60k
New Fiat Ducato base model	25k–40k
Nissan e-NV200 camper (2 berth)	59k
Second-hand Ford Tourneo base van	10k–40k
Cost of professional conversion	10k–40k

4 HOW MANY DO YOU NEED TO SLEEP/CARRY?

Another fundamental. If it's just you then it's easy. Life is so much simpler. You just throw it all in the back and enjoy living the way you want to.

Two is easy too, as you kind of hope there's some kind of agreement of sorts between you that makes the sleeping arrangements amicable and comfortable. Most camper vans – except perhaps the micro campers – sleep at least two.

It starts to get a little more difficult when you go beyond that.

The fact is, everyone is different and everyone's needs are different. And every family or group changes as time goes on. Kids don't stay kids forever. They have a tricky habit of growing up, getting bigger and growing out of bunk beds, hammocks and high-top sleeping platforms. Your little darlings might sleep on a Moses basket on the front seat for now, but it won't be too long until they need somewhere to stretch out, their own locker for clothes and their own space on the bike rack. That's life. Things change.

Camper vans

COUPLES AND SMALL KIDS
For two berth camper vans it is possible to add hammocks that fit across the front seat and fasten to the A pillar and window pillars, or that slip over swivel seats. These have a weight restriction of around 50kg, so are only really suitable for younger kids. They can also be used for storage, which can be useful when you want to fling off your clothes and dive into bed (and find all your clothes again the next morning).

FAMILIES WITH BIGGER KIDS
Unless you intend to use a pup tent or sleep in an awning (see Extra space, pages 127–130) then you'll need to look at four berth campers. When it comes to smaller camper vans that means looking at a pop top or high top with beds or hammocks 'upstairs'.

Joe, Sarah & Sebastian Kendall

'We've often found travelling around together in the van far more relaxing than being at home.'

Having originally started with a very small red converted post van, 'Posty', in which we journeyed one summer all the way to Croatia and back ... without air-con ... this fuelled the adventure-seeking genes inside us and we've not looked back.

When Posty retired, we decided a bit more space and insulation would be handy for year-round wild camping in Scotland. Our son Sebastian arrived a year or so later and spent his first overnight with us in February 2019 by the Crinan Canal, at three months old during an unseasonable warm spell. It was a great success and we've often found travelling around together in the van far more relaxing than being at home. The simple life.

After a week-long jaunt around the Isle of Harris completing various parts of the snorkel trail with a dog on a paddleboard in tow (yes, really), it was after a cosy night in the van at a white sandy Hebridean beach that I decided – unplanned of course – to propose. Well, at the end of a long walk to another remote beach, of course. And so the adventures continue and what we've found is that it's not only the overnight trips that are special. Any time in Minty gives us such joy, particularly on a soggy day at the table having lunch or warming up after a surf. Why would you own a car instead? Never understood that...

Many modern small van conversions include pop tops with a large double 'upstairs'. This is by far the most popular style of conversion for smaller vans as it adds two extra berths for a relatively small cost (£2k–£3k) in a van that can be driven every day.

LARGER VANS AND FAMILIES

Many larger van conversions are built for families and have four berths in all kinds of combinations, usually in long wheelbase models. Check out the following models for a family of four:

- Auto-Sleeper Fairford
- Auto-Trail Tribute
- Hymer Free
- Globecar Summit
- WildAx Solaris

Lots of European campers also offer four berths with the addition of a fixed bed in the rear, but this can restrict the living space up front, on the assumption that you will spend more time outside than in during the average European summer.

WARNING!

In vehicles manufactured after 2006, passengers must travel in designated travel seats. That means you can only travel with the same number of people as there are designated seats, irrespective of the number of berths. See pages 358–361 for more important information on seat belt law.

Hymer, among others, make a Fiat Ducato-based camper that has a pop top and sleeps four, with the added advantage of having a shower and full kitchen, plus a fixed bed and inside garage.

The only small classic VW that can sleep more than four currently is the Super Viking, which can sleep six. However, and this is something to watch for, the Super Viking only seats five. So who's the extra one?

Motorhomes

Motorhomes and larger conversions are a lot easier. In fact, many of them are aimed at the family market, with lounge areas that convert into beds or even drop-down beds that enable you all to sleep in layers. Drop-down beds on hydraulics are ever more common and allow for extra beds in smaller vehicles, but beware, as all the gubbins can add to your weight and reduce your payload.

If you intend to camp in the winter with more than two people, a larger van or motorhome will be infinitely more comfortable, since pop tops have little in the way of insulation.

MORE THAN FOUR

If you are looking at sleeping more than four then you'll need to consider a motorhome or a bespoke build that can fit you all in. As far as I know there are no factory-built van conversions that seat and sleep six. However, there are plenty of standard models of motorhomes that will safely seat and sleep six comfortably. This may include two above the cab, two in the dining area and two in the rear 'master bedroom', or involve drop-down beds.

Sleeping layouts

By now you will know that different campers and motorhomes have different layouts. The layout will always affect the way you live and sleep in any camper, even in the most spacious of vans. Some work well, some are OK while the kids are small, some are perfect for two but awful with four.

Danbury Surf, a three-quarter width bedded four berth camper.

CAMPER VAN: THE THREE-QUARTER-WIDTH ROCK AND ROLL

This is the 'industry standard' nowadays. It's the layout that's lasted because it's the most practical, giving a healthy compromise between space to sleep and storage space. It applies as much to vintage campers as it does to modern campers and is the adopted style of the T5 California, among many others. Some rock and roll beds are safer than others (see pages 265–270 for more).

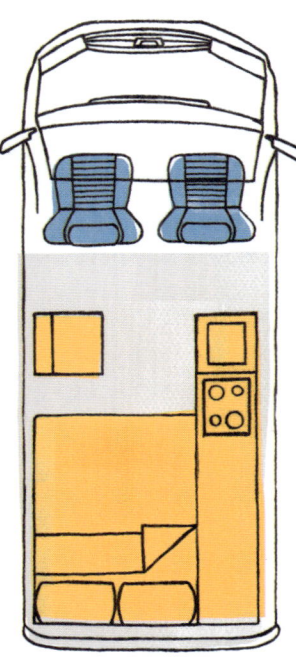

Three-quarter width
rock and roll

CAMPER VAN: THE FULL WIDTH ROCK AND ROLL

If you need sleeping and chilling space, this is a good layout to go for. However, the compromise is storage space, as your units will be at the front. In older vans it gives you the option of having three seats with belts in the back, and the two inertia reel belts.

VW Type 2 with full width bed

CAMPER VAN: REAR KITCHEN/SHOWER

This is a popular layout for couples who like smaller campers but don't want to give up the indoor plumbing. In early models it allowed for a rear kitchen and in modern conversions it allows for a kitchen plus loo and even a shower arrangement. It offers two single beds using the front swivel seats.

VAN CONVERSION: REAR 'LOUNGE'

This type of layout is only really possible in larger vans and van-derived motorhomes that have space enough for two side-facing bench seats in the back. These then turn into a big double bed. The greatest advantage of this layout is having both good space and the ability to open the rear doors to the outside. However, having a galley kitchen and shower in the middle of the camper can compromise the living space.

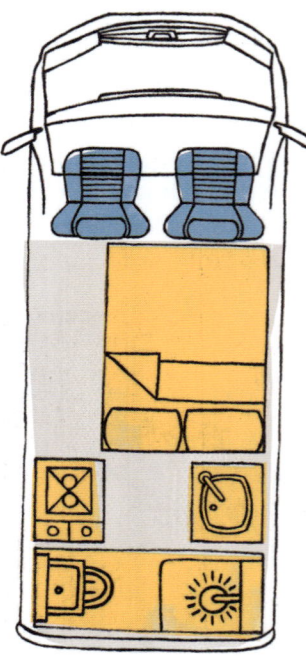

Rear kitchen/shower

VAN CONVERSION: REAR BUNKS WITH FRONT DOUBLE

Rear bunks are great if your van is wide enough to fit them in. However, unless you are driving something that's over 6ft wide, it might not be much good for grown-ups. However, kids will love them until they grow too lanky to fit any more (as kids do...).

Rear bunks with front double

VAN CONVERSION: DROP-DOWN BED

This is a bed that drops down from the ceiling over a living area or lower beds to add two more berths. Very useful in large vans to maximise space.

MOTORHOME AND LARGE VAN CONVERSION: FIXED BEDS

In recent years there has been a trend towards the fixed bed, in other words a bed that stays made up during the day. In large van conversions these are often able to swing upwards out of the way to allow bikes and kit to be stored while driving, while also keeping the bed made! Some conversions put the fixed bed above the garage at the back, giving lots of storage. Useful in vans over 6ft wide. VW's Grand California does this: it is a 'typical European' layout.

MOTORHOME: FIXED BEDS AND MASTER BEDROOM

In larger motorhomes the space is there to make master bedrooms that have fixed beds over garages. They may be separated from the living area by the bathroom, with a shower on one side and a loo on the other.

MOTORHOME: OVER-CAB BEDS, LUTON-STYLE

A-Class motorhomes and coachbuilt motorhomes often have over-cab bunks. They are useful if you want extra storage, as sleeping bags, pillows etc. can then be slung upstairs out of the way during the day. It also leaves space for more beds downstairs.

CLASSIC VAN: VIKING SPACEMAKER

The Viking Spacemaker roof was launched in 1975 and represented something novel and innovative at the time, which was an overhanging roof that could sleep three or four adults in a circular ring, or in beds around the central roof opening. They are somewhat of a rarity today but much loved.

SMALL CAMPER VAN: IN-CAB HAMMOCKS

For kids and luggage, a neat solution to needing extra space might be to consider an over-cab hammock. These are popular in VWs and add an extra bed for little ones, although they are only capable of carrying a certain amount of weight.

For more information on interiors of VW campers over the years, I recommend getting into the books of David and Cee Eccles.

Quick tip

Keep an eye on the payload of vans with drop-down beds, as the mechanics can add weight.

5 HOW DO YOU CAMP?

We all camp the same, don't we? We turn up, set up, cook, hang out, sleep, wake and do it all again. Well, yes, but no. Just as all camper vans are different, so are all camping experiences. If you know the type of places you are going and the type of camping you intend to do then it can really help you to decide what type of van is going to be right for you.

There is more to follow regarding campsites and camping later in the book, but for now, let's discuss camping styles and how they might affect your choice of camper van.

Glamping

This style of camping has become more common in recent years. But what does it mean? 'Glamping' is a bastardisation of 'glamour' and 'camping', and is designed to attract those who like their creature comforts to an activity that perhaps isn't always as comfortable as they may wish.

What does your average glamper drive? Something glamorous, obviously – probably vintage, maybe even a little quirky. That means it needs to be some kind of a classic. Perhaps not a VW. Perhaps something bigger, with crochet and bunting for sure. You'd like:

- plenty of space, for lounging around glamorously
- a shower and a toilet, because why else?
- a kitchen, for preparing glamorous snacks and Italian classic dishes
- retro looks and styling to make it ever so groovy
- lots of comforts and space so it's not like camping at all.

WHAT YOU NEED IS: a retrotastic 1980s A-Class? Maybe. Perhaps a Karmann Gipsy.

Festival camping

I don't know what type of festivals you're used to but the ones I've been to tend to be mucky affairs, with madness outside and a lot of rain. So, the perfect festival camper van needs to be a private space where you can get away from the chaos to reapply the lip gloss before venturing out again for more. It doesn't really have to be anything other than dry, comfortable and warm, perhaps with a fridge for keeping a few beers cool. You'd like:

- a Porta Potti, to save late-night trips to the festival portaloos
- a fridge, for keeping a few beers on ice
- a cooker, for putting on a brew first thing in the morning
- a very comfortable bed, for crashing out
- good curtains (or blackouts) for blocking the view for nosy neighbours.

While a VW classic will make you feel all cool and what not, a 4WD Bongo might stand a better chance of getting you out of there once the fat lady has sung.

WHAT YOU NEED IS: an overlander with chunky tyres for grip in the mud, or an all-wheel drive VW or T25 synchro to guarantee you'll get out of there. Basically, 4WD all the way.

Touring park camping

This is the kind of camping most of us will be used to. Touring parks are the kind of campsites that have a little of everything, so don't be surprised to find a few mobile homes, some caravans and an area for tents. You can also expect electric hook-up (EHU), hardstanding pitches, clean toilets and showers (we hope), and all mod cons. There may also be a shop. Basically, it's a very safe way of camping, with everything laid on. You'd like:

- a kitchenette
- beds
- an electric unit (for charging mobiles, tablets etc.)
- an awning if you need more space to spread out
- the kitchen sink, for a good-quality family holiday.

WHAT YOU NEED IS: any camper will do, to be honest. It all depends on the level of comfort you expect, the amount of space you need and how many of you there are. Most campsites allow you to add to your space by putting up an awning or a pup tent (see Extra space on pages 127–130 for more).

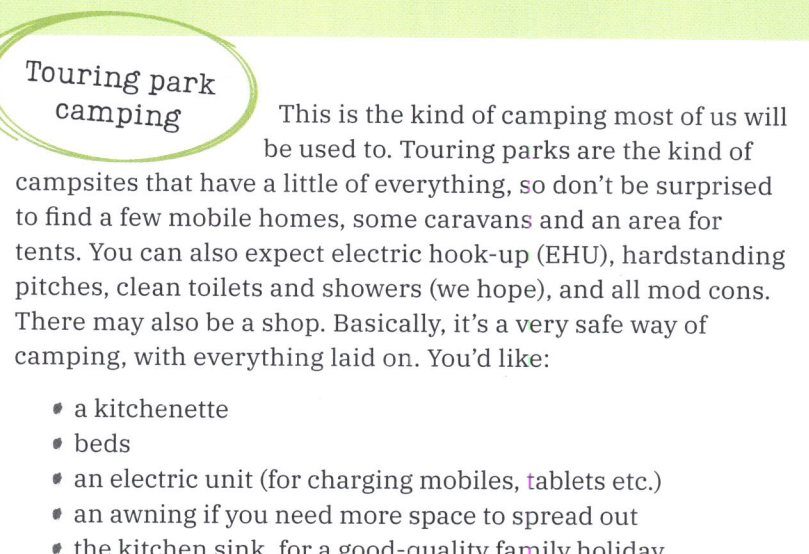

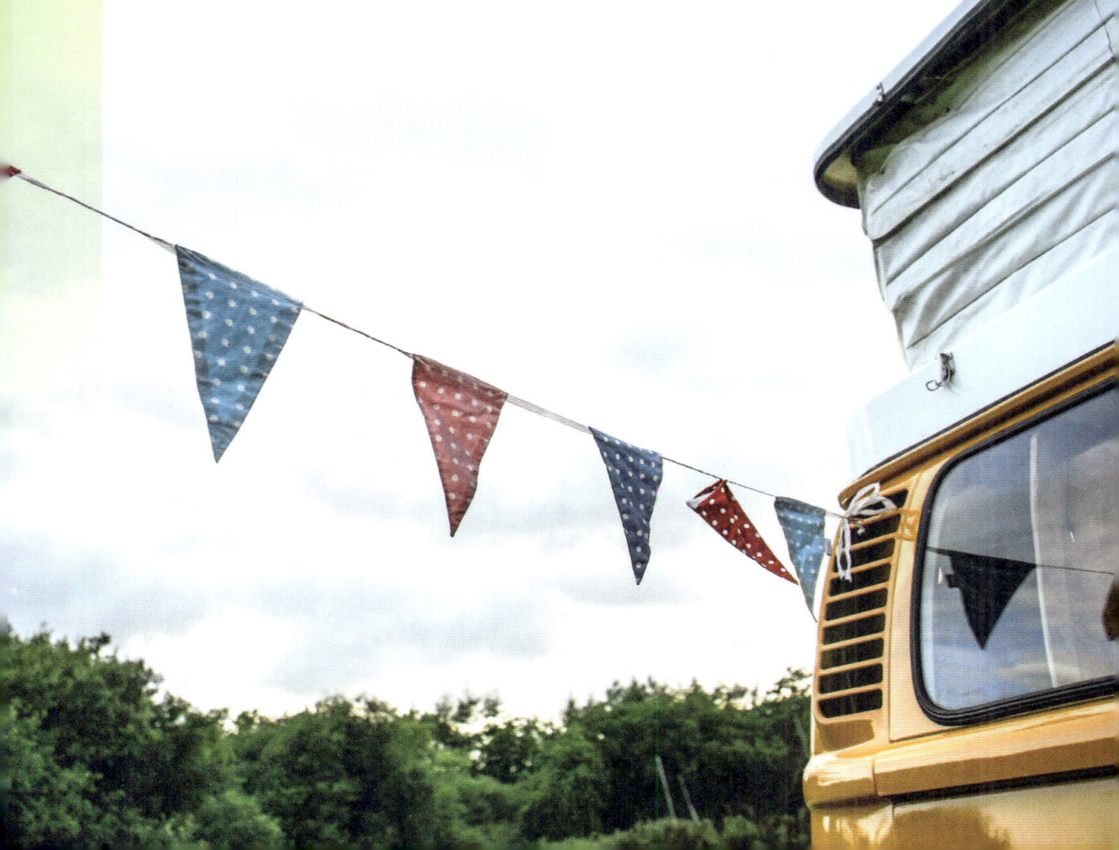

Small-site camping

Small sites are the non-corporate sites where it can be a bit rough and ready. These are the type of sites that appeal to the independently minded camper. They may be in a farmer's field or just in a great spot. The French would call it *camping à la ferme* or *camping au naturel* (which is not to be confused with being naked!). Again, any type of camper could be perfect for you, although bigger vans and large 'units' might struggle a little if there is no hardstanding.

If your van relies on having electric, then these kind of sites might not always be right, since they're often without electric, shops or much in the way of glamorous comfort. Best kind, IMHO. You'd like:

- the capability of being independent of electric
- a kitchen and a BBQ
- a fire pit (if allowed) for a genuine feeling of being 'out there'
- an awning or pup tent (for leaving gear) if you go out and about.

WHAT YOU NEED IS: anything goes, although big motorhomes might not last too long if electric is an issue and access to hardstanding is unavailable.

Stealth camping

As the name suggests, stealth camping is the type of camping you do under the radar, often in towns, pub car parks or at the side of the road but done in such a way as to avoid detection. The stealth camper van needs to be unassuming, without accoutrements (on the outside) and, for all intents and purposes, it must look like a standard van. You'd like:

- no windows, or blacked-out windows
- whatever you need inside – no one can see in anyway
- no bikes, roof racks or any kind of outside stuff
- no need for an awning.

WHAT YOU NEED IS: this is when the 'white van man'-type van comes into its own. Suits any home conversions without windows and converted tin top VWs without windows. Perfect for an ex AA Type 4 or blacked-out T5, large Sprinter or any large van.

Chloe Nash

'Having a van has given back my freedom, my adventure and my happiness.'

Throughout lockdown, like everybody I was starting to get frustrated with how dull life was becoming. Home workouts and healthy eating weren't filling the hole left by my adventures.

My weekends normally consist of hiking and wild camping trips in the Lake District, foreign travel or organising local community walks (as Local Walks with Chloe), but now all of my hobbies were on pause. I had wanted a van for years but couldn't afford one (due to funding my travel addiction), however I now had some spare cash so decided it was time to start researching. I originally wanted a VW Caddy but after lots of research it was clear I couldn't really afford one, so in the end I settled for a Berlingo and as soon as lockdown ended I purchased Brendá.

Every evening after work, with very little help, I spent hours in the van converting it. It's not yet complete but is liveable, and I now spend a lot of time sleeping in it. A couple of weeks ago I travelled to Lewis, Harris and Skye, and stayed in the van the whole trip. I am so happy that I went ahead because having a van has given back my freedom, my adventure and my happiness.

Getting a van has been the best thing I've ever done as I can now just pack a bag and go wherever I want. I believe this will also reduce my carbon footprint as I am less inclined to travel abroad every weekend. Visiting the Hebrides made me realise just how lucky we are to have the beautiful scenery in the UK. I never knew how beautiful Scotland was until I explored in my van.

Aires

Aires if the common name for *aires de camping car* (motorhome areas). This is camping in designated spaces and particularly applies if you're camping in Europe. The rules of *aires de camping* dictate that you must not spread out beyond your camper, which means that you can't put out tables, chairs and hammocks. That requires you to be self-contained. If you carry a lot of kit, camping on aires can be difficult, as everything needs to be packed away, even in night mode. With a family of four in a small camper, things can get tight. You'd like:

* to be self-contained
* a toilet
* ability to hook up
* to stay for 24–48 hours max.

WHAT YOU NEED IS: again, lots of campers are perfect for aire camping, although day vans might struggle if they rely on the extra space from a pup tent or awning to camp.

Passion/Britstop camping

Passion sites are camping spots in France available to self-contained motorhomes and campers at places like vineyards, farms, auberges and restaurants. As for aire camping, you need to be self-contained, as many sites don't have toilets, taps or electricity.

Britstops are the same deal but in the UK, and are largely pubs and farm shops. You'd like:

- the site to be free, but happy to spend on a meal or goods
- to be self-contained.

WHAT YOU NEED IS: big motorhomes are fine for these sorts of stops but you need to be self-contained and containable. If you can camp without toilets, water or electricity, then you'll love Passion sites and Britstops.

Wild camping

This is camping off-grid, out there, away from it all. This is where the camper van comes into its own, for my money. You've got everything you really need – heat, light, comfort – so there's no need for any of the extra glampy comforts like electricity or showers. Motorhomers who don't mind living without the hook-up are best placed to enjoy comforts in the wild – especially if it's Scotland, Ireland or somewhere that can get wet, wild, swarming with midges and generally uncomfortable in anything but a roomier vehicle. If there's no loo, you might have to take a spade or a Porta Potti. You'd like:

- to take everything you need (cooking gear, a Porta Potti, a spade)
- the ability to have a fire (fire pit/BBQ)
- a solar shower.

WHAT YOU NEED IS: a small van for getting down little lanes, plus water, solar and a Porta Potti so you don't have to despoil the countryside. A big van with everything on board. A motorhome with big enough water and waste tanks to live off-grid for a few days without filling up and solar panels for heating and energy.

Question 6 — WHAT DO YOU NEED UP TOP?

One of the first decisions you're going to face when you consider buying a camper is what sort of top it's got – or what sort of top you are going to need. There are various options and each has its advantages and its drawbacks.

Tin tops

This is a standard (low) metal roof on any van or camper. In the case of a VW, it'll be a van that still has its original roof. In the UK, classic VWs with tin tops are relatively rare, as many vans have had their roofs chopped off to make more room for a high top or a pop top. However, in later models, such as T25s (T3) T4s and T5s, the tin top is more common, simply because there are more base vans around than converted campers. It's the same for other types of vans, such as transits (UK) and modern transporter-style vans, although many manufacturers now offer high top options.

WHO WANTS A TIN TOP?

Tin top campers are great for couples, or singles and families who are happy to camp using a pup tent for kids or extra guests. In smaller vans, having a tin top usually means just one double bed in the back. Tin tops are also useful for people who want to camp stealthily in a vehicle that looks more like a work van than a camper.

WHAT'S SO GOOD ABOUT A TIN TOP?

The advantage of having a tin top is that it won't leak! They are more streamlined (and arguably more fuel efficient) and retain the original lines. However, they make standing up impossible, so you'll need to do everything sitting down, cooking included.

High tops

Small campers often have high roofs fitted, whereas larger vans are, more often than not, high roofed by default. Sprinters and Crafters are mostly made in high roof versions. High roofs on smaller vans are either added on after manufacture by camper conversion companies or are specified at the factory.

WHO WANTS A HIGH TOP?

High tops on smaller vans have one major advantage over other conversions or vans: they allow you to stand up. It might not seem a significant addition but it can make a huge difference, especially when it comes to cooking.

High top VW T25

High tops often have enough space in the roof for a secondary bed or 'upstairs' for small children or small adults, instantly turning your two berth into a four berth.

It is possible to convert standard tin top vans to high tops.

WHAT'S SO GOOD ABOUT A HIGH TOP?

Apart from the 'standing up' business, the high top roof offers more space for storage, meaning you can stow bedding, clothes, kit and all the stuff you like to carry in the roof – leaving the 'downstairs' tidy – as you drive.

WHY DON'T WE ALL DRIVE HIGH TOPS?

High tops can be tricky in side winds. They also produce more wind resistance than more aerodynamic shapes, which can affect speed and fuel consumption.

They can be a problem at some beauty spots, supermarkets, car parks and places where there are height restrictions. A standard smaller van with a pop top is likely to stand around 2m tall and will fit under most height barriers.

Pop tops

The pop top is the way many camper van builders add extra sleeping space without compromising the lines too much. The original roof is cut out and replaced with a fibreglass one that either pops up on struts or hinges at one side. This then forms a roof tent with bellows made from cloth or vinyl and, in some cases, solid panels.

WHO WANTS A POP TOP?

Pop tops and side elevating roofs are fantastic for families, as they double the sleeping capacity of an ordinary pop top van, adding options of either a double up top or bunks.

They also offer standing room for cooking and living for those who want extra space when they park up.

WHAT'S SO GOOD ABOUT A POP TOP?

Pop tops are great for adding space without adding height. They alter the profile of the van, but not as significantly as a high top does. Pop tops can also be retrofitted to most vans, which makes them perfect for the home conversion market. Pop tops also add to the value of a converted van.

WHY WOULDN'T YOU WANT A POP TOP?

The pop top, while creating space, only creates space when parked up and top popped. So they are great for turning a standard day van or tin top into a four berth camper van but useless if you want to increase the luggage carrying capacity of your van.

Pop tops won't always carry roof racks (although many will), so it's worth considering this if you intend to carry boards, bikes, top boxes or any of that stuff.

The transition between night mode, camping mode and drive mode can sometimes be a big hassle, especially if you travel with lots of kit and don't have extra space such as an awning or pup tents.

LARGE CONVERSIONS AND THE POP TOP

In the last 10 years, converters of big vans have come around to the idea of adding pop tops on big vehicles. It is, amazingly, one of the biggest advances in big van technology in recent years. Putting a pop top on a bigger van might not seem like rocket science, but it makes a huge difference to a family that wants a big-but-not-too-big van, needs to sleep four and requires a loo and shower. It's an excellent compromise, but remember that the pop top sides are canvas and allow heat to escape. They're also not particularly stealthy.

Day vans versus night vans

When is a camper van not a camper van? Day vans are vans that are used primarily for daytime activities – commuting, playing, transporting the kids around – but that also have sleeping and camping capabilities. So basically, it's a camper van without the kitchen, loo or shower.

This makes the van much more useful on a day-to-day basis, and with much more space than a standard camper, since less room is taken up with cupboards, sinks, storage etc. For those who want to camp occasionally but also need a vehicle that's practical for doing other things, it's a really useful option.

Some companies make removable camping pods containing a sink, cooker, fridge etc. so that there is space left in the van when you have pitched your tent. It means you have your own little portable camp kitchen that you can remove at any time.

Personally, I think day vans are the way to go if you camp and play on short hops and don't feel the need for lots of cupboard space or fancy gadgets.

Lindsay Freeth

'Being able to go on adventures and explore our amazing countryside at the weekends has been incredible for our physical and mental health.'

Our van, the Salty Dog (or 'Dogger' to its friends), is tiny but it gives us huge possibilities. We can explore anywhere we like, as near or far as we like, whenever we like. We got it in October 2018 and did work to insulate it, and built a bed and storage in it over the winter so we were ready to start exploring in Spring 2019. We knew we wanted/needed space inside for the stand-up paddle boards, a bed big enough for us both, and storage for fire stuff, wetsuits and clothes.

Being able to go on adventures and explore our amazing countryside at the weekends has been incredible for our physical and mental health. Being a summer beach bum, I find winter mentally really hard, but the winter of 2019 was made so much easier just by being able to escape in the van from the normality of the bleak English months. It gave us a sense of freedom and kept us in touch with nature and the elements. Although it was still sometimes cold and wet outside on our travels, it felt like a special holiday every time we went away.

Exploring is now a necessity in our lives and we are always planning our next adventure! Van life rocks, and Dogger just goes to show you don't need a big van and a big budget to enjoy van life and the benefits it brings.

Carrying gear/boards/kayaks/toys

WHY YOUR TOYS SHOULD DETERMINE HOW YOUR CAMPER ROLLS

If you're like me, and you love outdoor adventures, you'll need to consider toys and how you'll carry them when choosing your vehicle. In fact, I would say it is one of the most important factors in your decision, especially if you're planning on transporting bikes, boards and/or kayaks.

Bike racks

There are lots of bike racks on the market and there are a few ways of carrying them. Tow bar mounted racks can often carry four full-sized bikes, and an awful lot more weight, as you now find with ebikes – while rear mounted racks depend on the shape of the vehicle. Motorhome racks that bolt on to the rear panel of the van itself can often carry more weight than those that attach to the rear doors of a large van. In fact, often, large van racks are designed to carry just two bikes. Roof mounted racks also depend on the ability to carry a roof rack or to get access to the roof (on bigger vans).

If you are a family of four and want to travel with all your bikes, bear in mind that lots of racks, especially for older vans, only carry a couple of bikes. This is down to the fact that the racks sit on the rear tailgate so can't carry too much weight. Later models have fewer issues and can carry more weight.

Quick tips

If you want to open the rear doors of a van but need a bike rack then beware of the following:

● Door mounted racks can foul the sides of the van when open. Also, they may not be able to take the weight of ebikes.

● Towbar mounted bike racks may foul the rear doors of a van, so making them difficult to open unless the rack is removed.

● A device called a Van-Swing will enable you to move the bike rack out of the way and open rear doors. Very useful.

If a rear mounted carrier isn't an option then consider a tow bar mounted version. You'll need a tow bar for this, obviously, which is another consideration, as most vehicles don't come fitted as standard with them. They can also get in the way of rear barn doors unless you have a device to swing the bikes out of the way. That said, a tow bar offers versatility. You could tow a trailer to carry all your gear, or even a small car.

Roof mounting your bikes

This is pretty simple – if you can fit roof bars to your van. But some pop tops won't take roof bars unless you drill them because the pop top profile restricts access to the guttering. Also, consider the weight of the bikes. And don't forget about them when you go under low bridges.

Surf boards/kayaks/SUPs/windsurfers

Carrying surfboards is pretty straightforward if you can fit roof bars on your camper. The only potential issue is security, in which case you can invest in lockable straps or make sure your boards are locked away in the van when you aren't with it.

Westfalia supplies special brackets to fit roof bars on its pop tops, while products like Camper Van Culture's Load Rings allow you to strap boards down to pop tops without fitting specific roof bars.

If you're considering a high top then you may need to think about mounting J bars on the side of your roof to carry boards. Some of these sit on the gutter and fix to the roof itself, while others have to be adapted to bolt on to the roof itself. It's well worth doing your research before you buy any kit.

ROOF MOUNTING ON LARGE MOTORHOMES AND CAMPERS

Mounting gear on the roof gets harder the taller the vehicle and often means the addition of ladders. Telescopic ladders store away easily, making storing gear on the roof more secure. However, a permanent ladder means finding a way of securing your load or stopping people from climbing the ladder.

Another downside of having stuff on the roof is the height. Make sure you know what height you reach fully loaded. Low bridges may be a challenge. It may also mean that smaller vans can't get into car parks if there are height barriers.

For solo travellers, side loading roof bars (Thule make them) can be invaluable for kayaks and heavy boards. They enable you to load a kayak on to the rack and then load the rack on to the top of the van.

Awnings and sunshades

As I am writing this, a storm is blowing everything away outside, so it seems an inappropriate time to talk about awnings! Bad weather can cause all sorts of problems when it comes to awnings and sunshades, so now's the time to get clued up...

There are three types of awning:

- drive-away tent awnings, which add another room to your van
- fixed awnings that are permanently fixed to the van and provide shelter from the elements
- sunshades and tarpaulins, which are not fixed to the van but to the guttering or awning rail.

DRIVE-AWAY TENT AWNINGS

These awnings attach to your van, so that you walk out of the sliding door (or door) and into them, thus adding an extra room. You can drive away from them, leaving them up like a tent, or they can be fixed to the van (more about that in a moment). Drive-away awnings are useful for the family that doesn't have enough beds or sitting space in the van itself and can effectively double the living space of your van, since you can set up extra beds, table and chairs in them. As such, they are used mostly by those driving smaller vans.

Drive-away awnings come in various guises, with the most recent innovation being the SheltaPod (**www.sheltapod.com**), an easy-to-assemble awning that came into being thanks to a Kickstarter campaign and that actually looks very cool! (See more info below.)

AirBeam awnings are popular too, but tend to be heavy and take up a lot of space, even though they are doddle to put up. Some, like Vango's AirBeam Rhone, are huge and can cost upwards of £1,200.

Standard awnings with poles can attach to the side door or, in some cases, the rear doors. They are generally cheaper than AirBeams and don't get punctures. Expect to pay from about £250 to £800. They attach either with a pole that sits in the gutter (and gets clamped into place) or with some kind of permanently fixed rail that the awning slides into (although this can be a bit fiddly). Others rely on straps that go over the van (not great for pop tops).

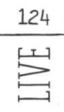

ERECTING A DRIVE-AWAY TENT AWNING

- In windy weather, make sure you peg out your guy ropes properly. Allowing an awning to blow away may cause damage to the van.
- Erect the awning with the van in place and level first, but make sure you leave enough space so that you can drive the van away.
- Don't put guy ropes in the way of the wheels if you intend to drive the van away.
- An awning skirt, which attaches to the side of the van between the wheels, can help stop draughts coming under the van and into the awning (see below).
- Be careful when you open the sliding door as it can foul an awning and rip it.
- Accurate recoupling is required to avoid slack joins and pools of water gathering.

FIXED AWNINGS

These kinds of awnings are the roll-out type and are attached to the van permanently. As such, they require a little extra care when in use. They can be erected with a combination of sides and extra sections to create an extra room for the van, but that does mean you won't be able to go anywhere in a hurry.

It may be interesting to note that the DVLA now requires the presence of an awning bar for a home conversion to be considered a motor caravan.

Also, it is really important to properly peg out your awning. When fully unfurled, they have a huge surface area. Allowing an awning to flap in the wind can cause damage to it and the van, which could ruin your trip. Most awnings come with some kind of strapping to use as an extra insurance policy.

ERECTING A FIXED AWNING

- If you're using your awning to shelter from rain, make sure one leg is lower than the other. That way, rain will run off to the lower end and won't gather in pools.
- If possible, put your back to the wind.
- Even if it's not very windy, peg out the legs to stop them from lifting.
- If it is windy, use straps to peg out the awning in addition to pegging the legs.
- If it gets really windy, wind it in!
- If you cannot put pegs into the ground (because it's hardstanding), strap the awning to the wheels of the van using ratchet straps.
- If you're using the awning as a sunshade, make sure you face your van the right way to get the benefit. By positioning your sliding door (and sunshade, if on that side) to the north you'll get the most shade. Face east and you'll get the most shade in the evening; west, the most in the morning. Facing south will give you the least shade.

Ashley

'I absolutely love my little van (named Little Vee) and so does everyone that sees it.'

My uncle Keith converted a van for my aunty, which I thought was just the coolest thing ever. When he told me it didn't even cost him £1,000 to do I thought it was something I wanted to do too. I'm 5ft 3in and have a teacup Yorkie, so I thought I'd go for a little van... I bought a Suzuki Carry, which had spent it's previous life delivering beer to a local pub. I made my dad get in the back and lay down in it when I went to view it, to check that more average-sized people would be able to sleep in it if needs be.

My plan was to build the van with help from my uncle. Unfortunately he wasn't very well and passed away before I really had the chance to get building. So, for the first two summers I just had a sofa bed and some boxes in the back. Last winter I decided it was time for me to crack on and make my van how I wanted it to be. So, I spent many an hour in the freezing cold garage getting it ready for the spring.

I absolutely love my little van (named Little Vee) and so does everyone that sees it. It's not the most professionally built camper in the world but I did it by myself and it enables me to go and do my thing whenever I want to.

Awning skirts

One really annoying thing about awnings is that wind blows under the van and into the awning, making the awning billow and everyone cold. The way to avoid this is to use an awning skirt that connects between the two wheels of the van and blocks out any moving air, although a surfboard will work just as well!

Toilet and shower tents

Aka the latrine. These are pretty useful if you have a Porta Potti and don't want it in the van while you sleep. Handily small and 'packawayable' for midnight visits, when the loo block is just a stroll too far away, or for when you're out in the wilds. They even come in pop-up form so you can wrestle them away when you've done your business. Now that's glamping.

SUNSHADES AND TARPAULINS

These are a super cheap option and can be very versatile, allowing, in some cases, any configuration of shade or shelter. Sunshades attach to the van either through a fixed awning rail or a rail that goes in the gutter and clamps to it. It's possible to make your own or use something like Olpro's retro sunshade (**www.olproshop.com**).

You can also use batwing tarps to create some kind of shelter, provided you have a way of connecting them securely to the van. They're useful for hot days or showers, and pack down small and neat so are easy to carry.

OTHER SHELTERS

Pup tents and event shelters

Pup tents are little tents that people take with them to stash gear, teenagers and snoring partners. They can be useful if you have kids who want privacy or if you have brought so much gear that you want to leave some of it behind when you go out for the day.

The same goes for an event shelter, with the added advantage that you can hang out underneath it, too, when it rains. If you have space in your van then it can be a useful addition if you regularly suffer from overpacking syndrome.

The SheltaPod

This is an extra room-cum-event shelter type of tent that can be used both as an event shelter and as an extra bedroom. Unlike most event shelters it can also be fitted with an inner tent to make a double skinned bedroom. Handy!

Other considerations when buying

Everyone has different needs and experiences, which means that the perfect van doesn't really exist. One size does not fit all and compromise is key. Some people can't live without a shower room while for others it is way down the list and other considerations are more important.

There are always things to think about, whether you're buying brand new, off the peg or second hand. Some might be relevant to you, others might not.

VENTILATION

If you're planning on travelling to hot places, ventilation is important so that you allow a through-draft on very hot days and nights. Windows that open wide and roof lights can be a real boon, but may affect the look of the exterior. Leaving the slider open can be a blessing on very hot nights, but only if used with a screen or net if there are insects.

Air-con is an option on lots of conversions and can be retrofitted.

HEAT RETENTION

If you're planning on travelling to cold places then it may be worth looking at double glazing for your windows. These offer more insulation than single-glazed windows, although insulated blackout blinds also help to retain heat.

SOLAR PANELS POSITION

If you carry boards, kayaks or roof boxes then check you can get them into a position on the roof rack so that they won't throw shade over your solar panels – it will make the panels much less effective.

ROOF RACK POSITION

Ensure you can open vents when boards, roof boxes or kayaks are on the roof.

FANS IN THE BATHROOM

Not only useful for extracting nasty niffs but also for covering up noises! Saves having to whistle.

TOILET EXTRACTORS

You can buy kits that vent smells from the chemical toilet to the outside of the van. Can be useful if it's hot! However, good, regular emptying and cleaning and proper (eco) chemical liquid will take care of a lot of those issues.

STORAGE

Garages can be extremely useful if you need to carry lots of kit (table and chairs, BBQs etc.), but they can reduce the living area to a dinette up front. Watch out for payload and ensure that you can carry the extra without falling foul of the law. The more space you have, the more payload you need.

COLD WEATHER

If you intend to use the van in the winter then look at getting a 'cold weather pack', which some dealers and manufacturers will provide. This usually consists of lagging for all the pipes and tanks underneath the van – you can do this yourself if need be. Some vans have water tanks inside the garage so that freezing water tanks aren't an issue.

Quick tip

Fold up sheets and duvets when you remove them in the morning so they are easy to put back on at night. This will save a lot of grief.

CONSTANT REASSESSMENT

Whenever I travel I always have a mini debrief on my return about what was useful and what was just using up space. This can be as simple as sorting clothes into piles of 'what I wore' and 'what I didn't wear' or even going through the whole van for things that you could lose if you need to free up space. Constant reassessment allows you to develop and get the best out of your van.

ALLOW SPACE FOR LAUNDRY

When you pack, ensure that you have space for laundry as you go through your clean stuff. Eventually, you'll find you have plenty of cupboard space but little left for dirty clothes – at which point it's time to go to the launderette.

CARRYING EBIKES

Standard bike racks, which hang off the rear doors of most vans, can take the weight of standard bikes but not usually ebikes. Bike racks that attach to a tow bar will. If you intend on travelling with ebikes, consider the cost of installing a tow bar (or make sure the van has one) and buying a tow bar bike rack (good news – they can also be used on the car).

Quick tip

Tow bar bike racks can impede access to the rear doors. Products like the Memo Van-Swing (pictured above) allow you to swing the bikes away from the vehicle, so allowing access to the rear doors.

BUYING BESPOKE

If you're going to a converter with a van or asking a converter to source one for you, you need to go through a number of stages to get to your finished vehicle. All converters follow more or less the same process, whether you buy an off the peg layout or have one made especially for you. It all takes time and everything has to happen in a certain order so that the process is as efficient as possible – so be prepared, because your bespoke conversion won't happen overnight.

If you're going to a dealer and ordering a motorhome off the peg you may still find there are choices to make, such as speccing the vehicle, colour schemes and winter packs.

The bespoke journey

Quick tip

Set your costs and agree a budget with the converter.

STAGE 1 YOU CHOOSE

Decide what kind of van you want. What sort of layout will suit? How many berths and driving seats will you need?

STAGE 2 FIND A CONVERTER

A really important decision. Finding someone local isn't always the right thing to do. Instead, focus on finding a converter who likes working on the type of vehicle you're buying, is affordable and who has a good reputation.

STAGE 3 BOOK IT

Any good converter is going to be working to long
lead times, so be prepared to wait. Talk to them,
decide on what you want (roughly), set a budget
and agree a timeline.

Quick tip

Read trade
magazines, talk to
owners, visit shows.
This isn't a decision
to be made
lightly.

STAGE 4 CHOOSE YOUR SPEC

Do you want heating? A bathroom? Cupboards?
A microwave? Lithium-ion batteries and induction heating?
Gas heating? What kind of layout and bed arrangement? What kind
of fridge? Captain seats? Skylights? Pop top?

STAGE 5 CHOOSE YOUR FINISHES

This is where you get down to the tiny details. Choose your head and
wall lining colour, seat finishes, the colour of your units and trim, plus
upholstery. If you're worried about resale, choose finishes you think
other people will like, usually something that's fairly neutral. Just
beware of falling into the beige trap.

STAGE 6 SOURCE AND STRIP THE BASE VEHICLE

Whether new or used, you vehicle needs to be stripped and prepped.
Any lining, floors or bulkheads (if they exist) need to be removed
before the basics can happen.

135

LIVE

STAGE 7 UPGRADE MECHANICAL

In the case of a classic camper van, you may need to undertake a lot of work to get your donor vehicle up to scratch. This could include rust treatment, welding, upgrading running gear or even going as far as a bare metal respray.

STAGE 8 PAINT

If the base vehicle isn't the right colour or your bumpers aren't colour coded, for example, it'll need to go to the paint shop to be repainted to your spec.

STAGE 9 MEASURE OUT THE LAYOUT

The converter will measure out where your units and services are being positioned. This involves either a lot of planning or following a pre-made template, and dictates what has to happen in the next stage.

STAGE 10 WINDOWS, OUTLETS AND ROOF

This is the bit where it gets worse before it gets better. Once the converter has worked out where everything has to go they'll need to cut holes in your precious van for the windows, skylights, pop top, fridge and heating vents,

toilet cassette and anything else you might need in the finished van. They'll do this with a jigsaw, and usually to a pre-formed template. Expect sparks.

STAGE 11 CAMPING ELECTRICS AND PLUMBING

Your camping electrics run on a separate circuit to your vehicle electrics and include lighting, power to the fridge, hob, interior and exterior lights, solar, 240V electric hook-up and leisure battery. It also includes a battery charger and split relay to charge the leisure battery from mains and the main vehicle battery when driving. The wiring looms go in before any of the interior fitting.

Similarly, the plumbing may go in at this stage, or at least a first fix including tanks, waste, filling and emptying points, and pipework to showers and sinks.

STAGE 12 INSULATION/LINING/FLOOR

Once the electrical looms are in, the van can be insulated inside the panels and lined with carpet liner or your choice of trim on all other surfaces, depending on the model and finish. The ply floor then goes in to provide a level surface from which to build.

STAGE 13 FURNITURE AND BEDS

Depending on your converter, the furniture carcases may be pre-built outside the van from panels that have been pre-cut by a CNC cutter to a specific van template. If they are bespoke, they may be built in situ and completely hand-built.

For smaller vans, cookers, water heaters and all accessories may be included in this build, in which case the entire unit can be lifted into place, fixed and connected.

STAGE 14 UPHOLSTERY

Seat and bed bases are recovered ready for fitting. Cushions that are making up the bed are cut and covered.

STAGE 15 FINAL FIXES

Furniture/drawers, cupboards doors, sinks, cookers fridges go in, facilities are connected, plumbing is connected.

STAGE 16 SEATS AND ROCK AND ROLL BEDS

Beds and captain seats are fixed with new upholstery, if necessary.

STAGE 17 FINAL EXTRAS QC AND FINAL POLISH

Any additional mechanical accessories (alloys, bespoke steering wheels etc.) are fitted, everything is tested to make sure it works and is safe to use, and cleaned ready for the customer. If necessary, gas and electric fittings are certified.

STAGE 18 YOU DRIVE AWAY

And the dream comes true. See you on the road!

Home conversions and re-registering a motorhome

If your camper van is home-converted then you may need to consider having it reclassified by DVLA as a motor caravan rather than its original vehicle type. There are a few reasons for this. First, it may affect your insurance, potentially allowing you to go to specialist insurers for cheaper quotes. Second, it will affect the speed at which your vehicle is permitted to travel on some roads (see pages 376–378). It may also affect the status of your MOT and the type of test you are required to have. Finally, it may affect you if the vehicle is over 3500 GVW because of rules about driver hours and the fitting of tachographs on vehicles that are still classed as goods vehicles.

THE RULES ON RE-REGISTERING A VEHICLE AS A MOTOR CARAVAN

You can reclassify your vehicle only if it currently falls into the following types on the V5C log book: ambulance, box van, goods, insulated van, light goods, light van, livestock carrier, Luton van, minibus, MPV (multi-purpose vehicle), panel van, specially fitted van, special mobile unit, van with side windows. If it's none of the above then the DVLA will not consider reclassifying it.

The reclassification must reflect how the vehicle appears in traffic. This means that 'stealth' campers (that look like standard vans) will not be reclassified.

THE HOOPS TO JUMP THROUGH TO RE-REGISTER

External features

The DVLA expects your vehicle to have at least some of the following to be reclassified:

- two or more windows on at least one side of the main body (not including windows on the driver or passenger doors) to provide a reasonable amount of daylight into the living accommodation
- a separate door that provides access to the living accommodation of the vehicle (excluding the driver and passenger doors)
- motor caravan-style graphics on both sides of the vehicle
- an awning bar attached to either side of the vehicle
- a high top roof (this does not include a pop top elevating roof).

NOTE: the DVLA requires photographic evidence of the completed conversion.

Internal features

The motor caravan classification defines a vehicle as being constructed to include living accommodation that contains at least the following internal equipment that is rigidly fixed to the living compartment, although the table top may be removed.

Seats and table (one example for both), which must have the following features:

- They must be an integral part of the vehicle living accommodation area, mounted independently of other items.
- A table mounting arrangement shall be secured as a permanent feature, although the table top may be detachable.
- Permanently secured seating must be fixed to the floor or side wall and available for use at the table.

Sleeping accommodation must be as follows:

- It must be an integral part of the vehicle living accommodation area.
- It can be either beds, or beds converted from seats.
- It must be secured as a permanent feature, either with the base structure of the vehicle floor or to the side wall, unless the sleeping accommodation is provided over the driver's cab compartment.

Damian & Nikki Maginn

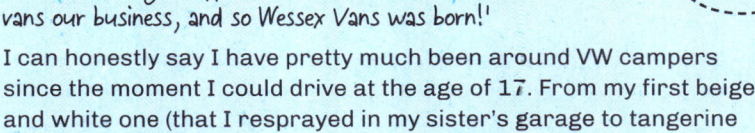

'We decided to get off the hamster wheel and make vans our business, and so Wessex Vans was born!'

I can honestly say I have pretty much been around VW campers since the moment I could drive at the age of 17. From my first beige and white one (that I resprayed in my sister's garage to tangerine and white) to the T6.1s we build at Wessex Vans today.

As an avid kite surfer and mountain biker, with a young family of twins to boot, I always needed space to get my kit and family (in that order) to wherever I was going. In 2011, myself and my friend, and now business partner, invested in a van each and outside of our day job, we spent time sprucing them up to our taste, lining and insulating them ourselves, adding alloys etc. They received a lot of attention within the water sport scene down at Poole Harbour and so we decided to sell them and do another! We sold 12 in a year privately between us and that was when we decided to get off the hamster wheel and make vans our business, and so Wessex Vans was born!

Little did we know nearly 10 years on we would have three units, 13 staff and be producing 25 vans a month. A wonderful ongoing journey of happy customers, many of whom have become friends. It has been a privilege to grow a lifestyle business that builds people's dreams for them to enjoy and make memories in. If Covid has taught me anything, making memories with the ones you care about is what matters most.

Cooking facilities must have the following:

- The conversion must have a minimum of a single ring cooking facility or microwave, which shall be secured directly to the vehicle floor or side wall as a permanent feature.
- The fuel reservoir must be secured in a storage cupboard or the reservoir secured to the vehicle structure.
- If the cooking facility is fuelled by gas having a remote fuel supply then the fuel supply pipe must be permanently secured to the vehicle structure.

Storage facilities must include the following:

- They can be a cupboard or a locker.
- They must form an integral part of the vehicle living accommodation, mounted independently of other items, unless incorporated below the seat, sleeping accommodation or cooker.
- They must be secured permanently to the vehicle floor or side wall, except when the storage facility is situated over the driver's cab compartment.

WHAT YOU NEED TO DO TO APPLY FOR A CHANGE OF CLASSIFICATION

You must write to the DVLA telling it what you require and providing evidence of the changes, including:

- A completed motor caravan conversion checklist.
- A V5C showing one of the applicable body types as above.
- Interior photos of each one of the required features with the bed and table in the use position – the photos must show that there are two or more windows providing daylight into the main living accommodation on at least one side of the main body.
- Exterior photos from the front, both sides and rear with the registration plates clearly visible.
- A photo showing the vehicle identification number (VIN) or the chassis number stamped on the plate attached to the original chassis or vehicle bodyshell.

You can find more information at **www.gov.uk/government/publications/registering-a-diy-caravan/converting-a-vehicle-into-a-motorhome**.

RENT BEFORE YOU BUY

This is the sagest piece of advice I am ever going to give you if you're looking to buy a camper van: for some, the reality of life in a tin box doesn't live up to the hype. And, let's face it, there has been a lot of hype. We've had 60 years of hype, as one generation after another finds its freedom at the wheel of a camper van. But it's not for everybody.

I hear stories from camper rental companies that, on occasion, campers are brought back before the due date by customers with tired eyes and mournful faces, who drop the keys back on the rental desk with a sigh, claiming it just wasn't for them.

It happens. Some people want more than what the camper van can offer. If you've known indoor plumbing, deeply filled hotel baths, pools, waiters and views overlooking the sea you might be a little disappointed with your camper and campsite. It's understandable.

When the rain lashes down and the neighbours are being bores, it can be tough living in a VW. I really hope it isn't like that for you because I believe that the good times are out there. It's just that there are times when it's hard to see through the mist and drizzle.

But hey, better to find out when you're just a few hundred quid down than when you've just handed over your life savings.

What to do then? Do you turn around and ask for your money back? By that time it's too late and you've got that sinking feeling that maybe, just maybe it isn't going to go well. I've had that. I get it every time I buy a camper. Yes, so things will go wrong, whatever you drive. Just make sure you're fit to cope.

So, my advice? Rent a van for a week, a weekend, a night. It really doesn't matter. Once you've parked up, got the kettle on and settled down for the night, you'll know. If, after a week you still love it, start saving for your own van.

Renting a camper

HOW TO AVOID A RENTAL CAMPER VAN DISASTER

- Book early – camper companies are busy!
- Choose wisely. Rent with a company that is well established, and have a back-up plan if things go wrong.
- Don't get overexcited. The more excited you are, the bigger the crash, if it comes. Keep steady. Hold your nerve. Enjoy the moment. Don't go potty.
- Go with a rental company that can provide you with a back-up vehicle if things go wrong. Ask questions. Make sure they'll look after you properly. Do they have roadside assistance? What happens if you break down?
- Get quotes from several companies. Don't go for the cheapest quote (as with everything in life).
- Do not overpack. Camper vans are small, so take the least you think you can get away with. I hear that lots of customers take everything – and I mean everything – when they rent a camper for the first time. This will only end in misery as you'll have to move everything each time you want to go to bed or make a brew. Take less, enjoy more.
- Make sure the rental has a bike rack or roof racks to carry bikes, boards and any other toys. Double-check.
- When the sun shines, make hay. By this I mean stop and take a few minute to smell the coffee. Park up. Put your feet up. Read a book. Enjoy the moment.
- Never underestimate the power of a good brew in a tense situation. Get the kettle on.
- Kick back and slack. Stop haring around. You won't hit 60mph if you try, so don't try. Learn to live at the pace of the van, not at the pace you're used to. Nothing wrong with underachieving. Achieve nothing.
- Make a plan and stick to it – but don't be overambitious. The moment you stray from your planned path is the moment things begin to go wrong. The freedom of the open road is all very well, but a little planning goes a long way. Go and see the stuff you've wanted to see for ages. Driving around looking for inspiration rarely lives up to expectation.

- Book into a really good campsite. Don't settle for anything less than something special. Disappointing campsites can kill your expectations stone dead. If the weather is looking iffy, book into a campsite with a bar, indoor pool, sheltered BBQ area or restaurant.
- If other people are the issue, find a good wild spot. Go somewhere you know, where it's certain you'll have a good time.

RENTAL COMPANIES

There are plenty of companies around, with new outfits springing up all the time. You only have to do a quick search on Google to realise that. As such, companies come and go, while some are better than others.

If you don't have a recommendation then it may pay to compare deals on aggregation sites or search sites where you can hire vehicles from owners directly. Start with the following:

www.quirkycampers.com
www.goboony.co.uk
www.camplify.co.uk
www.camptoo.co.uk

ACCESSIBLE CAMPERVANNING

If you have a disability or special needs there is no reason you shouldn't enjoy motorhoming just as much as the next person. In fact, compared with traditional holidays and travel, I would humbly suggest that an adapted camper van or motorhome might make all the difference. Why? One of the main reasons is because these vehicles can be modified to suit your exact needs. And because you can take the modifications with you (unlike any modifications you have at home), you've always got whatever you need while you're on the road: your perfect, built-for-you escape pod!

When you live with a disability, one of the most common difficulties with travelling is finding accommodation to suit your needs. It can sometimes feel like a mission to secure the right place to stay, in your desired location, within your price range AND for it to be suitable for your unique needs. That's where the adapted motorhome comes in.

'When I had my caravan made wheelchair accessible and modified to my own specifications it completely changed my views towards travel,'

says Karla Baker, a friend of mine I met through the Caravan and Motorhome Club. 'There's no longer any trepidation because I feel safe in the knowledge that wherever we go I'll have my own home-on-wheels with me, and it'll be as accessible as we've made it! This has given me the confidence to travel further afield, even caravanning off-grid on a white sandy beach in the Outer Hebrides.'

Fantastic, huh?

Is it right for you?

Karla and Stephen recommend hiring an accessible motorhome before committing to buying. Coachbuilt offers hire for people to try before they buy. It's a great way to see if it's the right lifestyle for you. You can get in touch at **www.coachbuiltgb.co.uk/motorhomes**.

Buying a van

Once you decide that it's the life for you (and why wouldn't it be?), there are a few things to think about when considering which camper to buy:

- Does it have the right sleeping arrangement?
- Is the toilet in an accessible position for you?
- Is there a sufficient amount of plug sockets, positioned where you can reach them?
- Is there enough storage for additional medical equipment?
- Does the fridge size suit you, especially if you need to take specialist food?
- Is there enough space in the places where you might need some help (the washroom, for example)?
- If you need the door widened for wheelchair access, is there anything on the inside that may make doing this more difficult/costly? A fuse box, heating supply or water pump, for example?
- Does it have the right heating system for you? If you suffer from asthma or other lung conditions you may prefer Alde wet central heating over dry blown air, for example.

Adapting a van

There are a number of companies that specialise in adapting motorhomes and camper vans in the UK, the best of which is Coachbuilt (see above). In general, manufacturers don't make their vehicles particularly wheelchair accessible off-the-shelf, but the majority of them are happy to fulfil accessibility requirements by honouring the warranty, even if extensive work is carried out. This means you can buy an off-the-shelf motorhome and have it adapted without affecting your rights.

THINGS TO CONSIDER

The main issues with living or touring in a camper for people with a disability are access, space, driving the vehicle and internal layout. A lot of these issues can be overcome with modifications, although funding them can be an issue in itself, as it's not a cheap thing to do. There is, however, an option for eligible people with disabilities to get the modifications tax-free, and to purchase the vehicle on finance.

Modifications you might expect to make include:

- grab rails
- wide-access door
- ceiling-track hoists
- hydraulic entry lift
- wet room
- layout adjustments
- slide-out systems
- profiling beds.

Karla & Stephen Baker

'Living with a disability can sometimes make you feel restricted, but I feel the total opposite when it comes to travelling. An adapted caravan, motorhome or camper van can give life spontaneity and freedom that a lot of people only dream of.'

READERS' DRIVES

Since getting a modified caravan back in 2017 our lives have completely changed. Gone are the days of searching for suitable places to stay, hoping that they'll actually somewhat resemble the accommodation described, because now we take our home-on-wheels with us on our travels. Having a wheelchair accessible caravan means that we no longer worry about compromising my needs and we're able to pack up and go wherever we want, whenever we want, safe in the knowledge that our accommodation will always be as accessible as we've made it. It's given us the freedom to visit the most incredible places across the UK and Europe and see some breathtaking sights, with one of our highlights being off-grid camping on a white sandy beach in the Outer Hebrides. Living with a disability can sometimes make you feel restricted, but I feel the total opposite when it comes to travelling. An adapted caravan, motorhome or camper van can give life spontaneity and freedom that a lot of people only dream of.

Insuring an adapted motorhome

When it comes to insuring a modified wheelchair accessible motorhome it is essential to make sure that the cost of conversion is included in the estimated value figure. You'll also need to make sure that the insurance provider is made fully aware that the camper van or caravan has been modified from its standard factory condition.

Accessible campsites

BEFORE YOU GO: WARNING!

• Make sure you have enough medical supplies (including spares) to last the trip.
• Check out the accessibility of the places you intend to visit or stay at overnight.
• If you're planning on going off-grid, make sure your battery/solar panel can run everything you need it to in a worst-case scenario.

In the same way that campsites vary in price, size and location, not all of them score highly on accessibility. But things are getting better. Although there is still work to be done, the majority of campsites are fairly accessible, and most site wardens are very friendly and willing to help make your stay as enjoyable as possible.

While some campsites still don't have wheelchair-friendly toilets or showers, there are many more installing them. Accessible washrooms usually have grab rails by the toilet and the shower, a lowered sink, an emergency pull-cord and a wet room-style shower with either a fold-down shower seat or a shower chair, and a moveable shower head.

A lot of campsites also enjoy level access to reception, an information room, laundry room and washing-up areas. Some may have lowered washing-up sinks that are ideal for wheelchair users.

Most campsites have accessibility information on their websites, but the Caravan and Motorhome Club (CAMC) and the Camping and Caravanning Club are both particularly good at this. The CAMC has a number of allocated 'disabled access' pitches on many of their club sites. These aren't much different to a standard pitch, but they're close to facilities.

There is no directory of accessible sites available but it is possible to search the CAMC website (**www.caravanclub.co.uk**) for accessibility options.

This section was compiled with the help of my friends Karla and Stephen Baker, who are known as Adventure Wheels to the motorhoming world.

BEFORE YOU GO

Make a list (or lists)

This book is full of lists. Each section has one. Why? Because they are useful and help to focus the mind on what is important. However, it is also vitally important to remember that lists have to be given an order of importance to make them useful. If you are the kind of person who cannot travel without stuff, put the stuff on your list. But do remember to debate the importance of any item before it goes on the list, not once it's in the van. By then, it will be too late and you'll risk travelling in an overcrowded van or else discarding the wrong stuff in a fit of overpacking frustration.

To this end, it may help to separate lists into lists, so that you can tell the difference between 'absolutely vital' and 'nice to have'.

Note: lists may also be location dependent, meaning, for example, that if you go somewhere without shops, restaurants or bars, you might need to pack additional food supplies.

LIST 1 — **Cannot travel without to avoid catastrophe.**
Bedding. Clothes. Prescriptions. Insurance. Money.

LIST 2 — **Can do without if pushed but better to have.**
Maps. Levelling chocks. Hoses.

LIST 3 — **Stuff you wish you had once or twice on a trip.**
Binoculars. Running shoes. Card games.

LIST 4 — **Luxury items that you only take when you know there's room.**
Smart clothes. Biscuits.

ONE MAN'S MEAT...

Please remember that my examples are based on how I feel about my stuff, and that I would consider a wetsuit and a surfboard above anything else if there was a chance I could score a few waves. You

might prefer to take guide books, binoculars, cameras – it'll be different for everyone, and even every time you go out. The point is to determine your priorities. If you'd die in a ditch without your Hawaiian shirt before you'd take a pillow, be my guest. It's your party.

Essential camping kit

What do you need? Ultimately it's up to you, but here are some very useful tips for things to pack.

- ☐ Clothes
- ☐ Wash gear (see pages 399–405)
- ☐ First aid kit (see pages 158–159)
- ☐ Sleeping gear (see pages 249–253)
- ☐ Food
- ☐ Cooking equipment (see pages 166–170)
- ☐ Van infrastructure (hoses, pegs, fridge, loo etc.)

Anything else is non-essential, although it might not seem like it. However, as someone who would consider a surfboard and wetsuit to be among the essentials, I understand that sometimes life demands more than just the basics of eating, sleeping and keeping warm.

ACCESSORIES: WILL THEY MAKE CAMPING EASIER?

Some bits of camping gear are, as we have established, essential – wet weather gear if you're off to the Hebrides, pegs for the awning, that kind of thing. However, even if they aren't absolutely essential, many items will help to make your life easier, provide a better night's sleep or make your space more effective.

There is a lot of camping gadgetry out there. It's like any other massive industry in the respect that there are always innovations for you to splurge on. Some of them are gimmicks, like musical pillows or blow-up gadget chairs, and it's up to you whether you consider them to be must-haves, and if you have the space to carry them.

The following list, inevitably, is short, because your van should provide you with basic cooking, washing, dining and sleeping facilities. Anything else is just being greedy.

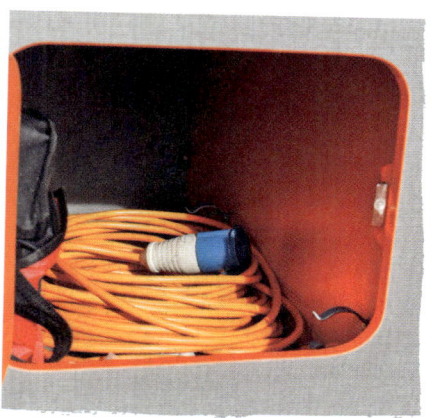

Electric hook-up cable

Electric hook-up – whether it's a 16 amp C-form cable or a complete hook-up kit – means you can connect to campsite electrics and enjoy mains lighting, recharging and running any on-board items such as fridges and cookers (some people have them) off the mains. If you're travelling to Europe, don't forget to take a two-pin European adaptor.

Levelling wedges

And possibly a spirit level. With a decent pair of levelling chocks you won't have to sleep on a slope. There's an art to getting it right and appreciation in a job well done. Your reward for using the spirit level? A great night's sleep.

Note: a glass of water on a flat surface will more than suffice in place of a spirit level.

Water hose

If you have an on-board water tank you'll need to be able to fill it up. A length of hose pays dividends, as many water points don't have them. Even if you have a portable water container it can be a pain to fill if you don't have at least a short length of hose.

Universal tap attachments

Carry a set of Hoselock adaptors as well as a universal attachment to fit your hose to any tap.

Short length of hose

For swilling out the portaloo. Avoid cross-contamination with your fresh water hose and store separately.

Water container

If you don't have an on-board water tank then you'll need to carry water in some way. Some jerry cans come with taps, while collapsible tanks pack away neatly.

Water storage

Many vans and motorhomes have a tank on board. If you don't, you'll have to carry one. Foldable and collapsible water containers are all very well but little replaces the aforementioned solid jerry can-type water container with a tap attachment. They won't puncture, are easy to carry and the tap makes it easy to pour.

Washing up bowl (or two)

Especially useful if you don't have a waste tank and your sink empties out under the van. Place your bowl under the outlet and empty it in the appropriate place to avoid despoiling the environment.

In winter, if there is a risk of below-zero temperatures, open your waste tank outlet and place the bowl underneath it. This ensures the water will freeze in the bowl, not the tank.

Head torch

Useful for cooking in the dark, walking to the pub, finding the loo or late-night hiking (aka being lost on a walk). Small enough to pack away tidily in the corner of a cupboard.

Map

Maps tell you everything you need to know about an area. They are wonderful sources of fascination and information. Map reading is both

a skill and a joy. I would urge everyone to learn how to navigate using maps.

Swiss Army knife

The only tool you'll ever need. Or so they say. Get a good one and you'll be able to do almost anything (almost). Don't bother with the one with two blades and a bottle opener. Go for the big one, with everything. It is a thing to cherish and use, and if it ever goes missing you'll likely be bereft. Know where it is at all times.

Slip-on shoes

While the fashion police might have something to say about them, slip-ons, such as Crocs, sandals or a pull-on Chelsea boot, can be a godsend to the camper. They're easy to pull on for those middle-of-the-night and early-morning wee visits, are light to carry and are comfortable to wear around the campsite.

In winter, wellies might be deemed essential for early morning walks through long and wet grass.

Decent weatherproof clothes

Don't scrimp on the waterproofs. And don't leave them at home. It's better to just leave them in the van so you'll always have them to hand if the heavens open while you're away in your van. Getting cold and wet is the first step to misery and is difficult to recover from. It can be dangerous, too.

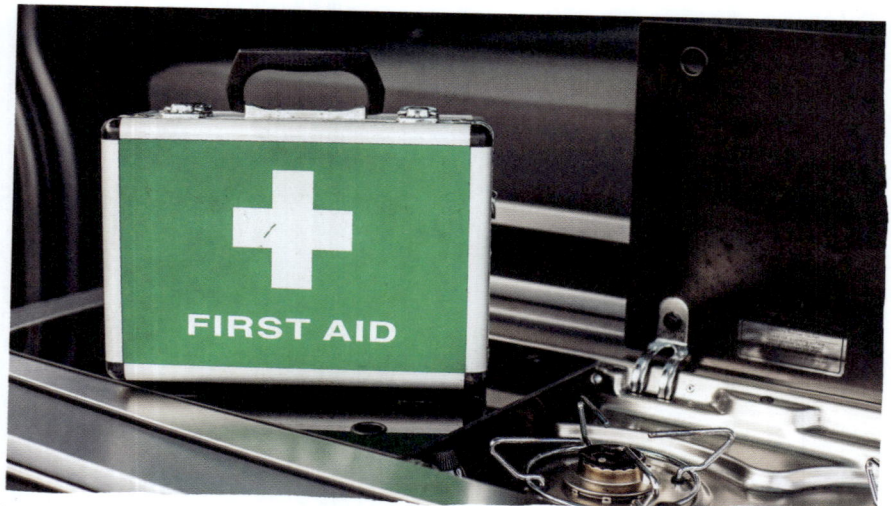

First aid kit

People hurt themselves camping. It's being out of the comfortable zone where nothing exciting ever happens that does it. We relax, let down our guard, enjoy a few glasses of prosecco and then trips, slips and falls catch us out. With any luck, the worst it'll be is a few cuts, stings and bruises. But it's still worth being ready to deal with any minor injuries – at least until you can get help.

A good first aid kit consists of the following:

- plasters
- scissors
- bandages
- gauze and lint for dressing wounds
- antiseptic cream for cuts and grazes
- antihistamine cream for bites and stings
- Sudocrem for cuts, sores and grazes
- Steri-Strips for larger cuts
- antibacterial hand wash
- insect repellent
- sun cream.

Loo paper and a folding spade

The spade is non-essential but can be useful if you get caught short. The loo paper, is, of course, vital to a happy trip. And there's nothing like walking across a muddy field with a roll of it early in the morning. Everyone knows where you're off to. No one minds.

Going wild? If you use a spade to bury your doings, make sure you do it at least 200m from any watercourses and NEVER use wet wipes (they won't break down).

An axe

If you need to cut kindling, chop logs or generally make any kind of fire, you're going to need an axe. I have a favourite, a light-weight double-edged billhook that's fantastic for making kindling, if a bit light for dropping trees.

PLEASE NOTE: Do not chop trees to make wood for your fire! Only ever burn deadwood, driftwood or logs you bring yourself.

Fire steel

Sometimes you lose your matches. Sometimes they get soggy. Sometimes you can't get a lighter to work. A fire steel is hard to lose, easy to use and very difficult to get wrong. I always keep one in my glove box.

EAT

ON-THE-ROAD EATS

Camping breaks life down into the essentials, and nothing more. You eat, sleep and play without distractions and interruptions, living simply, away from the vapid trappings of our everyday existence. No mortgage, no bills, no telly (for most of us), no shopping, no grooming regime, no crowds, no pressure, no crap.

It's the very best opportunity we'll ever get to take pleasure in the small things.

One of those, of course, is food. It doesn't have to be complicated or flashy, as long as it tastes good, is cooked with love and gets to be appreciated. On the campsite it becomes a part of the basic ritual of life. Everything stops and we gather to eat as one, in the open air.

But there's no need to make a big song and dance about it. Camping and camper van cooking should be simple, easy and done with as little fuss as possible. Of course it's nice to do showy feasts from time to time, but even they don't have to be over-fiddly and take hours. No one has to prove anything. All we want to do is eat

well and live well. The less you take and the more
you work within the limits, the happier you'll
be. You don't need flashy gadgets. You don't
need hundreds of pans. You don't need
electrical gizmos. All you really need
is fire, something to cook in and a very
sharp knife.

I love my food and I love to cook for
family and friends when I can. More often
than not, it's something at the end of the
day for Lizzy and me. It's almost always from
scratch and using the freshest ingredients we can
get our hands on. We don't coddle, engastrate or flash-
freeze on our camping trips and neither should you. Life is too short.
So don't bother with the cheffy shiz. This is camping, not *Masterchef*.

Quick tip

Remember the golden
rule: if it takes longer to
wash up than it does to eat
you've gone wrong somewhere.
Camping is supposed to be fun.
Relax. Take it easy. Grab a beer
from the cool box and go
back to basics.

EATING IN YOUR CAMPER VAN

Fresh, local and good for the planet

The recipes in this section are basic and tasty, almost always made fresh and easy enough for the weariest of camper van cooks to complete. They are mostly vegetarian or vegan, simply because that's the way I like to do things these days. I no longer cook with beef or processed chicken because of the environmental price, and I only cook with lamb or pork when I know the provenance. In a similar vein, I don't eat salmon any more because of the terrible environmental damage that salmon farming causes to the environment. I don't eat prawns because in some Asian fisheries, bycatch is as much as 98 per cent (which means 98 fish die needlessly for every two prawns you eat).

And that brings me on to where your food comes from.

Thankfully, getting in your van enables you to explore different foods, as well as places. Everywhere you go you'll find local specialities, ingredients and produce. Buy it as your first act of contributing to the local economy.

Reducing food miles is one way we can help to heal the planet, too, so, while I don't eat beef these days, buying local meat from the market is infinitely better for everyone than buying something vegetarian, like samphire, from Chile or Argentina.

Buying local helps local people. Going to a supermarket does not. So please don't stock up at Waitrose, Tesco or Lidl before you leave and then buy nothing locally when you're away – that's not what camper van living is about. Of course, it's hard to give up the convenience of doing a big shop all in

one go. But camping gives you the gift of time, so how about using it to stomp off to the local fishmongers, greengrocers, butchers and bakers to stock up on provisions? Put on your rucksack (no plastic bags please), swish a stick in the hedgerows as you go, buy what's local and fresh, and give yourself a break from the trolley pushing.

OK, so it might cost you a little more, but it benefits the places you go, allows you to interact with local shopkeepers (you might just learn a thing or two as well), contributes to the local economy and enables you to try something different, all while getting to eat fresh ingredients. Sounds healthy enough to me.

> ### Quick tip
>
> Stock up on a few staples before you set off. Then you'll always have enough in your store cupboard for a couple of emergency dishes.

Cooking kit

Cooking can be as simple or as complicated as you want to make it. I prefer it to be fuss-free, with lots of laughter, people poking their noses in, too much wine and kids running everywhere.

When it comes to kit, cook with a few well-chosen items instead of tons of gadgets and gizmos. There's not enough space anyway. Often, it's a compromise between portability and space when camping. It may also be a matter of cost. But buying cheap or lightweight camping kit doesn't always help when you're cooking in a van. We're not yomping over Dartmoor.

POTS AND PANS

Think of the size of your cooker rather than the size of your cupboard. If you use tall or small pans on a big ring, the heat goes up the sides of the pans and heats up the handles rather than the food in the pan. And vice versa. So, choose your pans for the cooker you travel with. Make sure you can get two on the hob at the same time.

Lightweight pans might seem like a good idea but they can burn food more easily than those with heavy bottoms. The heat, even when it's low, can often be too intense. A heavy bottom spreads the heat more evenly.

If you're using an induction hob then you'll need pans that work with it. Outwell's FEAST sets come in medium and large sizes, with three pans in each set and removable handles for storage. They also have a ferrous insert to be used with induction hobs and are lightweight, too. See **www.outwell.com**.

KNIVES

You can't cook without decent knives. and the sharper, the better. Don't settle for some rubbish serrated knife from a garage; bring your best knives, keep them sharp and slice with impunity. You'll need a large kitchen knife, a small veg knife and a bread knife.

Don't forgot the knife sharpener – a sharp knife is a happy knife.

VEG PEELER

You could use a knife, but why bother when a peeler is easier?

CHOPPING BOARDS

You don't need colour-coded boards for every eventuality. But I wouldn't travel with just one. Consider a couple of lightweight plastic boards – one for meat, one for veg.

STEAMER

Steaming veg is easier than boiling and the steaming baskets double up as strainers and colanders.

HEAVY DUTY SKILLET/FRYING PAN

Again, it's essential to have a decent frying pan for steaks and breakfasts. It doesn't have to be non-stick, although non-stick is good for pancakes and eggy bread.

SIEVE

Not just useful for sieving and draining veg , it can also be used to mash vegetables for soups.

MIXING BOWL

A couple of lightweight Tupperware bowls are useful for washing food, salads, serving and all kinds of other useful things, such as mixing and egg whisking. They also stack to save on space.

KNIVES AND FORKS NOT SPORKS

The spork (a spoon and fork combined) is good for nothing, other than saving space on micro camping adventures, although if you're eating a bowl of pasta it could be useful.

In my humble opinion, it's far better to carry proper cutlery in the van and eat properly, like civilised moho folk. It's camping, not the Dark Ages. If you can't carry proper cutlery, maybe because it's too heavy, invest in a set of lightweight titanium cutlery from the likes of **www.alpkit.com**. Please don't resort to using disposable plastic knives and forks, whatever you do!

MARSHMALLOW TOASTING FORK

No campfire is complete without toasting marshmallows.

COOKING SUNDRIES

- BBQ tongs
- Metal fish slice
- Spatula/wooden spoons
- Serving spoon
- Ladle
- Whisk
- Masher (useful for soups as well as spuds)
- Metal or bamboo skewers
- Grater

PLATES AND BOWLS

- **Melamine** won't break or scratch and is light. It also washes more easily than plastic. You can buy melamine picnic sets that are squared off. It might seem obvious, but when you're stuck for cupboard space, square plates and bowls can save a fair bit of space.
- **Traditional tin plates** can be useful as they won't break.
- **Bamboo** has become ever more popular of late. It's fast-growing, so relatively sustainable (even though it comes from China), and is light like melamine.

PLEASE PLEASE PLEASE don't resort to using disposables when you're camping. Even though it might save a bit of washing up, and even though they might be paper, they still take up space in landfill and are a waste of resources. Paper, once contaminated with food, cannot be recycled anyway.

BBQ THERMOMETER

If you worry about cooking meat right through, you'll need one of these. Temperatures of more than 75°C will ensure all bugs are killed by the cooking process, and 65°C is enough if you are cooking for at least 10 minutes.

KITCHEN ESSENTIALS

Don't forget the basic 'consumables'!

- **Cotton dish cloths**
- **Coconut scourers (can be composted)**
- **Tea towels**
- **Eco washing-up liquid**
- **Fire extinguisher**
- **Fire blanket**
- **Kitchen foil**

OTHER STUFF IT'S NICE TO HAVE

Paella pan

Get one as big as will fit into your cupboard. That might go against all I said above, but if you cook over a fire, it'll be really useful for cooking a big brekkie for everyone – not to mention my fantastic veggie paella (see page 240) – that one is a real treat.

Plancha

A flat, non-stick hot plate that can go over any heat (check for induction hobs). Great for cooking kebabs and breakfasts as well as searing steaks and veg. Also, they don't take up too much space.

Food cupboard staples

HERBS AND SPICES

The spice cupboard is a pretty important part of your kitchen equipment. Assembled with care and topped up regularly, it'll see you through any number of culinary adventures.

Start with:

- **Fennel seeds** – amazing with pork or fish.
- **Smoked paprika** – hot or sweet, great for flavouring meat and fish.
- **Dried rosemary/basil/ thyme/mint** – better fresh but handy to have.
- **Herbes de Provence** – useful for BBQs and lots of tomato-based dishes.
- **Ground turmeric/coriander/cumin/garam masala** – great for curries.
- **Ground cinnamon** – for both sweet and savoury dishes.
- **Nutmeg** – for sweet treats and Dauphinoise potatoes.

CONDIMENTS AND COOKING OILS

The only thing you really need to carry is some kind of cooking oil. Decanting oil into lightweight screw-top bottles can help to ensure you don't get spillages if bottles fall over in transit. Small drinks bottles can be useful, as they won't break and seal well. Buy in bulk and decant at home if you have the time.

Other condiments that are useful to have and don't take up much space include:

- Olive oil
- Vegetable oil
- Garlic
- Chillies
- Ginger
- Tomato ketchup
- English mustard powder/ wholegrain mustard
- White wine vinegar
- Soy sauce

DRY STAPLES

Absolutely essential! If you have rice, pasta or noodles, you can always eat, even if it's just a quick pasta and pesto. If you don't want to take a full bag, decant a smaller amount into Tupperware (or old plastic takeaway containers) – they're easy to stack and take up less room.
Start with:

- **Rice/pasta/cous cous** – fantastic staples.
- **Rice noodles** – buy them dry from a Chinese supermarket. Place in boiling water and leave for about 10 minutes before using. Easy, quick and good for you.
- **Risotto rice** – risotto is so easy and very versatile. Make it with just about anything for a super-filling meal.
- **Linguine** – flat spaghetti. Easy and quick – good with anything.
- **Chorizo** – lasts for ages.
- **Lentils** – last for a while, great for bulking up soups and stews.
- **White flour** – useful for making pittas and thickening coq au vin and other stews and soups.
- **Tinned foods** – tomatoes, coconut milk, chickpeas etc.

Washing up

No one likes washing up. I hate washing up with a passion, but, of course, even though I don't want to do it myself, I want it done properly. And there is a certain amount of etiquette to be observed, especially on campsites.

- Large plastic buckets with handles (trug buckets) are great for washing up – and easy to carry to the washing-up station.
- Use eco-friendly washing-up liquid.
- Soak difficult dishes and dirt-ingrained pans first while you wash the rest.
- Wash glasses first.
- Wash cups and mugs second.
- Wash plates third or swill out and fill up again with fresh water and suds.
- Wash pans last.
- Dry up as you go.
- Leave the washing area and sink tidier than when you got there. Wipe up any spillages and rinse away any food bits.
- If it takes you longer to wash up than to eat the food you've prepared, you've gone wrong somewhere.

COOKING METHODS AND HEAT SOURCES

Equipment

INDUCTION HOBS

More common in our homes than in vans, induction hobs use electric induction to create instant heat. They are massively versatile and only made possible by inverters that change your voltage to 220V. They do away with the need for fuel tanks or bottles, so removing the hassle of finding LPG stations or bottles.

The advantages of induction hobs are that they produce instant heat and cool very quickly, and present no danger of carbon monoxide (CO) poisoning. They are extremely efficient but draw a lot of power, so it is recommended you have either lots of solar to top up batteries, can run and charge on mains (from time to time) or carry two leisure batteries (minimum).

DIESEL BURNERS

This is another cooking device that does away with the need for separate fuel, as it runs off the diesel tank. It's not as controllable

Quick tip

When driving with a glass-topped sink or cooker, place a tea towel underneath it to stop it rattling.

as induction but can produce a good heat. The burner exhausts to the outside. Diesel burners can take time to warm up (minutes not seconds), which means meals need more time to plan and get ready. They require expert installation.

YOUR IN-VAN STOVE

A lot of today's smaller vans have a sink and burner combo with a collapsible tap. These save space where kitchen worktop area is limited and are neat, often with a glass top to provide more worktop space if needed.

Some larger vans and motorhomes have 'domestic style' cookers that have three gas rings and an electric hob plate (that only work when plugged in on site), as well as a grill and a small oven. They do take up space but can be useful if you like toast, need to cook for a crowd or just like to have a decent kitchen.

WARNING!
Don't close the lid on your cooker until the rings are cool — it can shatter your glass top.

All are available from manufacturers like Thetford, either as one-piece items or as separates. What you have in your van really depends on how you like to cook and what space you have. Burners come in twos, threes and singles, in a triangular array (left- or right-handed).

Something I always find amusing is that some manufacturers install the same cookers in their A-Class motorhomes (costing upwards of £80k) as someone might install in a home conversion.

COOKING TIPS

- If you use an induction hob, your pans must be compatible. Outwell's camping sets are 100 per cent compatible and still lightweight.
- When choosing pans for your van, ensure they fit on your rings. Choose steamers that are tall and slim and avoid huge frying pans or woks that won't fit (and may not fit in your cupboards either) – apart from the paella pan, if you've got space.
- If you cook with gas, ALWAYS make sure you have a CO alarm in the van.
- Never bring BBQs or fire pits into the van (or a tent), as they produce huge amounts of CO.
- BBQ gas points that allow you to attach an exterior BBQ are extremely useful in summer so you can BBQ outside. They also allow you to BBQ without using wood or charcoal in an area where fires are not permitted.
- If you're using a portable gas stove, please try to choose one that can be used with refillable gas canisters. Disposables require a huge amount of energy to recycle, and waste resources.

Fred & Karen Richards

'It really has and always will be like being teenagers again, escaping the system.'

It all started for us with a hand-painted 71 VW transporter panel van. We then home-converted a not so trusty 1982 T25 panel van, Frank. As the years have passed, several vans have come and gone, from a Renault Traffic to a T4, twice a T5 hence the second T4, to a now all-grown-up version in the form of a Ford Chausson 530.

It really has and always will be like being teenagers again, escaping the system. It started with just the two of us, then along came our daughter, now it's come full circle and it's just the two of us again. We have travelled and explored most of the UK over the years and across the Channel, allowing us to do so much, be it chasing the surf, to family trips in the peaks, the Lakes or the French Alps. Now, with all things Covid, the vans escapism is a true godsend. The van is social distancing personified, if that's what you want, or it can be the most social of things.

OUTDOOR COOKING

Cadac

The Cadac is a versatile piece of cooking kit that comes from South Africa. It's basically a single burner that runs straight from a gas canister (or BBQ gas point) with lots of interchangeable bits and pieces, such as a griddle, grill plate and the brilliant and very useful Skottel, a flattened wok. The Cadac can also be used as a BBQ in areas where you can't have fires.

Rocket stove

Rocket stoves work on the same principle as Kelly (or Ghillie) kettles. They use little fuel but burn it with lots of oxygen to make a fierce flame that burns bright and hot for as long as it gets fed. They squeeze a lot of heat out of a few twigs and therefore are particularly useful if there isn't much fuel in the way of dry logs to be had.

WARNING!

Disposable BBQs are wasteful and terrible for the environment. They are also extremely dangerous to use, as they emit heaps of carbon monoxide. In addition, they stay hot for long periods and are often the cause of bin fires or, if left on a beach, terrible injuries to people who step on them or on the sand where they have sat. They have also been known to cause wildfires. Please avoid them at all costs.

Cobb

The Cobb is a miracle, so they say. It's compact and neat and packs down small enough for most camping trips. It'll also do all kinds of great stuff, such as the legendary beer can chicken, which is what everyone cooked on it when they first came out. As time has gone on, they've become more and more versatile and now come in a gas version as well as the original cobblestone version.

Tripod and Dutch oven

A pot suspended over a fire is a truly time-honoured way of cooking. They can also be fully adjustable and hugely versatile.

- **The Roadii Grill** uses an old car wheel to contain the fire and a tripod with chains inside to control the height of the grill. It's very well thought out, works a treat and means your fire is off the ground. See **www.roadii.co.uk**.
- **The Kotlich** is a traditional Hungarian enamelled pot and tripod kit that's great for cooking stews but also comes with a suspended grill. The firepit has legs so it's off the ground. See **www.kotlichcooking. co.uk**.
- Cast-iron **Dutch ovens** are suitable for hanging from tripods and will also stand in a fire (they have little feet). The lid on a decent Dutch oven should also have a lip so you can shovel embers on top of it without them falling in the food. Good for making damper bread.

Frontier stove

This has to be the ultimate in outdoor cooking facilities. I say that in the way that invites something better to come along and take its place. But it's unlikely. Light, portable and about 10 times more efficient than cooking over an open fire, it's got a flue to remove unwanted smoke and can be packed down and carried away. Two pots fit comfortably on the top.

Frontier stove

Portable stoves

Portable worktop stoves are cheap, handy and produce a good heat, but rely on disposable canisters that make them wasteful and expensive to run. Better to find a cooker that uses reusable canisters or gas bottles.

Ghillie kettle/Kelly kettle

These little stoves are wonderful if you have the space and are looking to boil water in a hurry. They use virtually any dry fuel and very little of it, and boil water in just a few minutes. You can also cook on them if you need to with a range of accessories that turn the base into a simple cooker.

Solar cookers

There are a few of these on the market that use either a collapsible box or a parabolic mirror to direct heat towards the food. No need for any fuel, just sun. See **www.gosun.co**.

Removable kitchens

The idea of a removable pod that can be taken out of a transporter is nothing new. As we've already seen on page 40, the Camping Box was the first VW camper conversion. Removable kitchen pods make a lot of sense, especially if you use your van for weekend camping and weekday commuting or school runs. They can also be useful for putting out under an awning on a campsite or for making more space. In fact, a kitchen pod can turn a simple van into a camper.

Some versions are no more than buddy boxes that lock into rails in the floor and can then be removed for camping or used inside the van.

Others pull out from under the back seats so you can cook under the tailgate, while yet others swing out from the slider. Whatever the style the onus is on cooking outside, and that can only be a good thing. Check out Slidepods for more information: **www.slidepods.co.uk**.

Fuel for cooking (and heating)

Aside from wood for a fire and BBQ briquettes or cobble stones, there are a number of ways of generating heat for cooking.

THE SUN

Solar camping stoves are being developed all the time, but are only useful when the sun is shining. They often use parabolic mirrors to direct heat towards a cooking area.

ELECTRICITY

Lithium-ion batteries make it possible to have microwaves and induction hobs in vans. Previously impossible solutions are now available to all.

YOUR DIESEL TANK

See pages 176–177 for information on diesel burners. They can be useful and avoid the need for gas tanks or bottles, but they also take an age to warm up, so they're not very 'turn-off and onable'.

ISOBUTANE/BUTANE

This is the gas that comes in your standard blue Campingaz containers. It is available universally throughout Europe, burns well, provides a good heat and produces an easily adjustable flame.

It doesn't burn well at temperatures below 4°C and stops vaporising at −1°C, so it's not good for cold weather camping.

PROPANE/LPG

Propane gas, or LPG, is the main choice for motorhomes. It usually comes in red containers or grey and green for patio gas. Some motorhomes have on-board tanks that can be filled at filling stations. Propane won't stop vaporising until around −27°C, so it's the only option in colder climes.

GAS AND BBQ SAFETY

When cooking in a camper van or motorhome it's important to ensure that you use gas safely and understand the risks of cooking with BBQs.

- Do not cook in your van unless you have adequate ventilation. Keep a vent or door open .
- Make sure you turn off your gas supply at the cylinder (regulator) before you travel.
- If you suspect a leak, open all doors and windows, turn off the supply and get the help of an expert.
- If you suspect a flexible pipe or joint is leaking use a washing-up liquid and water solution on it. Gas will bubble through it.
- Get your gas equipment checked regularly by a qualified gas fitter.
- Change rubber gas hoses regularly for use with BBQs and stoves.
- Change cylinders in the open air, or at least with the doors wide open.
- If you have vents in the compartment where your gas is stored, make sure they are unobstructed. If you don't, get some fitted.
- Carry a fire extinguisher. Keep it nearby when cooking or using BBQs.
- Do not attempt to refill gas canisters unless they are specifically designed for the purpose.
- Don't use disposable BBQs in an enclosed space. NEVER light them in a van or motorhome. They give off lots of deadly CO fumes.

Open fires and BBQS

Having a fire is, some would say, an essential part of camping. A real fire takes us back to the days when fire was essential for preserving life. We feel good sitting in front of a real fire, staring into the embers, passing the time, telling stories, being the social creatures we are.

Unfortunately, we exist in a time when there are lots of rules about lighting fires in public. Fortunately, we also exist in a time when we are considerate to the natural world. Both of these facts conspire to mean that we can't, and don't, always light fires wherever we like. Some campsites do allow fires but these are few and far between. Often, in Europe, where fire danger poses a real risk to dry forest and habitats, BBQ are banned in all but the most controlled places. See **www.campfiresburning.org** for a list of sites in the UK where campfires are allowed.

FIRE PITS

There are times when fire pits may be allowed but lighting a fire on the ground is not. This is where owning a Roadii or Kotlich comes in useful, as they can double as fire pits. Some campsites will rent you a fire pit in order to preserve the grass on their fields.

Old washing machine drums make fantastic containers for flames at the campsite, if bulky to stash in your van. The way the tubs are made makes them ideal for fires as they draw plenty of air and let out a lot of heat. As long as you sit them well off the ground they can contain a fire nicely.

Gas BBQs

If you're travelling in Europe and staying on *aire de camping* sites or at campsites where open fires or BBQs are banned, then a gas BBQ, like a Cadac, can be very useful (and a lot safer).

Motorhomes with underslung tanks often have gas points for BBQs, which means you don't have to carry bottles. These are generally safe, although you

MUST remove the hose from the van connection before removing it from the BBQ.

FIRE SAFETY

As with many things, preparation is everything. Make sure you have enough tinder, kindling and fuel, that it is dry and that you have matches and/or a lighter that works. Also make sure you have a method of controlling your fire if it were to get out of hand. A fire blanket, extinguisher or, at the very least, a bucket of water, will do the job.

DO NOT be tempted to pour petrol, WD40, oil or any flammable substance on your fire to encourage it.

- Tinder is what you use to start the fire. It could be rolled-up newspaper, firelighters (no, it's not cheating to use these), dry grass or cotton wool.
- Kindling is the smaller twigs and finely chopped wood we use to get the fire going once the tinder is lit. Big kindling is useful as a halfway house before logs.
- Place the tinder at the bottom, position a few bits of light kindling on top and light the tinder. Add kindling as it catches, either in a square shape, narrowing as it piles up, or in a pyramid shape, and make sure there is adequate airflow. Don't add too much or you may smother the flames.
- Chopping logs in half makes them easier to light.
- Digging a fire pit and then encircling it with rocks creates a good pit in which to light your fire. It also helps to contain it should it get out of control.
- DO NOT light your fire anywhere near flammable items such as dry grass, fences, trees or peaty soil.
- Keep a bucket of water handy at all times in case your fire gets out of hand.
- If you're thinking of lighting a fire on grass, don't – it will kill it. If you must, at least dig out a sod of turf, light the fire in the hole and replace the sod afterwards, once the fire is fully out.
- Beware of lighting fires on stones or flint that may chip and explode under intense heat.
- NEVER LEAVE YOUR FIRE TO BURN OUT. If you have to depart, make sure you put it out completely and that the environment is put back exactly as it was.
- DO NOT leave mess, nails from old wood or litter.

Sammi Aplin

'My van is my opportunity.'

An opportunity to slow things down, saucepans of boiling water in place of the flick of a kettle, setting up the bed every night instead of jumping straight in, waiting for the sat nav to load and the condensation to clear, no alarms, early bed times. Breathing in the surrounding smells of barbecues, in the late September sun, believing and hoping summer will last forever. Taking us to our first surfing lesson, and an opportunity to dream about the tricks we might be able to do one day. The opportunity to wake up somewhere different every morning, the sense of freedom and adventure, the discussions of 'Where next?' Or 'Could we do this full time?' The opportunity to forget what day it is, forget the staff room number combination, forget brushing your hair. An opportunity to not dwell on the postponed wedding. Eating so much pasta that the occasional opportunity to eat at a pub is so very welcome. An opportunity to reminisce at the campsite he used to go to with his family. Seven years of waiting to see the beach I've always heard him talk about! The first time I've ever seen wild seals. The first time we've seen a pod of dolphins together. The coastal paths and opportunities to eat lunch while staring out to sea. Sharing stories and shower tokens with the couple next to us, welcoming the opportunity to sit around their fire. The opportunity to be covered in salt and sand. Wine glass at my feet, book in my hands. Picking blackberries to make a crumble, picking sloes to make sloe gin. An opportunity to be grateful for nature and her resources. The opportunity to connect with strangers, a big smile and wave on the road to fellow owners. On the road, the opportunity to play the music we both love.

COOLING

Keeping food cool is essential for food safety. Food that is 'likely to support the growth of pathogenic micro-organisms and toxins should be kept at a temperature of less than 8°C'. That's the official line from UK authorities on the subject. Those food types include dairy, fresh and cured meats, fish, prepared and cooked foods, and pastry or dough. The reason for this is that any toxins or pathogens in food are inactive below 8°C. Leaving 'at risk' foods (poultry, seafood and pork) above 8°C for any length of time could pose a risk to your health.

Of course, food also stays fresher, lasts longer and tastes better when it is cooled, not to mention you'll want to cool wine and beers for the evening.

Choosing a fridge

Fridges are vital pieces of equipment in a camper van or motorhome, for obvious reasons. They keep your milk fresh, stop your food from going off and chill your wine. But they can also kill your leisure battery, make you ill with carbon monoxide (if not serviced or vented properly), and can cost you an arm and a leg, if you get it wrong.

If you're planning a conversion or looking to buy a camper van, then you must think about the right fridge for you.

CAPACITY

Does it have enough capacity for all of you? Will you need to store food in a supplementary cool box or chiller if the fridge is small? If you like to go off-grid for days at a time then you'll need to ensure you have a fridge that can hold enough fresh food (or wine) for the time you'll be away, for all of you.

ACCESS

Can you get to the fridge easily? Fridges at eye level are much easier to access than those situated under the counter. Can you access the fridge when the bed is out?

POWER SOURCE

How does it work and what fuel does it require to power it? While fridges in small camper vans are usually around the 40l size, they can be as big as 150l in motorhomes. They can work off the gas, 12V, 240V or all three. Some fridges (compressor fridges) work off 12V only and use very little power, but can be a little noisy. See below for information on costs and power sources.

HOW CAMPING FRIDGES WORK

Motorhome and camper van owners can choose between three different cooling methods for their fridges. Depending on what type you go for, there is a choice of how you power your fridge, too – whether by gas, 12V or mains electricity via an electric hook-up.

Often, the determining factor in what type of fridge you get is the size of your conversion or the budget. The good news for old camper owners is that newer, more efficient fridges can be bought to replace the fridge from your original conversion, which may well be up to 50 years old! The bad news is that some fridges that use 12V can kill your leisure battery in a few hours.

Quick tip

If you park your camper or motorhome for long periods unused, clean your fridge thoroughly then crack open the door to allow air to circulate, which will help to prevent mould and bad smells developing.

Absorption fridges

This is the method that many camper van fridges work on. It relies on a concentrated ammonia solution being heated by a boiler, giving off a vapour that is then condensed and evaporated. The process draws heat out of the storage container (fridge), so cooling it.

ADVANTAGES

- Can be run on LPG or butane gas.
- Can be run on 12V (but usually only when you are driving) or 240V mains (only when the van is on site).
- Silent in operation.
- Cheaper than compressor fridges.
- Available in a range of 'standard' camper van sizes.
- Some 'three-way' fridges are designed to switch automatically between power sources but others are not. Automatic switching fridges mean you won't have to remember to switch the fridge over to a different power source when you set off or stop on site.

DISADVANTAGES

- Can only be run on 12v for short periods or when the vehicle is moving (and therefore charging the leisure battery).
- Will drain a leisure battery (and kill it) in a matter of hours.
- Must be vented externally to allow dangerous gas fumes from the boiler to escape.

Compressor fridges

Compressor fridges work by pushing a coolant, either as a gas or liquid, through a series of pipes that widen or narrow. The cooling works as the coolant is pumped around the system and warms up by pulling warmth out of the cooling compartment, then giving it out again as pipes narrow at the back of the fridge.

ADVANTAGES	DISADVANTAGES
• Powered by 12V electricity and don't pull a lot of current, therefore won't kill your leisure battery. • More efficient cooling, with the possibility of ice boxes. • Can also be run on solar power. • Easier to install. • No need for external ventilation as there are no fumes. • Modern compressor cool boxes (Dometic make a large range) are portable and can be used at home on 12V or 240V. Very useful if yours is a part-time camper.	• Can be noisier than absorption fridges. • More expensive than absorption fridges.

Portable thermoelectric coolers

Thermoelectric cooling relies on electricity to power elements that give off heat and cooling energy. These are then enhanced by heat exchangers and air fans to drop the temperature of a cool box to a temperature that is below the ambient temperature.

  Some cool boxes can be used with gas as well as 12V and 240V, so combining absorption and compression features. These cannot be used inside a camper on gas as they will not be sufficiently vented.

ADVANTAGES	DISADVANTAGES
• Portable and can be run on 12V or 240V. • Can be light and easy to carry. • Low-cost solution.	• Only cool to around 30°C below ambient temperature. In very hot climates, this may not be sufficient. • Cannot be used on gas power inside.

COOLING TIPS

- **Some campsites have freezers** where you can store your freezer packs overnight. Before you do, mark them with indelible pen to prove they are yours.
- If your campsite doesn't have a freezer, you can always **bury freezer packs in the freezer department** of the local supermarket and then come back for them later. It's a risk but worth it. Bury them deep though, in less popular foods, like frozen gooseberries.
- If you're short of space, **freeze bottles of water (or milk) before you go** and place them in the fridge or cool box. They'll help to bring down the temperature more quickly, so putting less demand on the fridge. If you use milk to do this, it'll help it to keep longer.
- If your fridge isn't working or too full, **cool your wine in a river or rock pool.** Just remember not to let it drift away...

RECIPES

Top 10 tips for camper van cooking:

1 Put butter in jam jars to stop it melting or getting messy.

2 Take a spare portable gas burner if you want fish and don't want to cook it in the van.

3 Take melamine plates. They won't break if you hit a speed bump.

4 Take basics you can't get anywhere but home: tea bags … Marmite … Worcestershire sauce.

5 Consider off-the-ground grills-cum-fire pits for campsites where you can't light fires but want to cook on an open flame.

6 Don't forget the marshmallows if you're travelling with kids. It's the rules!

7 Use a tea towel on your legs if you're using tin plates! They will burn your knees if your dinner is hot and you wear shorts.

8 Don't overpack your cupboards or you'll have to take everything out to find anything.

9 If you can't think of anything to cook, don't panic. That's what hot smoked paprika is for.

10 Check you have enough gas before you start a stew.

BREAKFAST

A camping breakfast sets you up for the day, gets you ready for adventures to come and stokes the fires of your boilers.

This section contains four of my favourite ways to wake up: kipper kedgeree is a traditional breakfast that you can have at any time of the day, while a shakshouka is a delicious hash that won't leave you wanting. It's the same for the tortilla. As for the home-made granola, it's just lovely. Make it before you go and you'll never be short of something. I eat it with soya yogurt for a vegan treat. It's gluten-free, too, unlike lots of bought granola, and can be zero-waste if you buy the ingredients at your local waste-free shop.

Craster kipper kedgeree

FOR 2

2 fillets of Craster kipper (or any
    other kipper)
A knob of butter
1 onion, diced
A sprinkle of chilli flakes
1 heaped tsp curry powder

120g of basmati rice
2 eggs
1 tbsp chopped fresh parsley
2 lemon wedges
Seasoning

METHOD

In a saucepan, boil around 350ml water. When boiling, remove from
the heat and 'jug' the kipper fillets by placing them in the water and
leaving them for 6 minutes. After 6 minutes, remove the fillets, flake
them with a fork and leave them aside (covered so they stay warm).
Save the water in another mug.

In the empty pan, melt the butter and fry off the chopped onions until
soft over a low heat. Add the chilli flakes and the curry powder and stir.

Add the rice and mix
well while still on a low
heat, then add 300ml
of the water saved from
jugging the kippers.
Put the lid on and allow
to simmer for around
10–12 minutes.

Meanwhile, boil the eggs
in another pan until they
are soft boiled (around
6 minutes). Drain, leave
to cool slightly, then peel
and slice them. When
the rice is cooked, take it
off the heat and add the
kippers and the parsley
and squeeze the lemon
wedges over it. Mix and
season. Serve in bowls.

Gluten-free granola with cinnamon and orange

ABOUT 12 SERVINGS

160g of coconut oil
160g of runny honey
Zest of 1 orange
1 tsp ground cinnamon
500g jumbo gluten-free
  oats

100g each of pecans and whole
  almonds
50g each of pumpkin seeds and
  sunflower seeds
100g each of sultanas, chopped
  dried mango, and chopped dates

METHOD

Preheat the oven to about 150°C (slightly lower for a fan oven).
Melt the coconut oil (if cool) in a large mixing bowl over a bain-marie
and mix it with the honey, orange zest and cinnamon (this will help it
to stay runny while you mix the oats and nuts). Add the oats, nuts and
seeds, and mix well to coat everything with the honey and oil. Line
a large baking tray with baking paper and spread the mixture out,
pressing it lightly into the tray (like you might with flapjack).
This helps with making clusters.

Cook for an hour until it's golden, stirring it and turning it over
gently a couple of times during the cooking time. Once it's cooked,
mix with the dried fruit and lay out on a tray to cool. As it cools it
will start to crisp up.

Once it's completely cool, store it in an airtight container until it's
time to go. Serve with yogurt and some fresh fruit for a super-nutty
brekkie on the road. YUM!

Super-fast shakshouka

FOR 3 (OR MORE)

A dash of olive oil
1 small red onion, finely chopped
1 orange (or red) pepper, finely
    chopped
4 cloves of garlic, finely chopped
1 tsp ground cumin
1 tsp sweet smoked paprika
1 400g tin of chopped tomatoes
A handful of young leaf spinach
3 eggs (more if you want to
    feed more)
A small handful of fresh coriander
50–100g of feta cheese,
    chopped into cubes
Seasoning
Pittas, toasted, to serve

METHOD

In a skillet or large frying pan, heat up a dash of olive oil over a
medium heat. Cook the onions and peppers for about 10 minutes,
or until the onion becomes translucent. Add the garlic, cumin and
paprika, and stir well. Next, add the chopped tomatoes, mix the
whole lot together, lower the heat and cook for another few minutes.
Season with black pepper and a little salt.

Next, add the spinach, allow it to wilt a little and then stir it in.
Cook for a minute or so more, then make three (or four if feeding
more) little dips in the mixture. Crack an egg into each dip and then
cook for a few more minutes until the whites are cooked. Cover with
a plate for a couple of minutes if the whites aren't cooking quickly
enough. When the whites are cooked but the yolks are still a little
runny, remove from the heat, scatter with coriander and feta and
then serve, with toasted pittas.

Tortilla deluxe

FOR 4

1 red pepper
1 large white onion
2 cloves of garlic, finely chopped
A good glug of olive oil
2 large waxy potatoes

4 eggs
A small handful of fresh parsley,
   finely chopped
Seasoning
Salad, to serve

METHOD

Chop the red pepper, onion and garlic, then cook for a couple of minutes in a non-stick frying pan with a glug of oil. While that's doing, slice the potatoes thinly – and when I say thin, I mean about 3–4mm, no thicker. Remove the peppers and onions to a plate and put to one side, add more oil to the pan and then cook the spuds for about 10 minutes, on a lowish heat, covered, being careful not to burn them. Add the peppers and onions back to the pan and then cook a little more until the potato is cooked.

Meanwhile, whisk up the eggs with seasoning in a bowl, add the parsley, and, when you are happy the spuds are done, pour the eggs into the pan. Turn up the heat for a minute or so to allow it to cook a little around the edges before turning down the heat again and cooking for around 6–7 minutes.

Now, run a spatula around the edges of the tortilla to release it from the pan. Put a plate on top of the pan and turn the two upside down to release the tortilla. When it's safely out, slide it back into the pan so that it's cooked side up. Cook for another 6 minutes or so. Serve with salad and a smile.

P.S. if you're afraid of doing the turning bit, do the top under the grill, but it's risky and fun to do it the proper way.

SANDWICHES AND SNACKS

Never underestimate the power of a good snack. Usually, on the road, I eat rice cakes with goat's cheese, mayo and cucumber for lunch, but that's not much of a recipe, so I have included a couple of my favourite bits and bobs here. The crab sandwich is to die for. The dahl can be stored in the fridge and brought out when needed and the recipe for home-made pittas can be used to accompany curries. The goat's cheeses bites are an easy treat for every day, too.

And yes, you are worth it.

Crab sandwich to die for

When in West Penwith (or just about anywhere on the UK coast), it would be rude not to have a fabulous crab sandwich lunch. Pick up a dressed crab from the local crab shack, mix up some sauce, lob it on a doorstep with some greenery and you've got a crab sarnie to die for. Make it with tiger bread, because it's the best bread for sarnies (I first discovered it in St Ives in the 1990s).

FOR 2 HUNGRY WEEKEND ADVENTURERS.
MAKES 2 DOORSTEP SARNIES

3 tsp mayonnaise
2 tsp tomato ketchup
A pinch of cayenne pepper
A pinch of smoked paprika
A squeeze of lemon

4 doorstep slices of tiger bread
1 dressed crab
½ avocado, sliced
A handful of watercress
Ground black pepper to season

METHOD

In a bowl, mix the mayonnaise, ketchup, spices, pepper and lemon juice before slathering both sides of the bread with it. Mix the brown and white crab meat together and spread on the bread. Add the sliced avocado and watercress then pop the top slice on... easy!

Dahl and fresh pittas

FOR THE DAHL (FOR MORE PEOPLE, SIMPLY DOUBLE THE MAIN INGREDIENTS, EXCEPT FOR THE SPICES!)

1 small red onion, finely chopped

A good glug of olive oil

1 garlic clove, finely chopped

A small knob of fresh ginger, finely chopped

A sprinkle of chilli flakes

½ tsp each of curry powder, ground coriander and ground turmeric

A vegetable stock cube or 1 tsp bouillon powder

2 cups of water

1 cup of red lentils

A small bunch of fresh coriander, to serve

Seasoning

METHOD

In a small pan, soften the onion over a gentle heat with olive oil. When soft, add the garlic, ginger and chilli flakes and cook for a couple of minutes. Then add the curry powder, coriander and turmeric, and stir for a couple of minutes more to make a paste.

Next, add the vegetable stock cube or bouillon powder and water. Dissolve the stock cube or powder, then add the lentils. Bring to a simmer and let it bubble away for 25 minutes, checking that there is enough water and stirring every few minutes. If the lentils start to get too thick and dry, add more water. Season to taste with salt and pepper and top with fresh coriander to serve.

FOR THE FRESH PITTAS

1 sachet (7g) of fast-action dry yeast	1 tsp salt
1 cup of all-purpose flour, plus extra for dusting	1 tsp olive oil, plus extra for greasing
1 tbsp fennel seeds	⅓ cup of warm water

METHOD

Mix the sachet of yeast with the flour, fennel, salt and oil. Add the water and mix in a bowl until you get a slightly wet dough. Knead a little on a floured surface then return to the (cleaned) bowl, lined with a little more olive oil. Cover it with a tea towel and leave in the warmest place in your van for 30 minutes.

To cook, cut the dough into two and roll out into two flatbreads of about 1–2cm thickness. Cook for around 5 minutes on the BBQ or griddle, or until the bread begins to puff up or brown nicely, flipping them over halfway through.

Goat's cheese and honey appetisers

FOR 2

2–3 tbsp olive oil
8 very thinly sliced rounds of
  slightly stale bread
8 slices of goat's cheese
A dollop of runny honey

A small bunch of fresh thyme,
  finely chopped
A dollop of fig jam (or similar
  chutney or jam) for each slice

METHOD

Pour the olive oil on to a plate. Dip each slice of bread into the oil on both sides, very briefly, so as to coat it but not soak it. Place the slices on a medium griddle or on the BBQ, but not on the hottest part (you want to toast them, not set light to them!). When you've got some nice lines on them, turn them over. Next, place the goat's cheese on top of each, drizzle with honey, sprinkle with thyme and, if you can, cover to allow the goat's cheese to melt a little while the bottom is doing. Be quick though!

When the toast is ready on the bottom, remove it from the heat and dollop a little of your jam or chutney of choice on the top before serving to your adoring other half, who will love this little pre-meal treat before you go on to impress them with the main course!

SALADS

Salads come in all shapes and sizes. The following are my favourites. Grapefruit adds a zing that, when combined with fennel, makes for a great, fresh flavour. On the other hand, grilling avocados lets them take on new possibilities, so let this recipe be just the start. The salsa can be used for fajitas and curries, too, if you like something different.

Amanda's amazeballs Asian-style salad

Amanda brought out this salad on a recipe testing night for this book round at her house. Shamefully, as it was tipping down, we sat around the kitchen table while her 1978 Westfalia languished in the garage, unstarted. But, she assured me, this recipe was devised on a trip, in the sunshine, on vacation, somewhere on a campsite in the middle of nowhere.

And it still tastes OK in the rain. Good enough for us then.

FOR 4

For the dressing
1 tbsp lime juice
1.5 tbsp fish sauce
1 tbsp caster sugar
1 clove of garlic, finely chopped
1.5 tbsp rice vinegar (or white or red wine vinegar)
1 fresh red chilli, deseeded and finely chopped
1 tbsp water

For the salad
¼ red cabbage, finely sliced
¼ white cabbage, finely sliced
2 small carrots, grated
A handful of fresh coriander, chopped
A handful of fresh mint leaves, chopped
A handful of chopped salted peanuts

METHOD

For the salad dressing, place all the ingredients in a bowl and stir well (or put in a jam jar and shake!). Leave for a few minutes to allow the sugar to dissolve, then stir (or shake) again.

For the salad, simply toss all the ingredients together in a large bowl (except the peanuts, if you want to allow people to add their own) then stir in the dressing. Voilà!

Fennel and grapefruit salad

If you like sharp and zesty salads then you'll like this. It's quick and easy, and very fresh and fruity. It's simple, too, and goes great with just about any kind of meat or fish. Or how about with some grilled halloumi and some more fresh mint and basil? That's going to take you on a taste adventure!

FOR 2

1 fennel bulb
1 large beetroot
6 cherry tomatoes
4 spring onions
1 red grapefruit
A handful each of fresh
    mint and basil, chopped

A handful of pine nuts, pumpkin
    seeds and sunflower seeds
A handful of pea shoots (or rocket)
A drizzle of olive oil
1 tsp icing sugar
Seasoning
Optional extra: griddled halloumi

METHOD

Finely slice the fennel and beetroot, halve the tomatoes, shred the spring onions, and cut the grapefruit into chunks (removing as much of the pith as you can). Catch as much of the grapefruit juice as you can in a glass – it'll become part of the dressing. Put it all in a bowl – along with half of the herbs, the nuts and seeds, pea shoots or rocket – and mix. Then add half of the icing sugar and toss with a drizzle of olive oil.

Add the rest of the herbs to the glass of grapefruit juice, along with the remaining icing sugar, and mix. Season to taste with salt and pepper.

If serving with griddled halloumi, drizzle the cheese with the herb and juice mix before placing on top of the salad. If not, just add the herb and juice mix to the salad and toss to combine..

Warm avocado with fig and honey salsa

This is a really simple and quick recipe for a light lunch or salad snack.

FOR 1

1 avocado, deseeded and
   quartered (skin on)
4 ripe figs, chopped
2 cloves of garlic, finely chopped
2 tomatoes, chopped

2 spring onions, finely chopped
1 tbsp olive oil
1 tbsp lime juice
Seasoning
2 tsp runny honey, for drizzling

METHOD

Heat up the BBQ or a griddle pan on the hob. Cook the avocado on each side for 5 minutes or so, on a high heat, until you get nice tiger stripes on it from the BBQ or pan.

Meanwhile, mix up the figs, garlic, tomatoes and spring onions in a bowl. Mix well with the oil and lime juice.

Once the avocado is ready, take it off the grill and put it on to a plate. Spoon the salsa over it and then season lightly with salt and black pepper. Drizzle the honey over the lot.

SOUPS

Like a good dahl, a decent soup can be made at home, stored in a good Tupperware dish in the fridge and brought out on cold days. They can also be made fresh in the van, even without any fancy whizzers. These recipes were made for winter, for days when the rain's lashing down and there's not much else to do but comfort slurp.

The original pea souper

This is a version of the classic Austrian 'pea soup with frankfurters' using mushy peas instead of real peas. It's just as good and twice as easy.

FOR 4 CAMPERS IN NEED OF A CLEAR VIEW OF THE ROUTE AHEAD...

A knob of butter

2 shallots, finely chopped

1 carrot, chopped into cubes
   of about 1cm

1 stick of celery, chopped

1 clove of garlic, finely chopped
   or crushed

1 bay leaf

2 300g tins of mushy peas

300ml chicken stock

6 frankfurters, chopped into
   2.5cm pieces

Seasoning

Dash of double cream, to serve

½ fresh chilli, finely chopped,
   to serve

METHOD

In a large saucepan, melt the butter and sauté the shallots, carrot and celery. When the onion is translucent, add the chopped garlic and the bay leaf. Sauté for another minute or so. Add the tins of peas and mix in. Add the stock and stir to mix in well. Bring to a gentle boil and then simmer for about 15 minutes. Add the chopped frankfurters and season to taste. Simmer for a further 5 minutes, stirring gently but being careful not to break up the frankfurters. Serve in bowl (or tin mugs) and add a little cream and a sprinkle of chilli.

Spicy pumpkin soup

FOR 4

50g butter
1 tsp vegetable oil
1 red onion, diced
1 tsp ground ginger
A pinch of chilli flakes
1 clove of garlic
1 vegetable stock cube

1 star anise
1 small pumpkin
Seasoning
A dollop of soured cream, to serve
A few fresh coriander leaves,
   to garnish if you wish

METHOD

Melt the butter in a large saucepan. Add the oil and soften the onions. Add the ground ginger, chilli flakes and garlic. Meanwhile, make about 1.5l of hot stock using boiling water and the stock cube. Add the star anise to the stock.

Cut the top of the pumpkin off, remove the seeds and scrape out as much of the flesh as you can. When the onions have softened, add the pumpkin flesh to the pan and mix it all up well, keeping it on a medium heat. Make sure that the onions and spices cover the flesh. Cook for a few minutes. Add enough stock to just cover the flesh of the pumpkin and then simmer for 10–15 minutes or until the flesh has cooked through and starts to break apart.

Remove the pan from the heat and mash the contents gently to break down as much of the pumpkin as possible. This will make a really rustic soup. If you want to make a smooth soup, pour the soup into a sieve a little at a time over a mixing bowl and press the flesh through the sieve with the back of a wooden spoon until all the liquid has come out.

Season to taste and serve with a dollop of soured cream in each, and perhaps a little coriander to garnish.

Thick and spicy cauliflower soup

FOR 2

2 tbsp oil
1 small white onion, finely chopped
1 fresh red chilli, finely chopped
4 cloves of garlic, finely chopped
1 small cauliflower, cut into florets
    (discard the core and leaves)
1 tsp ground cumin
1 tsp ground coriander

1 400ml tin of coconut milk
A small handful of fresh coriander,
    finely chopped, reserving a few
    leaves for a garnish (if liked)
Seasoning
100ml soured cream, to serve
Crusty sourdough and butter,
    to serve

METHOD

First, heat the oil over a medium heat in a saucepan. Add the chopped onion and fry off for a few minutes until it gets soft. Next, add three-quarters of the chilli and all the garlic. Continue to fry for a minute or so more. Add the chopped cauliflower to the pan and fry off a little more (about 4 minutes), stirring until it is coated with oil and beginning to cook. Add the cumin and coriander and stir until everything is coated. Add the coconut milk, stir and bring to a gentle simmer, making sure the cauliflower florets are covered in liquid. Simmer for 15 minutes, until the cauliflower starts to break up. Add the chopped coriander.

At this point, if you were at home, you'd whizz the whole thing up in a whizzer, but seeing as you are camping, and you probably don't have a whizzer, you can simply mash it really well with a potato masher until all the big pieces of cauliflower have broken down. This will give you a lovely, chunky and rustic soup.

Season to taste with plenty of salt and pepper and stir in most of the soured cream just before serving. Garnish with a little dollop of the remaining soured cream, the remaining chilli and coriander, and serve with crusty sourdough and butter.

Beery Suffolk onion soup

30g butter
A glug of olive oil
4 white onions, sliced into rings
1 tsp sugar
4 large cloves of garlic, finely
 chopped

1 bottle of dark ale (I used
 Nethergate Old Growler)
4 thick slices of French bread
Gruyère and Cheddar cheese
 (grated)
Seasoning
Sprig of fresh parsley, to garnish

METHOD

Heat a big-ish saucepan. Melt the butter and add a glug of olive oil.
Add the sliced onions and cook slowly until sweated. After about
15 minutes, add the sugar and garlic. Continue to cook over a low heat
until the onions begin to brown and caramelise, another 15 minutes
or so. Don't let the onions burn, but do allow them to brown. After
about 30 minutes, deglaze the pan (get all the brown bits off the
bottom of the pan) with a splash of water, then add the beer and
bring to a simmer for another 15 minutes or so. Season to taste.

While the onions and beer are slowly becoming one great big pan
of loveliness, grill both sides of the French bread then cover them
with most of the grated cheese and grill a bit more until the cheese
melts and browns a little.

To serve, place two slices of bread in a bowl and ladle over the soup.
Sprinkle the remaining grated cheese on the top and garnish with a
sprig of parsley (if you're feeling fancy). How's that? Ooh la la!

BBQ

Everyone has their favourite way of doing a BBQ. Mine is to slap on a bunch of fresh veg and let them cook away until they are tender, then fluff them up with basil and lemon for a heavenly, Mediterranean vibe. As for the falafel burgers... well, if you don't eat meat they are a great alternative and very easy to make. Actually, even if you do eat meat, give them a go. They're a planet-friendly alternative.

BBQ vegetables with a Mediterranean flavour

FOR 2 (OR 4, IF USED AS A SIDE)

1 aubergine
1 courgette
1 red pepper
1 green pepper
1 large onion, sliced
1 chicory bulb
10 cherry tomatoes
8 asparagus stalks
4 small baby leeks

For the dressing
A small bunch of fresh basil
Juice of 1 lemon
1 tbsp pine nuts
1 clove of garlic, finely chopped
A dash of olive oil
Seasoning

METHOD

Fire up the BBQ. Slice the aubergine, courgette and peppers lengthways. Quarter the onion. Cut the chicory in half lengthways. Put the tomatoes on to a skewer to keep them together.

When the BBQ is ready, place all the veg on the grill, including the asparagus and baby leeks, and allow to cook and chargrill slightly so that you get nice griddle lines; don't let it burn.

Meanwhile, chop the basil and mix with the lemon juice, pine nuts, garlic and olive oil to make a dressing, and season to taste.

When the veg is ready, put it into a big bowl and drizzle with the dressing. Serve immediately.

Herby falafel burgers with mint and lime yogurt and fresh rocket

MAKES 4 BURGERS

1 400g tin of chickpeas
1 tbsp olive oil, plus more for frying
1 medium red onion, finely chopped
2 cloves of garlic, crushed
1 heaped tbsp each of finely chopped fresh coriander, dill and parsley
A pinch of chilli flakes
1 tsp ground cumin

1 egg
Flour, for dusting
1 heaped tbsp finely chopped fresh mint
1 small pot (150g) plain yogurt
1 lime
4 medium pittas
Fresh rocket
Seasoning

METHOD

Drain the chickpeas. In a mixing bowl, crush the chickpeas with a potato masher (or similar) until they break up.
Add the tbsp of oil, onion, garlic , fresh coriander, dill and parsley, chilli flakes and cumin, and season. Mix well and season a little with salt and pepper.
Add the egg and mix together without working it too much. Divide the mixture into four.

Dust a plate lightly with flour and then shape each portion of the mixture into a patty. If you have a burger press, use that. If not, use your hands. Place the patties on to the plate and then dust again to ensure there is flour on both sides. Put in the fridge for 30 minutes.

Meanwhile, mix the finely chopped mint into the yogurt, along with a squeeze of ½ lime.

After 30 minutes, fry the patties in a couple of dashes of olive oil in a frying pan on a medium heat for about 5 minutes each side (or until golden and crispy).

Toast (or dry fry) the pittas. Cut each one open and stuff with the rocket. Place a burger in it and drizzle with the yogurt, finishing off with another squeeze of lime. Eat – and imagine you're just off to dance to your favourite music in a muddy field!!!

STOVETOP SUPPERS

The main event!!! These simple veggie recipes can all be cooked in a van without too much trouble or mess. And they are all delicious. Thinking of giving up meat for the sake of your health and the planet? Try a cauliflower steak instead! If you need a stonking cuzza but without the cruelty, my butternut squash curry will send you in all the right directions. And if you want a celebration of all things vegetable, try my vegetable paella. It's just as good as the meaty version!

Mushroom stroganoff

FOR TWO

A glug of oil
2 small white onions, finely chopped
2 large cloves of garlic, finely chopped
500g mushrooms, sliced
1 tsp English mustard
1 tsp paprika
1 tsp dried thyme

1 tbsp plain flour
300ml vegetable stock
2 tbsp crème fraiche or soured cream
Seasoning
Cooked white long grain rice for two, to serve

METHOD

First, heat the oil over a medium heat in a saucepan. Add the onion and fry off for a few minutes, until soft. Next, add the garlic and fry off for a few more minutes. Add the mushrooms and cook until the juices flow out of them and they are cooked (about 5 minutes). Add the mustard, paprika and thyme and stir. Sprinkle the flour over the top of the ingredients and then stir in. Next, add the stock and stir well to avoid any lumps. Season well. Cook for another 5 minutes or so until the sauce thickens to a good gloopy consistency and then remove from the heat. Stir in the crème fraiche or soured cream. Serve with the white rice.

Butternut squash, apricot, chickpea and chard curry

Even if you can't find a roadside stall selling squashes, it's worth trying this recipe if you like creamy, hearty, one-pot wonders. And the great thing about most of the ingredients is that you can usually find them without packaging in the supermarket! Brilliant. If you can't get chard, use spinach or green beans.

FOR 2

1 tbsp rapeseed or sunflower oil
1 red onion, diced
1 clove of garlic, peeled
A pinch of chilli flakes
1 tsp ground ginger
1 tsp ground coriander
1 tsp ground cumin
1 tsp turmeric
4 or 5 curry leaves
1 butternut squash, peeled and
    cut into 2.5cm chunks
1 400ml tin of chickpeas, drained
1 400ml tin of coconut milk
8 dried apricots, chopped
A handful of fresh chard leaves,
    chopped
Seasoning
A small handful of chopped fresh
    coriander, to garnish
1 tbsp flaked almonds, to sprinkle
    on top
Cooked jasmine rice, to serve

METHOD

Heat a sauce pan over a medium heat. Add the oil and the onion. Cook the onions until soft, then add the garlic and chilli flakes and cook for a minute or so. Add the spices and curry leaves, and

stir to coat the onion. Add the butternut squash and chickpeas, and stir so everything is coated with spices and onion.

Next, add the coconut milk and chopped apricots and bring to the boil before simmering for about 20 minutes, stirring occasionally to avoid sticking. Season. After 20 minutes or when the squash is tender, remove from the heat and add the chopped chard leaves. Allow them to wilt before serving. Serve with the fresh coriander to garnish, a sprinkling of flaked almonds, and jasmine rice.

Easy ratatouille

FOR 2 (OR 1, WITH PLENTY LEFT OVER)

Several glugs of olive oil
1 aubergine, diced
1 yellow pepper, diced
1 courgette, diced
1 large onion, sliced
A few sprigs of fresh thyme
1 clove of garlic, finely chopped
1 tbsp red wine vinegar
1 tsp sugar
4 tomatoes, cored and diced
Seasoning
A small bunch of fresh basil,
    to serve
A few parmesan shavings
    (do this with a veg peeler),
    to serve

METHOD

Heat a glug of olive oil in a medium saucepan, on a medium heat. Throw in the aubergine and cook, stirring regularly and gently, until it starts to brown (about 8 minutes). Add the yellow pepper and continue cooking for another 5 minutes or so, still stirring occasionally. Add the courgette and cook for another 5 minutes (still stirring). Put all the veg aside in a bowl.

Add another glug of olive oil to the now empty pan, along with the onion. Soften for a few minutes and then add the sprigs of thyme, chopped garlic and a couple of twists of black pepper. Cook for another 5 minutes. Add the red wine vinegar, sugar and tomatoes. Cook for another 5 minutes, stirring gently and occasionally. When the tomatoes start to break down, fish out the thyme sprigs, then return the rest of the veg to the pan and cook to heat through thoroughly for another couple of minutes.

Serve in bowls with a few torn basil leaves and parmesan shavings. Season to taste.

Goat's cheese frittata

If you fancy eggs but don't want them fried, boiled or scrambled, the frittata is a great way to serve them up. It's quick, easy and produces very little washing up, making it perfect for cooking in a camper.

FOR 2 HUNGRY CAMPERS

A dash of oil
1 large red pepper, sliced
4 spring onions, finely chopped
8 cherry tomatoes, halved

6 large eggs
1 tbsp chopped fresh thyme
Ground black pepper
120g goat's cheese, crumbled

METHOD

In a good, non-stick frying pan, heat a dash of oil. Add the pepper and spring onions and cook for a few minutes, until soft. Add the cherry tomatoes and cook for a few minutes more.

Meanwhile, crack the eggs into a bowl and mix with the fresh thyme and a twist of black pepper.

Spread out the contents of the pan evenly, then pour on the egg mixture and add the crumbed goat's cheese. Cook over a lowish heat for 5 minutes or so, then place under a preheated grill until the top is golden brown. Serve immediately.

Cauliflower steaks with peas and almonds

This is really easy and very adaptable. Cauliflower steaks can be griddled or cooked on the BBQ, as long as they are cooked slowly so that they cook through.

FOR 2

1 cauliflower to make
  2 x 2.5cm cauliflower steaks
Olive oil, for frying
1 tsp paprika
1 tsp ground turmeric
½ cup of peas
Seasoning

A small handful of chopped
  fresh coriander, to garnish
1 tbsp flaked almonds, to garnish
A pinch of chilli flakes, to garnish
  (optional)
1 lemon, cut into wedges, for
  squeezing over (optional)

METHOD

Cut 2 steaks from the cauliflower by cutting it exactly in half, starting at the stalk, with all the leaves already taken off, then cutting around a 2.5cm steak from the inside. Drizzle the steaks on one side with olive oil and then dust with half of the paprika and turmeric. Season with black pepper and salt.

Place the steaks oiled side down in a preheated frying pan on a medium heat. Drizzle the uppermost side with oil and dust with the rest of the paprika and turmeric, and season. After about 5 minutes, check the steaks underneath. If they are browning nicely, turn them over (carefully) and cook for a further 5 minutes.

After the steaks have been cooking for a total of 10 minutes (5 minutes on each side), check them for tenderness. If they are tender enough that you can easily push a fork into the stalk, to its middle or further, then they are ready. If not, lower the heat and give them another 5 minutes on each side. Meanwhile, heat the garden peas in a small saucepan.

When the steaks are ready, serve with the peas, garnish with fresh coriander, flaked almonds and chilli flakes (if using) then serve with lemon wedges for squeezing over each steak, if liked.

Easy vegetarian paella with oyster mushrooms

FOR 4

2 tbsp olive oil
1 large onion, chopped
4 cloves of garlic, chopped
1 red pepper, diced
150g oyster mushrooms
    (or button mushrooms, if
    oyster ones aren't available)
1 tbsp paprika
300g short grain or paella rice

800ml vegetable stock
10 French green beans, chopped
    into 2cm lengths
1 courgette, diced
1 cup of peas
Seasoning
Chopped fresh parsley, to garnish
    (optional)

METHOD

Heat the oil in a large non-stick frying pan or paella dish, if you have one. Add the onion and cook on a low-ish heat for a few minutes, until it begins to go translucent. Add the garlic, pepper and mushrooms and continue to cook over a low-ish heat for a further 5 minutes, stirring regularly to keep from sticking/burning.

Add the paprika to the pan and give it a good stir. Cook for a minute or so, then add the rice and stir the whole lot together. Season with pepper and a little salt. Add about half the stock and stir gently, making sure the stock covers everything. Allow to simmer for about 10 minutes, making sure that the rice doesn't absorb all the stock (if it's looking dry, add more stock).

Add the remainder of the stock. Add the French beans, courgette and peas, making sure everything is covered with stock. At this stage, if it's looking dry (it should be very moist, with liquid bubbling), add more water a little at a time and stir gently.

Cook for another 10 minutes, until the rice has lost its crunch and is properly cooked. Garnish with fresh parsley, if you have it. Serve.

SLEEP

GETTING COMFY

Sleeping is what this section is all about. And that means getting a good night's sleep. It's not as easy as it might sound. What is it that's going to keep you awake at night? Is it your pitch? Your camper's cushions? Your kids? The temperature?

Let this section help you. The following pages cover everything sleep related, from foam density to sleeping bag ratings and what makes a good or bad pitch. So drift away and let the sounds of the night transport you into a world of sweet dreams, cosy snoozes and happy awakenings.

What was that noise?

GETTING A GOOD NIGHT'S SLEEP

What keeps you awake at night?

Before we move on to the nitty-gritty of getting a good night's sleep, let's ponder a moment how best to go about *not* getting a good night's sleep. Sometimes, no matter how hard you try, the world conspires to test you with things out of your control. Despite the comfiest bed, the cosiest duvet and the best companion, you still can't get a good night's sleep. It might not be your fault. But, equally, it might be.

Here, to start us off, are a few of the rookie mistakes (and how to avoid them) that could keep you up.

PARKING UP LATE AT NIGHT UNAWARE OF YOUR EXACT LOCATION

If you don't know exactly where you're parking it stands to reason that you won't know what's likely to keep you awake. The only solution is to pitch up in daylight. How to achieve this? It's not always easy but route planning and booking ahead helps. Sometimes, though, you just have to take your chances.

- Plan your overnights and get there before dark.
- Book ahead if it's unavoidable and check late arrival rules.

GETTING COLD

You only need one cold night to ensure you remember to pack your sleeping bag. If there's a danger you might run out of the door without your sleeping kit, make sure you have a spare blanket or two in the van at all times. If the heating fails, you run out of gas, the EHU fails or you pack the wrong duvet, at least you'll have a back-up plan.

- Always carry spare bedding.
- Ensure you always have enough gas to last, especially if you're staying in a cold location.

PARKING UP NEXT TO THE NOISY CAMPERS

This is hard to avoid. You can't always judge a book by its cover and it's not always easy to tell who is going to keep you awake and who isn't. If you worry about kids screaming, check into an adults-only campsite. If you want to camp alone, find a nice CL (Certificated Location) with plenty of space. If you want to avoid being kept up all night by the ravers, avoid popular summer sites. Also, check with the owners what the noise policy is before you pitch.

In some places, like *aire de camping* sites, you can often be at the mercy of your fellow campers. The good news, though, is that you can always leave the next day. It's only one night.

WEATHER EVENTS

You can't stop bad weather, but you can mitigate against it. Today, there is little excuse for not knowing bad weather is on the way, so if you get caught out, it's generally because you weren't prepared.

When bad weather is forecast
there are plenty of options.

- Plan an escape route if things
  get really bad.
- Put away any awnings, pup
  tents or washing.
- Bring in bags and all
  equipment (see below).
- In extreme situations, move
  to higher ground.
- Close and secure all windows and doors.
- Make sure all blackouts/blinds are secure.

ANIMALS KEEPING YOU AWAKE

You might find you're kept awake by animal noises outside. It could
be farm animals, wild animals or just some curious badgers.

- Park away from field boundaries if there is livestock.
- Don't leave rubbish outside that attracts animals.
- Clean up BBQs and food before you go to bed.
- Check for burrows or setts before you pitch up.

LEAVING BAGS OUT OR AWNINGS FLAPPING

Flapping bin bags, noisy awnings and improperly secured items have ruined
many a good night's sleep. Make sure it's all sorted before you turn in.

- Secure bikes and valuables to avoid fear of theft.
- Bring rubbish bags in to prevent flapping and animals getting
  into them.
- Secure awnings properly so they don't flap around.

FLYING TROUBLES

Insects are the most likely thing to keep you awake at night, especially
if they are biting. In Scotland, for example, midges can wreak havoc at
dusk if there is no wind.

- Close windows and doors well before dusk.
- Don't leave lights on inside and doors open – insects will flock in!
- If you leave doors open for ventilation, fit fly screens.
- Keep all your limbs under the blankets.

Sleeping bags, duvets, liners

Sleeping bags are vital pieces of camping equipment. Even if you don't use a sleeping bag, getting the right duvet is just as important. Get it wrong and you'll be sweating or shivering all night. Get it right and you'll be sleeping like a baby.

After a little research, I concluded that it is more important to get something that's warmer than you need if you're unsure. You can always make a hot sleeping bag cooler by opening the zip a bit, but you can't make a cold sleeping bag warmer unless you put on more clothing or add a blanket.

WHAT YOU NEED TO KNOW ABOUT SLEEPING BAGS

Sleeping bags are temperature rated. These are set by a European Standard (EN13537), so all sleeping bags must conform to the same standards and the standards must be set in a predetermined laboratory standard test. The ratings are as follows, and they refer to someone with clothes on.

Upper limit/maximum rating. This is the highest temperature at which you can sleep comfortably without sweating (based on a standard man (25 years old, with a height of 1.73m and a weight of 73kg).

The comfort rating. This is the temperature at which a standard woman (25 years old, with a height of 1.60m and a weight of 60kg) can have a comfortable night's sleep.

Lower limit/minimum rating. This is the lowest temperature at which a standard man can have a comfortable night's sleep.

Extreme rating. This is the point at which the standard woman is protected from hypothermia.

Quick tip

If you wear nothing at night, keep a pair of shorts and a T-shirt (and slip-on shoes) handy at night in case of emergencies or wee events (if you haven't got a loo).

- These ratings are given for the person with clothes on, although the kinds of clothes are not specified. Assume it's a pair of long johns and a T-shirt.
- When it comes to standard, it's also safe to assume that if you are on the slimmer side then you may feel the cold more.
- Men and women react to temperature in different ways, which is why the ratings are specified for both. Women generally feel the cold more.

PYJAMAS?

Because sleeping bags, as we now know, are rated for a clothed body, if you like wearing thick pyjamas, or perhaps a onesie, to bed, your bag may make you warmer than 'standard'. However, if you prefer sleeping in the buff, you should look at a bag that's more highly rated than you might otherwise choose.

WHAT BAG SHAPE TO GO FOR

The shape and style of your sleeping bag will determine how warm it is. The rule is that the more air there is inside the bag, the cooler it will be.

- **Standard/rectangular shapes** are standard in that they will fulfil your needs but may not be as warm as a mummy-shaped bag. But, on the plus side, you can zip two of them together to make a double bag. Handy, but not always.
- **Lozenge shapes** don't have the awkward corners of a standard bag shape, so still allow you to move about with a little extra warmth.
- **Mummy shapes** are the daddy – they get warm quicker and stay warm longer. This is because there is less chance of colder air circulating, especially if you zip up tight and keep your head inside the hood. The shape can be restrictive for those who like to move about in the night, though.

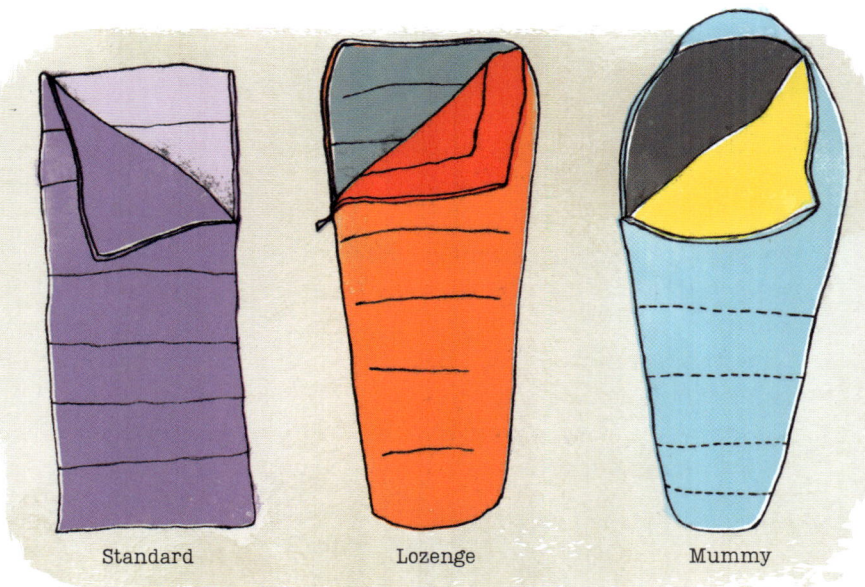

Standard   Lozenge   Mummy

For extra warmth and comfort, sleeping bag liners add another layer and make it easier for you to keep your bag clean. You also get the added benefit of sleeping in a cotton sheet.

WHAT SEASON BAG TO GO FOR

To make it a little easier to choose, camping stores divide their bags into seasons. These are set out below. Remember, though, that the temperature ratings still apply here. So, when choosing your bag, you still need to think about when you'll be using it and what the limits are you expect it to cope with. Keep in mind that the extreme limit is less about comfort and more about survival.

- **One-season bags** are for use in a hot climate or indoor use.
- **Two-season bags** will see you through, as long as the temperature remains above 9°C. Basically, you're looking at a normal British summer night.
- **Three-season bags** are for temperatures as low as 0°C and can be used from early spring to late autumn.
- **Four-season bags** are designed for winter backpacking or climbing. Useful for people who really feel the cold, but rarely useful in a well-insulated van.

LOOKING AFTER YOUR SLEEPING BAG

You might think that stashing your bag away into its stuff sack is the best way to store it – but it isn't, apparently. The more compressed you make your bag, the more it's going to lose its insulating properties

over time. So, while it's OK to stuff it for short trips, store it in a larger bag between trips. If you fold and roll your bag the same way each time you'll stop the inner fabric becoming creased and working less efficiently.

DARN THE SAVING SPACE, GO FOR A DUVET

Very wise choice! A duvet is a far more civilised way of sleeping (especially with a friend), although you'll need to carry a bottom sheet too. The only downside is the bulk of them. Even so, you still need to be mindful of the tog rating (don't worry; it's actually a lot less complicated than sleeping bags).

What's the tog rating?

The tog is a measure of thermal resistance. That means it's all about how a duvet contains heat. So, for the layman, the thermal resistance in togs is equal to 10 times the temperature difference (in °C) between the two surfaces of a material, when the flow of heat is equal to 1W per square metre (eh?).

And that, in turn, translates as:

Summer duvet	4.5 tog
Spring or autumn duvet	9.0–10.5 tog
Winter duvet	12.0–13.5 tog

If you want my advice, I'd say go for more togs than you think you'll need. You can always stick a leg out if you get too hot.

Fly screens and mosquito nets

On balmy nights it's a real pleasure to sleep with the tailgate or sliding door open and allow a gentle breeze to cool you while you snooze away. It's almost a prerequisite of any camper van dream. It's hot. You can't sleep. You open the doors and listen to the sounds of the night. Everything is wonderful ... until the insects find you. Then you'll spend the rest of the night either swatting mozzies in the dark or scratching at your bites.

The solution, of course, is to fit fly screens or mozzie nets to your van. They can almost always be retrofitted and are available for all types of modern campers. They can be extremely useful when travelling to areas where midges are prevalent.

- Choose from full screens for sliding doors to tailgate screens.
- Most skylights also have insect screens fitted these days, which means you can enjoy air circulation without the security risk of having the doors open.
- If you don't want to go to that kind of expense, you can always use a standard mozzie net in the van. They're generally cheap and will protect the bed only.

Condensation

Having condensation inside your van won't stop you from getting a good night's sleep – unless it drips on you – because it is just a by-product of sleeping in a tin and glass box. But stopping it makes for a more pleasant experience all round and means you don't have to wipe the windows down each morning.

Condensation is a common problem that affects all camper vans and motorhomes. It can cause real issues if the water hangs around for a while and begins to corrode the bodywork. If you allow it to happen a lot – especially in older vehicles – it could well kill them.

WHY CONDENSATION OCCURS

Whenever there are differences in temperature and moisture, condensation will occur. So, when you are cosy inside the van and breathing out hot, moist air, the likelihood is that you'll create condensation if the outside temperature is cooler. You'll find it happens a lot more on cold nights.

Condensation can also be caused by high moisture content in the interior air of the van – by wet towels, using a shower, damp wetsuits, whatever. As long as there is a difference, it will happen.

STOPPING CONDENSATION

Allowing air to circulate by opening a window or two will let the moist air escape, evening up the difference between outside and in. Insulating the van and windows also helps, as the insulation provides a protective heat-proof barrier between the two temperatures. Insulation also helps to keep the van warm and to stop warm air escaping through the thin metal sides of the van.

STOPPING WINDSCREEN CONDENSATION

The windscreen is the place where you are most likely to get condensation. This is because it's a large area that isn't usually insulated. It's a pain to wake up every morning and have to wipe away gallons of condensation from a big windscreen, so anything you can do to reduce it is worthwhile.

Thermo screens that you can stick to the window interiors are a great idea and stop a certain amount of condensation. Buy them or make them yourself with bubble wrap or foam insulation. However, a more effective way to make use of thermo screens is to mount them on the outside of the van, so stopping the warmth of the van (and a nice warm windscreen) from having direct contact with cold air outside.

Blocking out the daylight

Blocking out the light is kind of essential when it comes to getting a decent night's sleep. Or at least sleeping in once the sun has come up. So, getting the right curtains is important. They're also the first and most important soft furnishings you'll have to decide on.

Curtains can be decorative, blackouts or both. Most modern coachbuilt motorhomes have some kind of blinds and fly screens already installed, so curtains are usually no more than a decoration to soften the edges a little. But for most campers, proper curtains are the way to go.

You can choose to match the interior and be damned by what light-stopping properties they might have, perhaps lining them and hoping that helps, or you could go the full hog and make sure they are fully blackout lined.

Blackout curtains and blinds are available for most vans from the following places:

- Kiravans (**www.kiravans.co.uk**) – makes blackout kits for most modern VWs.
- VW Camper Curtains Ltd (**www.vwcampercurtains.co.uk**) – makes curtains for classic VWs.

BLACKOUT CURTAIN TIPS

- Magnets sewn into the linings of curtains can help to stop them from flapping about and letting in light.
- Tie-backs are essential to stop curtains from flapping about as you drive.
- Most classic camper vans and many modern motorhomes and vans use Silent Gliss single curtain track and runners, along with end stoppers and hooks for curtains and shower curtains. They are widely available online.
- Velcro strips can be used to hold curtains together to stop light from coming in.
- Single-lined curtains are unlikely to stop light from waking you.
- Double-lined curtains will stop more light, but unless they are designed to be blackouts, they will still let light in.
- Blinds are more efficient than curtains – and also have thermal properties – but are not as pretty.
- Blinds that are retrofitted in cassettes can be clipped into the windows of Ducatos, Crafters and Sprinters, and can take up space in the window surrounds. However, they're easy to fit and use. They have thermal qualities, too.

Quick tip

Bungee cord washing lines can be used to hold down exterior thermo mats if windy. Clip each end to the door and wrap around the mats on the windscreen, keeping them in place with the wing mirrors.

THERMO MATS

These are blackouts that also have thermal qualities. They can be used inside the van (and are fixed using suction cups) or outside, over the front windscreen. If using outside thermal blinds, they are fixed by tucking the ends into the van doors.

Thermo mats can be really effective against condensation and light pollution, as well as providing extra thermal insulation. However, they can flap about in high winds (unlike thermal blinds used on the inside of windows).

- Front and rear thermo mats are available for all makes of campers from **www.rainbowscreens.co.uk**.
- Inside thermo mats are available for all makes of campers from **www.thecampercoshop.com**.
- Cassettes with thermal blinds that fit into your windows are available from **www.rainbow-conversions.co.uk**.

Levelling wedges and chocks

Levelling wedges are wedges that you drive on to in order to level up the van. Chocks are blocks that keep you from rolling away, once up on your chocks.

Wedges are small but vital. This is because not all ground is level, and many campsite pitches are far from level. If you've ever tried to sleep on an incline, even a mild one, then you'll know it's not the way to get a good night's sleep. At best, you'll spend all night tossing and turning. At worst, you'll end up in a heap on one side of the van. If you have nylon sleeping bags, leather seats or even satin sheets (God forbid), it gets worse and you may even slide off the bed altogether.

Levelling also affects cooking, eating and everything else in the van, so it's important to get it right.

The size of the wedges you need is usually determined by the size of the van. Longer wheelbase vehicles generally need taller wedges, as the height difference between back and front wheels is greater than those with short wheelbases.

Use chocks to lock the vehicle in place.

Levelling can be done with the aid of a spirit level, by eye or with a glass of water on a flat surface. How thoroughly you do this depends on how you sleep, whether or not you can be bothered, or if you have a pernickety assistant.

HAND BRAKES, SWIVEL SEATS AND WEDGES

If you have a swivelling driver's seat and a handbrake that needs to be depressed to operate the swivel you might need a little help getting on wedges, staying there and swivelling the seats. (Vans with floppy handbrakes won't have this trouble.)

How to operate a swivel seat on wedges

1 Drive up on to the wedges and set your heights.

2 Pull on the handbrake.

3 Keep your foot firmly on the foot brake and stop the engine.

4 Get off the seat, keeping your foot firmly on the brake and hanging on to the steering wheel. DO NOT LET YOUR FOOT OFF THE BRAKE.

5 Get an assistant to release the handbrake and swivel the seat, then pull on the handbrake again.

6 Release the footbrake and step down. Sleep like a baby.

John Midgley

'We love our van. We love the escapes it gives us.'

I love my van (technically it's our van). It's an escape pod. It's an adventure van. It takes us to places we wouldn't go otherwise. It allows us to travel with our little family of three, my wife Nicola and little dog called Peggy.

Our van is called Ruben. He's a 17 plate red VW T6. Not fancy, pimped or lowered, and covered in extra bits. Functional and comfortable. We designed the layout with a local converter, choosing every bit from floor to walls to seating. It's a tweak on the traditional VW rock and roll layout, but with a king-sized bed!

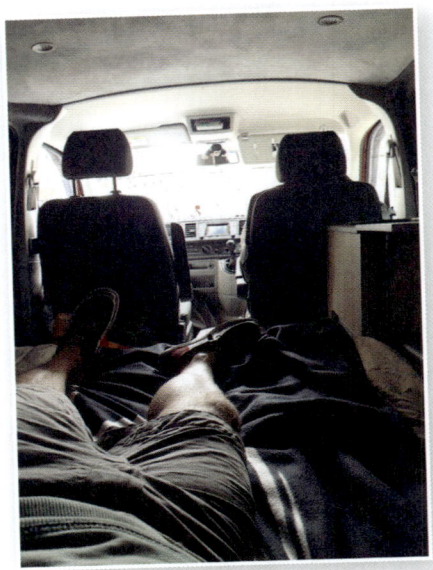

Ruben replaced a coachbuilt Swift Suntor called Stanley. Stanley was a bit old when we got him and a bit too bulky for remote Welsh or Cornish lanes. He did a couple of trips to Europe and loved it there. The luxury of a walk-in shower is missed, but the fuel bill and not getting into car parks is not.

Ruben has taken us to Belgium, the Netherlands, Germany, Austria, Italy and back through France. To wild Northumbria and the Hebrides. The magic is wherever he takes us feels like home. Wild storms on Anglesey and we close the door, and cocoon ourselves in, knowing we're not going to wake up with a

face of tent. In the 38°C heat of the Netherlands and the island of Texel, he provided safe shade for us all. Cool water for the dog and maybe some beers for us – then into the heart of Amsterdam, hidden away in an underground car park, he can sleep while we explore the city.

He's also my escape pod. For me and my boards. Weekend trips to the coast with a surfboard, a paddle board and a belly board or three. Sleeping comfortably, warm, wetsuit drying up front, waking with the surprise of a board bag cuddle. I can zoom to the beach late at night and be ready for an all-day session in the waves. I can get changed for a surf or post-surf without flashing at the locals! I can make a warm drink or some food in winter. I can sit and watch and relax!

I've also used my van during lockdown. Just crawling on to the bed took me to far-off places. A sanctuary away from digital and social distractions. Outside, I was in lockdown on our driveway. Inside, I was visiting Brugge ... or climbing a mountain near Innsbruck ... or simply eating imaginary fish and chips in Bridlington! An escape and release.

In short, we love our van. We love the escapes it gives us. We love the flexibility to go where we want (Covid-19 lockdown aside!). I can't wait to go on more and further-afield travels.

THE CAMPER VAN BED DEPARTMENT

What you sleep on is as important as what you sleep under when it comes to getting a good night's kip. You won't have much of a choice if you're buying second hand and beds, cushions and mattresses are already in place, but it is possible to buy foam cushions cut to size and have them re-covered to suit the interior or how you like to sleep if things aren't quite right for you. There are also a couple of checks to do before you buy, or to make your bed safer once you have bought.

Rock and roll beds

Rock and roll beds are beds that turn from travel seats into beds, and vice versa. They are common in most small van conversions and also in some larger conversions.

If you're buying or converting a van, the bed may well be the most important piece of equipment to consider, both from a safety and comfort point of view. There are lots of different types to go for, with many options ranging from fully crash tested. 100 per cent compliant, touch-of-a-button, British-made steel constructions to wood and hinges kits that look decidedly un-crash ready.

Rock and roll beds for standard-sized camper vans generally come in two sizes: full width and three-quarter width.

FULL WIDTH BED

Full width beds are fantastic for families that have children who like to creep in with parents in the night. They're great for the whole family to lay about in, and even better if you like a lot of space to sleep in.

The drawback is that space is quite limited for other stuff – like cupboards, cookers and sinks. It means all your stuff is going to be up front, out of the way of the bed as it swings forward.

THREE-QUARTER WIDTH BED

The three-quarter width bed is something of a standard when it comes to smaller camper vans. This

is because it enables a full set of units to be installed along one side of the van, so allowing for plenty of worktop and under-cupboard space, for clothes, kit, cooking gear and fridges.

ROCK AND ROLL SAFETY AND COMPLIANCE

Rock and roll was never supposed to be governed by rules and legislation. But sadly it is, especially when it comes to rock and roll beds. Actually, it's no bad thing. We are responsible for our passengers' safety as well as our own.

Rock and roll beds are not only an important part of the camping set-up of many camper vans, but they're also a vital part of the seating arrangements. That means they have two important functions to fulfil: sleeping and seating.

The EU dictates that new motorcaravans (camper vans) sold in the EU need to be type approved, which includes testing and assessment against EU standards for seat belts, anchorage points for the seat belts, and the strength of seats and their mountings. In the UK, following

Brexit, this has become a provisional UK-type approval for M-rated vehicles (passenger vehicles) but this does not cover the habitation parts of a leisure vehicle.

The standard to look for is the NCC (National Caravan Council) Manufacturers' Approval Scheme. This imposes a strict inspection regime on manufacturers to provide consumer protection over and above the requirements of the British/European standards. Every unit that has been approved is licensed to carry an NCC Approved Badge. A certificate is also issued to the consumer detailing the specification of the model that was inspected and approved.

When it comes to converting existing vans with rock and roll beds into motorcaravans, the seats are not subject to the same demands, although they are subject to road vehicles regulations demanding similar standards for seat belts and anchorage points, but not of seat mounting strength.

What this says is: 'a motor vehicle, and all its parts and accessories; the number of passengers carried, and the manner in which any passengers are carried in or on a vehicle; and the weight, distribution, packing and adjustment of the load of a vehicle, to be at all times such that no danger is caused, or is likely to be caused, to any person in or on a vehicle or on a road.' ('Carriage of Passengers in a Horsebox', UK Department for Transport.)

BED-MAKING TIPS

- If your bed cushions also make up seat cushions, you MUST ensure that the cushions are fixed to the seat base, otherwise they can slip – and be dangerous – if you have to brake suddenly.
- If your cushions have knee supports, turn them around and put them under your head. Much better than having them under your bum, in the middle of the night.
- If your bed is made up of lots of small cushions, draw a map of your bed and the way it is supposed to be set up. Tape it to the inside of one of your cupboards. Try it out before you go.

Pull and crash tests

Some rock and roll beds are subject to testing. This is often a 'pull test', where the seat is pulled by a mechanism that exerts similar forces on the seat as it would receive if a vehicle were to stop very suddenly (crash). Depending on the number of passengers a seat is designed to carry, rock and roll beds get pull tested for 3 (one person), 7 (two people) or 11 tonnes (three people). This is a test of the strength of the seat and seat belts, not necessarily of the loading points of the seat (where it fixes to the chassis).

Some manufacturers also send their bed frames off for 'in-vehicle' crash testing, which actually tests the strength of the mountings as well as the seat itself. Often, these manufacturers add extra strengthening to the chassis to be able to cope with high loads.

Other manufacturers also test their seats with 'sled tests', in which the seats are tested on sleds that move backward and forwards, so creating a more 'realistic' scenario.

PUTTING SAFETY FIRST

There are lots of rock and roll beds on the market. Some are pull tested, some in-vehicle tested, few are sled tested. Many are compliant. Only you can make big decisions about the integrity and safety of the products you put in your van. However, if it were me making those decisions, I would go for the most rigorously tested and approved design I could afford. It's precious cargo aboard.

MAKES OF ROCK AND ROLL BEDS

Reimo rock and roll beds (**www.reimo.com**) (Reimo is an approved VW converter based in Germany with a base in the UK) are engineered

differently and run on runners that are bonded to the vehicle's floor, so spreading the load over the entire floor rather than on a small number of mounting points.

BEBB rock and roll beds (**www.bebb.co.uk**) are tested in-vehicle and come supplied with extra strengthening.

RIB altair beds from Scopema (**www.scopema.com**) are considered to be among the best rock and roll beds and also come with extra chassis strengthening. Unlike other beds, they turn over, so you sleep on the underside of the seat, allowing for a completely flat bed, while at the same time still enjoying sculpted seats.

Titan beds (**www.titanbeds.co.uk**) are easy to use and sturdy. They are also M1 pull tested.

NOTE: in the UK, there can be differing restrictions on seats in vehicles in M or N classes depending on the DVLA category.

BEDS MADE FROM OTHER SEATS

Lots of motorhomes and camper vans have beds made up in all sorts of ways: from table tops, seat cushions, extra pieces and pull-out bits. Some take a little getting used to, others not so much. Remember that any seats without seat belts, that are side facing and not type approved, cannot be used while driving.

Fixed beds

In recent years, particularly in Europe, there has been a trend towards 'fixed' beds. These are beds that stay made all day. Often, they are made slightly higher than a normal bed to allow for garage space below. This is the height of luxury, if I'm honest, but it can take up space that might be used for living in smaller conversions.

MAKE BEDTIME EASY

You may think that making a bed each night won't be a hassle, but it can be, no matter how quickly you can do it. If you're the type who needs to tumble into bed at the end of a busy day, it may be wise to have a fixed bed, if you can live with the compromise on space, or at least have the ability to live in the van with the bed down on busy days. If bedtime is a hassle on day one of your trip it will be a hundred times the hassle on day 10, when you're cream-crackered and half-full of vino tinto.

The advantages are clear: you can simply crawl into a fixed bed at night – no putting on sheets or zipping up sleeping bags or moving boxes. And on top of it all, you get to sleep on a real mattress.

DOWNSIDES: Fixed beds take up living space.
UPSIDES: You don't have to make the bed every night and get to sleep on a real mattress.

ABOVE-CAB BEDS (LUTON)

Luton cab motorhomes are those with a large area above the cab for a fixed bed. They are very useful if you need to keep living space clear or if there are more than two travelling. Kids love them.

DOWNSIDES: Climbing up a ladder, headroom is limited.
UPSIDES: Kids love them.

DROP-DOWN BEDS

Beds that rise and fall are nothing particularly new in motorhomes. A lot of A-Class motorhomes make use of the space above the driver's seats to fit a bed that stays made and drops down at night. Often, the driver and passenger seat have to be moved to make this work but the principle is simple.

In recent years, drop-down beds have been installed in large van conversions as well as motorhomes. These simply drop from the ceiling on straps or motorised lifts. This way, two beds can be made to take up the same space as one.

Some motorhomes have beds that rise and fall to allow for more or less space in the garage.

DOWNSIDES: They take up space in the roof of the van.
UPSIDES: You can fit an extra bed in a smaller space.

Comfort and your bedding foam

Buying foam for a conversion or looking at beds for a conversion? This section is for you.

The first thing to remember is that comfort is relative. Bony bottomed people are going to need softer, thicker seating than someone with natural padding. The only way of knowing what's right for you is to try it.

The second thing to remember is to think about what your cushions are to be used for predominantly. Are they to be for seating or bedding?

UNDERSTANDING FOAM GRADES

Bedding and seating foam is graded by FOAM TYPE, DENSITY, HARDNESS and VOLUME. On your search for a decent night's sleep you may come across foam grades such as 3 INCH V38/200 or the heady combination of a classic 4 INCH R40/180. You lucky people. Let's explain...

Foam type

This is the basic name for any particular type of foam.

- **V is for foam that is 'heavy domestic and contract quality'.**
  A quality foam that is best suited for sitting and seat cushions and will last well. Generally 30 per cent cheaper than Reflex (see below) and better suited to sitting than sleeping.
- **R is for Reflex, a brand name.** This is a very high-quality latex foam that will retain its properties over time. The best quality for sleeping.
- **CMHR is for 'Combustion Modified High Resilience Foam'.**
  It includes a lot of melamine for flame retardancy. It can tend to powder over time and retain moisture, so isn't recommended for camper vans.
- **RECON is reconditioned foam.** It's made up from all the off-cuts. Generally poor wearing, very heavy and not much use to anyone, although it is cheap. Avoid.

Foam density

This is the weight of the foam in kilograms per cubic metre. The higher the number, the higher the density. A high-density foam will last longer and be of better quality. Expect to see density of around 38–40 for a decent foam.

Hardness

This is measured in Newtons. It's all about comfort. Typical foams for campers come in at anywhere between 135 and 200 Newtons, depending on the comfort required.

The rules for choosing foam based on hardness:

- If you're sitting more than sleeping, use a high-density V grade foam. If it's less firm, go for extra thickness. V40/200 at 3 inches is a good bet for camper van cushions.
- If you're sleeping more than sitting, use a thicker, but less firm, Reflex foam. Try something like an R38/150 at 5 inches for a cosy night.

Volume

This is basically the thickness of the foam, with increased volume offering you more support. However, after a certain point, volume is pointless, as a dense foam can have the same support at 3 inches thick as at 4 inches thick, depending on how you use it.

CHOOSING FOAM OR MATTRESSES FOR YOUR HOME CONVERSION

When the time comes to work out how big your bed is going to be in your home conversion, stick, if you can, to standard sizes, especially if you're looking at mattresses. While foam can be cut to size easily, it is generally extremely expensive to stray from standard bed sizes for some materials.

So, when planning your bed, stick to the following:

Sizing up your bed foam (in cm)	
90 x 190	single
122 x 200/190	small double
135 x 200/190	standard double
150 x 200	king size
180 x 200	super king

MEMORY FOAM EXTRAS

Lots of campers like to top up their standard cushions with memory foam toppers, with the idea that a little extra comfort can make an uncomfortable bed more comfortable. And it can. However, in the camper van context, it does have limitations.

Memory foam moulds to your shape and cradles you in your sleep. It works very well in everyday life but its main property – that its hardness is determined by temperature – can work against it.

Between room temperature and body temperature, memory foam will halve its hardness – it doesn't like the cold. So, if you're creeping back from the pub to a cold van, it could well feel like sleeping on cardboard until your body temperature has warmed it up a bit.

If memory foam is part of a multi-layered cushion (and therefore underneath a cushion cover as well as a sheet or a sleeping bag), it'll take longer to heat up through your covers (if at all) and so longer to be effective (if at all). In addition, memory foam requires three-way fabric to be truly effective and mould to your body shape – this won't work so well through a vinyl covering.

TOP TIP FOR UNCOMFY MATTRESSES

If your camper van bed is uneven, lumpy or just uncomfortable, you can make it less so by adding a sleeping mat or thick duvet to it underneath your sheet. Sleeping mats are often super light, self-inflating (to a point) and surprisingly comfy. Adding one to an existing bed should help to remove the lumps and bumps. As an added bonus, they roll up small and can easily be stowed.

OVERNIGHTING

Planning overnights

Not everyone likes to plan their trip down to the tiniest detail, but it can help to have a rough idea of where you might stay from one night to the next. If you are touring it can become like a job to work out where to stay, with lots of resources needed to plan ahead, even if it's just an hour.

The issue we are trying to avoid here is getting to the end of the day and not having anywhere suitable to stay. It does happen. To prevent this, here are some tips for advance overnight planning:

- Get your first night sorted out, at the very least, in advance, in a campsite where you can spend a little time getting used to living in your van again. Get there before dark and leave as late as possible so as to not be in a rush. Set the speed and tone of the weeks to come.

- If you're planning on wild camping, make sure you know where you'll be able to fill up and empty so you're not tempted to empty waste on the fly. This is NOT good. Find campsite alternatives that you can head to when you need that wash and brush-up.

- Look at the options for aires or motorhome stopovers so that you have somewhere to go if you get moved on or can't find anything suitable.

- Plan on taking a couple of days 'off' every week or so to give yourself a chance to stop and rest. If you're continually on the move, it can be tiring packing up day after day. Having a morning when you can leave the bed out can be a tonic!

- Remember that you can always move if you don't like a site. Have a spare up your sleeve in case it turns out to be a disaster.

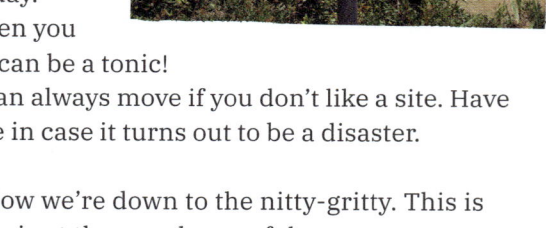

But where to overnight? Now we're down to the nitty-gritty. This is what it's all about. Sleeping is at the very heart of the camper van or motorhome experience. Without it, the camper van would just be … well … a van. Overnighting is the *raison d'être* of this cult we call camper van.

Of course, everyone is different and we all have different wants, needs and desires. But at the heart of it is the idea of freedom, of waking up somewhere new, of the endless possibilities given to you by a new day, of escaping to somewhere other than humdrum, of exploration and finding new experiences, places and things, and of appreciating the outdoors.

For those new to campervanning or motorhoming, I'd like to spend the next 20 or so pages going through the options for you. I think it's important to know what's open to you, so you can make your own choices about what you aspire to, feel comfortable with or simply like the sound of. I'll go through all the possibilities and explain the pros and cons. I hope it won't offend you if I point out some of the basic stuff,

especially if you already camp regularly, but it's important to get it right. Staying in the wrong kind of place can make or break a trip.

Of course, the best thing about your motorhome or camper van is that you can up sticks and move on to somewhere better if you don't like it. The secret, though, is to know what you like and head there first.

And that's what this section is all about.

Michelle

'We love being in there so much we sometimes just sit in the van on the drive, still in awe of what we've got.'

So, back in 2014, my hubby Simon decided it was his turn to have his dream car and that turned out to be a VW T5. We got it home and I couldn't really understand why we needed something so big for two of us and our little dog, who by the way hated it! We bought private plates and the van was named 'Ella' by hubby, because she was a 'Ella've a lot of money'...! 'It' was now officially a 'she'.

Our first proper trip out was for New Year and we headed to the Lakes after packing then repacking stuff, finding homes for everything and just getting used to our little engine house on wheels. We had the best time, and I still can't stop saying it's the best thing we've ever done. We've been to Europe, we've been to Canada skiing, but none of those trips ever created as much excitement as when I'm getting the van packed up ready for a weekend away.

Being able to cook and live in our little van without the worry of the weather outside is just awesome. The dog will not let me pack up without her being with me – it's not enough just to sit watching me through the window, she has to come with me no matter how big or small the job. We love being in there so much we sometimes just sit in the van on the drive, still in awe of what we've got. It's just awesome.

Campsites

Campsites come in all shapes and sizes. Big, small, quirky, wild, manicured, regimented, noisy, quiet, boring, whatever. Every one of them is different. However, we can generally class them in types, so at least you know what to expect. Sort of.

Holiday/ touring parks

These are the giants of the leisure industry. Usually owned by large companies or groups, like Hoseasons, Parkdean or Haven, they often have a mix of camping, touring (pitches for caravans and motorhomes) and chalets (mobile homes). Lots of these kinds of parks have attractions and activities and may have pools, bars, restaurants, a golf course, amusements, whatever. You may find that camping pitches are limited. In any case, expect to be among families, kids and the whole of humanity in its many forms and all of its wondrous beauty.

PROS: Lots for everyone to do. Fun for the kids.
CONS: Not everyone likes big sites with lots of chalets and mobile homes.

Club sites

There are two camping and caravanning clubs in the UK.

The Camping and Caravanning Club is the oldest. It began life in 1901 as the Association of Cycle Campers and today welcomes campers, caravans, camper vans and motorhomes. It offers insurance, online booking, a network of sites and help and advice, plus discounts.

The Caravan and Motorhome Club used to be just the Caravan Club, but changed the name in 2018 to reflect the changing landscape. Again, it offers travel advice, and travel and insurance packages and cover, and has a network of club sites and affiliate sites.

The advantage of staying on club sites is that the experience is often very similar from site to site. You are guaranteed a good washroom experience, checking in is generally on the same terms and the approach is similar. They also have a 6m rule, which guarantees distance between you and your neighbour. Sometimes, however, they can be a little too regimented regarding their rules for how you pitch.

PROS: Well-organised sites, with wardens, good-quality showers and washrooms, and often extra facilities. Great for wash and brush-up days. Good locations. Guaranteed experience.
CONS: Can be a little regimented and may feel corporate. You may feel surrounded by white boxes.

Small/ independent sites

Lots of campers like to turn their backs on the kind of 'civilised' camping you might find at a club site and go for a more natural camping experience. Sites may be on a working farm or just because it's someone's dream to own a nice campsite. Often gems, sometimes basic, occasionally in spectacular locations.

When you want to see countryside or beach out of your camper van window rather than a sea of mobile homes and static caravans, the small site is the way to go. This is camping as it should be (if you ask me), the way I remember it from when I was a boy, except the shower blocks and facilities have been upgraded.

These are the kinds of sites that people revere and talk about on forums. If you find a good one, keep it to yourself. They may not have a website. They may not have online booking. You may be required just to turn up.

Check websites like **www.pitchup.com**, **www.campsited .com**, **www.coolcamping.com** and **www.campsites.co.uk** for the best UK and European selection.

PROS: Camping how it should be. In a field, away from the trappings of modern life.
CONS: You might not get wifi.

Certificated Locations

(CARAVAN AND MOTORHOME CLUB)/ CERTIFICATED SITES (CAMPING AND CARAVANNING CLUB)

These are small, privately run sites that are allowed to offer pitches for up to five units (or 10 tents if a Camping and Caravanning Club Certificated Site). There are thousands of them all over the UK. Often located on farms or run as a side business. You'll need to be a member of a club to use them, which makes it all the more worthwhile joining. It is often advisable to book in advance (often just call ahead). These sites are commonly out of the way, in interesting places where big sites wouldn't be allowed. For more see **www.caravanclub.co.uk** and **www. campingandcaravanningclub.co.uk**.

PROS: Great locations on private land, often secluded and quiet with just a few other campers.
CONS: Fewer facilities than bigger sites. Directories show what facilities are available. May need to have your own loo.

Themed camping

One way to make yourself feel comfortable on a campsite is to hang out with people who think like you. Of course, you can't ever tell if you're going to get on with your neighbours before you arrive at a site, but you can increase the chances by going to sites where your kind might gather. Whatever your kind is.

ADULTS ONLY

So you don't like kids? That's OK. Other people don't like them either. And it may be best if you all stick together so you can find a little peace and quiet on your just-for-grown-ups campsite. It's a shame that some sites prefer not to hear the joyous laughter of healthy, outdoor children, but that's the way it is.

PROS: If you're allergic to kids, this is your kind of camping.
CONS: If you have kids, you can't go.

NATURIST CLUBS AND SITES

There is something beautiful about going wild when you're going wild. I'm not a naturist but I see nothing wrong with stripping off and baring all. If your camping experiences include wanting to let the sun see the whole of you, then there are lots of options, with more in Europe than in the UK (perhaps for obvious reasons – i.e. the weather!).

See **www.naturist.guide** for a list of naturist campsites and review in the UK and Europe.

Alan Rogers, providers of guide books and camping directories, has a list of naturist campsites all over Europe **www.alanrogers.com**.

PROS: If you want to be among naked people, there's no better way to camp.
CONS: Are there any? For naturists, perfect. Weather dependent.

Pop-up summer sites Some campsites pop up in the summertime only, so taking advantage of the 28-day rule (in the UK) that allows campsites to have a temporary licence. These can often be just for camper vans and motorhomes, as they have no real facilities or share facilities with a shop, bar or café. Some people call them aires.

PROS: It's normally about the location, so they're situated in great places.

CONS: In my experience, they offer few facilities other than loos and water, if that.

Campsite alternatives

AIRES AND OVERNIGHTS

'Aires' is the common (UK) name for *aires de camping car* (motor-home area). These are overnight parking places that are specifically designated for motorhomes and camper vans. The system is prevalent in France, although it's spreading across Europe, with guides now available for France, Belgium, Germany, Italy, Spain, Portugal, the Netherlands and Luxembourg from **www.vicariousbooks.co.uk**.

The idea is that local councils (or private individuals) provide an overnight stop for self-contained motorhomes. Tents and caravans are not allowed, neither is putting out tables and chairs or awnings. Most aires have fresh water

and facilities for emptying waste water and toilet tanks – these are known as service points. Some have electricity. Some charge for the privilege and others don't. Some provide showers and toilets, others just the basics – a parking place and somewhere to empty the Porta Potti. Local police often make daily rounds and take number plates to ensure no one abuses the system.

I understand why the French have aires. They offer a neat solution to some problems. With designated places, they can police who stays overnight and control illegal camping on the roadside or at beauty spots (they are using a similar technique in the Scottish Islands). They also go some way to controlling the flow of traffic through busy summer resorts by signposting the aires via quiet routes or placing them on the edge of town. It works. The system also works to attract people to a town and gives them a reason to visit – if there's a cheap place to stay, people will come and spend money in the town.

Aires post–Covid

In the wake of the Covid-19 pandemic and the motorhome traffic it brought, particularly in Scotland, more and more aires are in existence and being proposed. A campaign group called CAMpRA has been working hard to influence councils to open aires and has provided lots of useful information to help.

The National Trust, Forestry Commission and Scottish Forestry have been trialling overnighting on selected properties. Watch this space, but the news is good for the future.

Find new aires on SearchforSites: **www.searchforsites.co.uk**.
Find overnights on Park4Night: **www.park4night.com**.
Find out more about CAMpRA here: **www.campra.org.uk**.

BRITSTOPS

These are the British version of the highly popular France Passion scheme that puts producers, cafés, restaurants and bars in touch with motorhomers. The hosts offer a free night (and often no facilities)

on their land in exchange for a simple hello. There is no obligation to buy anything, although if you stay in a pub car park you know where you'll end up.

The guide costs £32 or so and gives you a year's worth of 'invitations' to stay on more than 1,000 sites across the UK and Ireland. Locations vary, but they are mostly pubs. The guide includes details of the number of spaces, whether you have to call ahead and if there are any facilities.

There is no charge for staying, only the obligation that you will say hello and goodbye as you leave. To take advantage of the scheme you must be self-contained and have the current guide.

Buy your Britstops Guide from **www.britstops.com**. There are similar schemes in Italy and Spain. Buy the guides, including France Passion, from **www.vicariousbooks.co.uk**.

Wild or free camping

This is camping off-grid, away from campsites or alternatives, freely and in the wild. It's the Shangri-La of the camping world and lots of camper van and motorhome owners aspire to it.

In Scotland, wild camping is legal, although the right to roam does not actually extend to vehicles. However, it is largely tolerated in many places, despite issues in the past. Some places, like the Trossachs National Park, now have bookable wild camping permits that must be purchased online in order to control antisocial behaviour at many precious sites. In recent times, there has been much made of wild camping, caused by those who choose to abuse the right. During the summer of 2020 and 2021, places that are usually open to wild camping (in tents primarily) were shut down as a result of antisocial behaviour and the sheer numbers of people wanting to get out and into the countryside.

The idea is great, but in practice it may not be.

I love 'free' or 'off-site' camping. I've done it regularly ever since I started sleeping in vans. Sometimes, in winter, it was a necessity. I slept in boatyards, on quaysides, among dunes and in pub car parks

just to be able to go for an early surf. And it was brilliant fun. I still do it now. But the fact remains that wild camping is illegal in England and Wales. And, unless we realise that we must respect the countryside and leave it nicer than how we found it, we'll forever forfeit any rights we may have.

The **Caravan Sites and Control of Development Act 1960** makes it a civil offence to pitch your tent or park your camper without permission on someone else's land or to operate a caravan site or campsite without a licence. There are exceptions (for clubs and societies and for licensed gatherings) but on the whole the Act means that you are causing an offence by camping on unlicensed sites without permission.

Landowners, even the ones who don't mind, are restricted by the amount of time that they can allow anyone to camp on their land, even with permission. They may allow one caravan, motorhome or camper van to stay overnight, for no more than two nights in succession and for no more than 28 days in any 12-month period.

Wild camping is a civil offence, which means that it is a matter for the courts, not the police. You make your own choices, but it is as well to remember that parking up on the hard shoulder or in a lay-by (that is a part of the public highway) means that the police do have the power to move you on, if they consider you are causing an obstruction. Although in my experience, a policeman in a good mood would rather see you snatch a few hours' kip than drive tired.

At the time of writing, trespass – wild camping on other's land without permission – is a civil offence, but the government is making moves to make it illegal, which means the police will have the power to remove and arrest you if a complaint is made against you.

OVERNIGHTING ON THE SIDE OF THE ROAD

How many times have you found a beautiful parking spot – an esplanade or lay-by or car park – only to find you can't stay for the night because of the 'no overnight parking' signs? It's infuriating. But is it legally enforceable?

There seems to be plenty of information, and everywhere is different, but essentially, if you're not causing

an obstruction and are parked legally, it may not be enforceable. However, as is the case in parts of Scotland, if there is evidence of the local bylaw or traffic regulation order on the sign, then it may be. Traffic regulation orders are legal documents that restrict or prohibit use of the highway network. They can be concerned with parking and prohibition of certain types of vehicles and may be enforceable with fines.

This may be the case when councils decide to ban overnighting in camper vans at hotspots, car parks and in places where residents have complained about antisocial behaviour and mess (or just don't like motorhomes), or there have been historic problems with narrow streets, overcrowding or disrespectful overnighting. It may also be that some councils don't want you staying in their towns and spending money in their shops. The best thing to do? Go somewhere else!

THE RULES OF WILD CAMPING

This is simple. Please follow these rules:

- Leave it nicer than it was when you arrived. Take your litter home. If you can, pick up others' litter and take it home, too. You'll make a good impression.
- Do not empty tanks of any type anywhere you are not authorised. Take it with you until you are able to dispose of it properly.
- If you can, get permission from the landowner.
- Do not light fires or BBQs unless you know it is approved by the landowner.
- Arrive late and leave early.
- Don't set up camp, hang out washing or get out all your tables and chairs and windbreaks etc. Others might see it as preparing to stay a long time.
- Don't pitch up near houses or block anyone's views.
- Be prepared to defend your right to wild camp by ensuring others don't break the rules either.
- Don't play loud music or act in an unsociable way.
- If you're asked to move on, do it with a smile.

WILD CAMPING IN NATIONAL PARKS

There are areas in some national parks where it is legal to wild camp. However, that's for the tented folk. If you want to camp in a van, you risk being moved on by the rangers. In the summer of 2020, several

national parks banned wild camping because of the numbers of people doing it and the fact that some of them left a mess.

WILD CAMPING IN SCOTLAND

The promised land! Or is it? The Land Reform (Scotland) Act 2003 makes wild camping legal on public access land in the country. It's a truly liberating thing, but it isn't without its problems.

The Act makes no mention of motorhomes or camper vans and it is safe to assume that wild camping is legal. The Scottish Outdoor Access Code also makes no mention of wild camping in vehicles.

If there was one recurring story in the motorhome world in 2020, it was that wild campers – and we get lumped in with that lot – have been making a big mess in Scotland (as mentioned earlier). This is due to overcrowding and lack of care. What will happen – as has happened in Loch Lomond and the Trossachs National Park – is that hotspots get zoned and wild campers will require a permit. The best way to avoid this is if we all follow the wild camping rules outlined above.

WILD CAMPING IN EUROPE

In my experience, wild camping is easier in Spain and France than in the UK, with Spain marginally ahead in terms of ease. France's aire system takes care of a lot of the problems it has had in the past with wild camping (mess and disrespect) by encouraging it in organised areas. There are still places where wild camping is tolerated, but in some areas – for example the Côte d'Azur – local bylaws have made it virtually impossible to stay in beach-side car parks or in lay-bys. Don't be surprised if you get the knock in the night.

In Spain, I have free-camped all along the north coast without any problems. Wild camping is tolerated at many spots and has become a part of life at some surf destinations – even though it may not be strictly legal. There are laws that prohibit camping within 200m of the beach and in other places, such as near military zones, national parks and plenty of other places. Some regions ban wild camping altogether while others allow it as long as there are no more than three units, fewer than 10 people and you stay no more than three days. Whatever the rules and how you interpret them, respect is always the order of the day.

In Scandinavian countries, including Norway and Sweden, the individual has certain rights to roam and gain access to land. In fact, as a nation with rights of access and the right to commune with nature embedded in its culture and laws, Norway has some of the most liberal access laws of any country. However, it also comes with rules, such as not camping within 150m of a house or on uncultivated land, in young forest or where it may cause environmental damage.

For more information, ask Google. There are plenty of sites offering suggestions for wild camping spots in almost every country.

Final tip: leave it nicer.

Going off-grid: tips for managing your resources

If you're travelling off-grid, or even just taking a few days away from campsites by camping on aires or at smaller sites with fewer facilities, it can pay to learn how to manage your resources. What I am referring to here is emptying, filling and cooking. I would include food in this, but it's really up to you.

GAS

If you cook, heat and run fridges on gas, it pays to get to know how much you are likely to use on cold nights (when you're likely to use more) so you have some idea of how many days your tanks or bottles will last for the weather you expect to encounter. Ensure you are full before you set off or at least try to plan when you might be able to exchange bottles or fill up with LPG on your journey. Filling with LPG can sometimes be a challenge, so use **www.mylpg.com** to work out your next fill, and keep an eye on your levels.

- Run gas-powered fridges on low settings to conserve gas.
- Run heating a few degrees colder to help conserve gas.
- Cook quick meals to conserve gas.
- Plan your refills and keep an eye on levels.

WATER

If you have an on-board tank you should have a level indicator that tells you how much you have left. This is fine if you know you can get more water but not so handy if you need to conserve it. Using less water when washing up, flushing the loo less and doing all you can to conserve water means you'll need to fill up less often.

- Don't leave taps running while cleaning your teeth or washing your hands.
- Use less water to wash up.
- Don't run taps when washing your hands.

WASTE

Chemical toilets cannot be emptied in the wild. This means you need to make sure you don't overfill your toilet and have space enough for a few days. Going for a nature wee or stepping outside to go in the night will help. Avoiding using too much water to flush will help to conserve fresh supplies.

- Line the loo with paper to avoid needing lots of water to flush the bowl clean.
- Wee in the wild when you can to avoid unnecessary filling.
- Never empty your loo in the wild.

Grey waste

In most motorhomes that have both fresh and waste tanks, the waste tank is smaller than the fresh tank. This is on the assumption that not all of the fresh water ends up in the waste tank. Since it's not good form to empty waste into the wild, it's a good idea to stop your waste tank from overflowing by managing what you put into it, how much fresh water you send to it and how much fresh water you lose elsewhere.

Places to stay en route

Got a long way to go? Then better plan for a stop along the way. There are some options open to you, however each one comes with caveats. Nothing is ever simple. If you stay in a public place then it will either be the police or the local authority who has the responsibility for that space. They have different powers, but ultimately both can move you on, wherever you are. Be prepared to be moved on if you don't have permission to stay. The last thing to do is have a glass of wine with supper. If the police come knocking and don't like the smell of you, you could end up spending the rest of the night in jail, or worse.

CAR PARKS AND MOTORWAY SERVICES

Every car park is different and has different rules. Some motorway services will slap a ticket on you if you don't buy a ticket for time over 2 hours (supermarkets can do this, too).

Now, I'm not saying that these are legal or not legal, but I have never paid one, having written, on several occasions to the issuing 'authority' (usually just the car park owners), to declare that I had stopped because I was in danger of crashing – this seems a very reasonable response to a big 'invoice'. In the UK these 'fines' aren't issued by the police or local councils and are usually just 'invoices'.

TRUCK STOPS

Looking for a good brekkie? This is the place to stop. Just be careful, park away from traffic, don't block anyone in. As with any park-up, lock your doors and windows and keep everything out of sight.

STEALTH CAMPING

Some campers don't look like campers. That enables them to go under the radar of the authorities and stay in places other campers wouldn't even consider. It's at your own risk. But the same applies: if you get moved on, go. If you have a drink, be prepared for the consequences.

PITCH PERFECT: THE BEST UK CAMPSITES

What's your idea of a perfect campsite? Views?
Proximity to water? A pub? Ease with which you can get to a city?

Everyone's idea of perfect is different. It all depends on what
criteria you use to judge a site. Often, it's just how a place *feels* that's
important. It doesn't matter if places are a little ramshackle if the
views are great and the owner is lovely. Guide books can't always
tell you this.

The following is a list of campsites rated on what is special about
them, with an honest description of why they're special, to give you
a good idea of what to expect. It's by no means exhaustive, as I haven't
included sites I haven't been to or don't like. If you want comprehensive
then I suggest checking out the following guide books:

- *Cool Camping Britain: A hand-picked selection of exceptional
  campsites*, James Warner Smith & Jonathan Knight (Punk
  Publishing, 2020)
- *Tiny Campsites: 80 small but perfect places to pitch,* Dixe Wills
  (AA Publishing, 2017)
- *Touring Europe in a Caravan, Motorhome or Tent*, Katie Walters
  (The Caravan and Motorhome Club 2022)

Scotland

1 BEST FOR CAMPING ON LOCH LOMOND

Luss Caravan and Campsite

Luss, Loch Lomond,
  Argyll & Bute, G83 8NT
www.lusscampsite.co.uk
01436 860 658

This site consists of 90 pitches
of glorious lochside camping.
Gets busy and can get midgey.
Book early for a pitch next to
the loch.

2 BEST FOR AN OVERNIGHT EN ROUTE TO OBAN

Ardfern Motorhome Park

Barrfada Farm, Ardfern,
  Argyll, PA31 8QN
www.ardfernmotorhomepark.com
ardfernmotorhomepark
  @gmail.com
07949 494 492

Tucked away down a little
offshoot, by the sea, away from
the A816, it's got everything a
motorhome stopover should have.
It's cheap, too, and has a decent
loo and nice, simple facilities.
An aire in the Highlands.
Go for it.

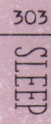

3 BEST FOR DIVERS AND JUMPING-OFF EXPLORERS

Oban Caravan & Camping Park

Gallanachmore Farm, Gallanach
  Road, Oban, Argyll, PA34 4QH
www.obancaravanpark.com
info@obancaravanpark.com
01631 562 425

Just 3.1 miles from Oban and
yet a world away. With views
over to the Isle of Kerrera, it's a
beautiful and tranquil site that's
a short walk from the Puffin Dive
Centre. Perfect for overnights on
the way somewhere or even as
a base for a holiday. But then,
with the Western Isles just a
boat ride away, why linger?

4 BEST FOR GOING ON SAFARI

Blair Drummond Caravan Park & Shepherd Huts

Blair Drummond, By Stirling,
  FK9 4UP
www.blairdrummondcaravan
  park.co.uk
office@blairdrummondcaravan
  park.co.uk
01786 841 208

A walled campsite in lovely
surroundings near Blair
Drummond Safari Park.
No animal noises reported.

Oban Caravan & Camping Park

5 BEST FOR EXPLORING LOCH KATRINE AND THE TROSSACHS

Loch Katrine Aire

Trossachs Pier, Loch Katrine,
  Stirling, FK17 8HZ
www.lochkatrine.com
enquiries@lochkatrine.com
01877 376 315/6

Loch Katrine is fabulous. A wonderful place for a walk or cycle and to see where Victorian Glasgow got its water (and where it still does). Favoured by Sir Walter Scott and Queen Vic. Stay over in the car park at Loch Katrine with toilet, showers, chemical waste disposal point, electric hook-up, recycling and visitor wifi.

6 BEST FOR EXPLORING THE RIVER TAY

Maragowan Caravan Club Site

Aberfeldy Road, Killin, Stirling,
  FK21 8TN
www.caravanclub.co.uk
enquiries@haughtonhouse.co.uk
01567 820 245

Brilliantly situated site on the banks of River Lochay, a little downstream from Killin on the A827 at the western end of Loch Tay.

7 BEST FOR VIEWS OF SKYE

Sands Caravan & Camping

Gairloch, Wester Ross, IV21 2DL
www.sandscaravanand
  camping.co.uk
info@sandscaravanand
  camping.co.uk
01445 712 152

Pitches in the dunes near Gairloch, overlooking Skye. Amazing beaches nearby in this touring park in the wilderness of Wester Ross.

8 BEST FOR HIGHLAND WILDERNESS

Kinlochewe Caravan Club Site

Kinlochewe, Achnasheen, IV22 2PA
www.caravanclub.co.uk
info@sandscaravanand
  camping.co.uk
01445 760 239

Another oasis of Caravan and Motorhome calm in a wild, open landscape near Torridon.

9 BEST FOR THE BEALACH NA BA PASS

Applecross Campsite

Strathcarron, Ross-Shire,
 IV54 8ND
www.visitapplecross.com/
 accommodation/camping
enquiries@visitapplecross.com
01520 744 268

A small, family-run site in the centre of Applecross, the village at the bottom of the pass. Busy, so book ahead in peak periods. Just a short walk from the walled garden café and situated at the heart of this stunning hideaway in the wilderness.

10 BEST FOR SEAL WATCHING

Borve Camping & Caravan Site

104a Borve, Isle of Barra, HS9 5XR
www.barracamping.co.uk
donald@barracamping.co.uk
07530 265 531

Seriously, one of the best-situated campsites I have ever had the pleasure of waking up in. Great views and nice, clean facilities. Nice owner. Dodgy wifi at the far end, but does that really matter when you can watch the local seals bask on the rocks below?

11 BEST FOR EXPLORING NORTH UIST

Balranald Hebridean Holidays

Hougharry, North Uist,
 Outer Hebrides, HS6 5DL
www.balranaldhebridean
 holidays.com
info@balranaldhebridean
 holidays.com
01876 510 304
 or 07748 267 996

A lovely little site with two hardstanding pitches with electric. It's just about 20m from a gorgeous, west-facing white-sand beach. Perfect for watching the sun go down.

12 BEST FOR WILD-LIFE SPOTTING ON ARRAN

Seal Shore Camping and Touring Site

Kildonan, Isle of Arran,
 KA27 8SE
www.campingarran.com
enquiries@campingarran.com
01770 820 320

Amazing site right on the shore. It's small, so book ahead to avoid disappointment. Snorkelling and fresh fish in season. Nice hotel bar next door. Book it!

13 BEST FOR WHISKY

Lochranza Caravan & Camping Site

Lochranza, Isle of Arran, KA27 8HL
www.arran-campsite.com
info@arran-campsite.com
01770 830 273

Nice, open site that's handy for the north, for walks to Fairy Dell and the Lochranza Distillery.

14 BEST FOR EXPLORING LEWIS

Eilean Fraoich Campsite

77A North Shawbost, Isle of Lewis, HS2 9BQ
www.eileanfraoich.co.uk
01851 710 504

A neat and tidy site on the wilder side of Lewis. Handy for Callanaish and the north coast. One of only a handful of sites on Lewis.

15 BEST FOR THE MACHAIR IN HARRIS

Horgabost Campsite

Horgabost Township, Isle of Harris, HS3 3HR
www.horgabostcampsite.co.uk
01859 550 386

A brilliantly located site overlooking the beach at Horgabost. Popular but still lovely.

16 BEST FOR HARRIS
WILD CAMPING

West Harris Trust Camping Spots

www.westharristrust.org

The West Harris Trust was set up in 2010 to revitalise the villages along the west coast of Harris. This has led to a positive attitude towards motorhomers looking for places to wild camp. It's a great thing for the community to do and we all applaud it. However, let's not forget that staying here is a privilege not a right, by keeping it clean and tidy and ensuring we leave it well and make donations when asked for.

Camping spots can be found at:

Seilebost School

Isle of Harris, HS3 3HP
01859 503 900

Nightly fee including hook-up.

Talla na Mara

Pairc Niseaboist,
 Isle of Harris,
 HS3 3AE
01859 503 900

Nightly fee including hook-up.

Pairc Niseaboist

Pairc Niseaboist,
 Isle of Harris,
 HS3 3AE
01859 503 901

Quieter spots linked to Talla na Mara site. £5 donation. Not suitable for awnings or tents.

Losgaintir, Seilebost and Niseaboist

Sites off A859
01859 503 900

Six Trust camping spots. Fantastic views. Marked with a small sign.

17 BEST FOR FAIRY POOL AND THE CUILLINS

Glenbrittle Campsite & Cafe

Glenbrittle, Isle of Skye, IV47 8TA
www.dunvegancastle.com/
  glenbrittle/campsite
01478 640 404

Perfect base for exploring the Cuillin Mountains, the Fairy Pools and southern Skye. Right on the beach. A wild camping experience, in the wilds, but with facilities and a coffee machine.

18 BEST FOR MOUNTAIN BIKING

Lidalia Touring Caravan Park

Old Station Road, Moss Road,
  Newcastleton, Scottish Borders,
  TD9 0RU
www.lidalia.co.uk
info@lidalia.co.uk
01387 375 587

A small, friendly site with great showers just a minute's cycle from the 7stanes route at Newcastleton. Even in January it was busy with motorhomers and caravanners, so perhaps book early. Just be careful how you reverse on to your pitch: we took off the corner of the grass. Sorry about that Eddie.

19 BEST FOR A WASH AND BRUSH-UP STOP AND A NIGHT OUT*

Melrose Gibson Park Caravan Club Site

High Street, Melrose,
  Scottish Borders, TD6 9RY
www.caravanclub.co.uk
01896 822 969

A well-manicured, friendly, 58-pitch club site with smart uniforms and loos. Also close to town, restaurants, shops and the rugby club. A great stop at which to refresh and fuel up for the next adventure. A short drive from Innerleithen and Glentress 7stanes centres.

*Nights out limited to a few cosy pubs.

20 BEST FOR BOOK LOVERS

Garlieston Lodge Campsite

Burnside Lane, Garlieston,
  Wigtownshire, DG8 8BP
www.garliestonlodge.co.uk
01988 600 641

Adults-only Camping and Caravanning Club Certified Location site with five pitches for caravans and motorhomes and a further three for tents set around a small fishing lake. Traffic-light system for the single loo and shower so you won't stand outside for ages! Close to Wigtown, the book capital of Scotland.

21 BEST FOR SUBTROPICAL GARDENS

New England Bay Caravan Club Site

Port Logan, Stranraer,
 Dumfries and Galloway,
 DG9 9NX
www.caravanclub.co.uk
01776 860 275

Situated right on the water overlooking Luce Bay and the Mull of Galloway, a Caravan and Motorhome Club site with excellent facilities, direct access to the beach and big, private pitches. Just a short drive from the Logan Botanic Garden.

22 BEST FOR THE CITY

Edinburgh Caravan Club Site

35–37 Marine Drive, Edinburgh,
 East Lothian, EH4 5EN
www.caravanclub.co.uk
01313 126 874

A vast and orderly site. Handy for Edinburgh and VERY friendly staff. There are buses into the city from here.

23 BEST FOR KINTYRE AND WATERSPORT

Carradale Bay Caravan and Motorhome Club Site

Carradale, Campbeltown,
 Argyll & Bute, PA28 6QG
www.caravanclub.co.uk
info@carradalebay.com
01583 431 665

I loved Carradale. It felt spacious and light, with big pitches and lovely views of the sea. Friendly owner, too, who clearly loves camping. All in all, a favourite site that's in the middle of Kintyre and adjacent to the beach for watersports lovers.

24 BEST FOR BALMORAL

Motorhome Parking Balmoral Castle

Balmoral Coach Park, Ballater,
 Aberdeenshire, AB35 5TL
www.park4night.com/lieu/
 23236//ballater-a93/united-
 kingdom/aberdeenshire#.
 Y15CWy2l2X0

There are six motorhome parking spaces at Balmoral. They're close together, but free. Great if you plan to visit the castle but I can't see why else you'd want to use them. Not level.

25 BEST FOR SNOWSPORTS

Braemar Caravan Park

Glenshee Road, Braemar,
 Aberdeenshire, AB35 5YQ
www.braemarcaravanpark.co.uk
info@braemarcaravanpark.co.uk
01339 741 373

A big, popular site on the road
to Glenshee Ski Centre.

26 BEST FOR SPEYSIDE

Grantown-on-Spey Caravan Site

Seafield Avenue, Grantown-on-
 Spey, Highlands, PH26 3JQ
www.caravanscotland.com
warden@caravanscotland.com
01479 872 474

A popular, tidy park on the edges
of Grantown-on-Spey, with great
views from the loos on the park's
lofty edges.

27 BEST FOR BEING FURTHEST NORTH

Dunnet Bay Caravan Club Site

A836, Dunnet, Thurso, Highlands,
 KW14 8XD
www.caravanclub.co.uk
01847 821 319

Top of the world! A neat and tidy
site on the machair above the
beach at Dunnet Bay.

28 BEST FOR PITCHING ON THE BEACH

Portsoy Links Caravan Park

Links Road, Portsoy,
 Aberdeenshire, AB45 2RQ
www.portsoylinks.org
contact@portsoylinks.org
01261 842 695

Portsoy Community Enterprise
runs this great little campsite
right on the beach at Portsoy.
The village is lovely, the harbour
ancient and the community spirit
inspiring. There's a traditional
boatbuilding festival in June
each year, plus a community
'boat shed' where it's possible
to learn boatbuilding skills.

29 BEST FOR REMOTENESS

Kinlochbervie Loch Clash Campervan Stopover

Loch Clash Pier, Kinlochbervie,
 Sutherland, IV27 4RR
www.klbcompany.com/loch-
 clash-stopover
grahamandlynn@theuphouse
 .co.uk

Great spot on the quayside at
Bervie in a truly remote corner
of north-west Scotland.

Sango Sands Oasis

31 BEST FOR NORTHERN BEACHES

Sango Sands Oasis

Sango Bay, Durness, Sutherland, IV27 4PZ
www.sangosands.com
stay@sangosands.com
07838 381 065

Amazing views and direct beach access, plus a good pub on site and an automatic petrol station. Best fill-up. Best campsite for miles and miles.

30 BEST FOR WANDERING LONELY SHORES

Invercaimbe Caravan and Camping Site

Invercaimbe Croft, Arisaig, PH39 4NT
www.facebook.com/Invercaimbe-Caravan-Site-256438287736152/
invercaimbe@btinternet.com
07919 872 309

Awesome campsite right on the sea at Arisaig.

32 BEST FOR LOCH ACCESS AND FORT WILLIAM

Bunree Caravan Club Site

Onich, Fort William, Highlands, PH33 6SE
www.caravanclub.co.uk
enquiries@haughtonhouse.co.uk
01855 821 283

Absolutely stunning location on the shores of Loch Linnhe. Fish from your pitch! Less than 20 minutes to Fort William.

England and Wales

1 BEST FOR CULTURE, ART AND BEACHES

Ayr Holiday Park

Alexandra Road,
  St Ives, Cornwall,
  TR26 1EJ
www.ayrholiday
  park.co.uk
recept@ayrholiday
  park.co.uk
01736 795 855

Few campsites
have locations like
this, overlooking St
Ives and Portmeor
beach. Book early!

Ayr Holiday Park

2 BEST FOR HADRIAN'S WALL

Herding Hill Farm Camping and Glamping Site

Herding Hill Farm,
  Shield Hill,
  Haltwhistle,
  Northumberland,
  NE49 9NW
www.herdinghillfarm
  .co.uk
bookings@herdinghill
  farm.co.uk
01434 320 175

A lovely site right on
the wall and a short
walk from a pub
– awesome!

3 BEST FOR WHITEWATER AND TEESIDE

White Water Park Club Campsite

Tees Barrage,
  Stockton-on-Tees,
  County Durham,
  TS18 2QW
www.caravanclub
  .co.uk
01642 634 880

A site that's right
next to the Tees
Barrage. Handy for
Middlesbrough and
the east coast.

SLEEP

4 BEST FOR THE CHEVIOT HILLS

The Boe Rigg Campsite

Charlton, Hexham, NE48 1PE
www.theboerigg.co.uk
hi@theboerigg.co.uk
01434 240663

The Boe Rigg, just outside Hexham in the Cheviot Hills, is our kind of place. There are rooms, plus camping, an excellent restaurant and bar, and very friendly staff. Go see them, say hello and wish that every campsite could be like this.

5 BEST FOR ROBIN HOOD'S BAY

Hooks House Farm Campsite

Robin Hood's Bay, Whitby, North Yorkshire, YO22 4PE
www.hookshousefarm.co.uk
(01947) 880283

Small vans and motorhomes only at this well-placed site in Robin Hood's Bay.

6 BEST FOR WALKING AND THE LAKES

Chapel House Farm Campsite

Chapel House Farm, Borrowdale, Cumbria, CA125XG
www.chapelhousefarm
campsite.co.uk
chapelhousefarmcampsite
@gmail.com
01768 777 256

A small site in the heart of Borrowdale. Amazing base for walking.

7 BEST FOR DERWENTWATER

Keswick Camping and Caravanning Site

Crow Park Road, Keswick, Cumbria, CA12 5EP
www.campingand
caravanningclub.co.uk
01768 772392

Nice, friendly site on the banks of the Derwentwater. Open all year so perfect for winter wanderings.

8
BEST FOR LAKES WINDERMERE AND CONISTON

Coniston Park Coppice Site

Park Gate, Coniston, Cumbria,
 LA21 8LA
www.caravanclub.co.uk
015394 41555

A big site with plenty of
hardstanding among the trees,
great facilities and lakeside
access for small craft and
rubber duckies.

9
BEST FOR WELSH SUNSETS

Cae Du Campsite at Tywyn

Rhosllefain, Tywyn, Gwynedd,
 LL36 9ND
www.visitmidwales.co.uk
01654 711234

Open fires, friendly farmer
and an amazing location.

10
BEST FOR BARMOUTH AND ABERDOVEY

Nyth Robin

Panteidal, Aberdovey,
 Gwynedd, LL35 0RG
www.nythrobin.co.uk
hello@nythrobin.co.uk
07731 783 534

Quiet and secluded yet right
on the main road, and good,
clean facilities.

Wood Farm

11
BEST FOR FOSSIL HUNTING ON THE BEACH

Wood Farm Camping and Caravanning

Axminster Rd, Charmouth,
 Bridport, DT6 6BT
www.caravanclub.co.uk
01297 560697

A big site in the rolling hills
behind Charmouth Beach. Luckily
it's terraced, with good pitches
and a pool. Yes, a pool! Very handy
for fossil hunting on the beach.

12 BEST FOR A GOOD SEASIDE HOLIDAY

Southwold Camping & Caravan Site

Ferry Road, Southwold, Suffolk,
  IP18 6ND
www.southwoldcamping.com
01502 722 486

Council-owned and very popular.
Make a booking and then take
your place at this lovely campsite
south of the seaside town of
Southwold.

13 BEST FOR THE HARTLAND PENINSULA

Stoke Barton Farm and Campsite

Stoke Barton Farm, Stoke
  Barton, Hartland, Bideford,
  North Devon, EX39 6DU
www.westcountry-camping
  .co.uk
01237 441 238

A gem of a site on a working
farm just a short walk from
Hartland Quay and Abbey.

14 BEST FOR TINTAGEL

Trewethett Farm Caravan Club Site

Trethevy, Tintagel, Cornwall,
  PL34 0BQ
www.caravanclub.co.uk
01840 770 222

Another top spot for a site, on the
cliff top above Rocky Valley and
just a short drive from Tintagel.

15 BEST FOR BUDE

Cerenety Eco Campsite

Lynstone Lane, Bude,
  Cornwall, EX23 0LR
www.cerenetycampsite.co.uk
cerenetycampsite@hotmail.com
07789 718 446

An eco campsite in a quiet
location between Bude's
canal and the coast.

16 BEST FOR NORTH NORFOLK

Blue Skies Campsite

Stiffkey Road, Wells-next-the-Sea,
  Norfolk, NR23 1QB
www.blueskiescampsite.co.uk
Info@blueskiescampsite.co.uk
07557 021 660

A campsite that will make you
smile as you drive past and decide
to pull a U-turn. Sunny, friendly
and fun (and bigger than it looks).

17 BEST FOR SAMPHIRE AND THE MARSHES

High Sand Creek Camp Site

Greenway, Stiffkey, Norfolk,
 NR23 1QF
www.highsandcreekcampsites
 tiffkey.co.uk
01328 830 235

Another darling of the Cool
Camping scene. Rightly so, as it's
on the creek and just a dash from
the marshes. Great sunsets, too,
as it's on a gently sloping field.

18 BEST FOR THE DALES

Kettlewell Camping

Conistone Road, Kettlewell,
 North Yorkshire, BD23 5RE
www.kettlewellcamping
 .co.uk
07930 379 079

Traditional camping in
Wharfedale, just outside
Kettlewell, in the glorious
Yorkshire Dales.

19 BEST FOR YORK

York Rowntree Park Caravan Club Site

Terry Avenue, York, North
 Yorkshire, YO23 1JQ
www.caravanclub.co.uk
01904 658 997

One of the club's most popular
sites. Open all year, although if
there's a lot of rain, watch out.
The reception isn't built on stilts
for nothing. Great location.

20 BEST FOR CHATSWORTH HOUSE AND THE PEAKS

Chatsworth Park Caravan Club Site

Baslow, Bakewell, Derbyshire,
 DE45 1PN
www.caravanclub.co.uk
01246 582 226

A great site in a walled garden
on a posh estate. Love it? Yeah!

21 BEST FOR THE THAMES

Hurley Riverside Park

Hurley, Berkshire, SL6 5NE
www.hurleyriversidepark.co.uk
01628 823 501

A formal campsite between
Bisham and Henley with all the
trimmings, but, and it's a great
big, fantastic but, it's on the river!

22 BEST FOR THE DART AND DEVON

River Dart Country Park and Campsite

River Dart Country Park,
  Ashburton, Devon, TQ13 7NP
www.riverdart.co.uk
01364 652 511

A family-friendly campsite and holiday park with loads of activities for the kids and plenty to do for the grown-ups, too. Right on the river.

23 BEST FOR SURF

Newgale Campsite

Wood Hill, Newgale,
  Haverfordwest, SA62 6AS
www.newgalecampsite.co.uk
bookings@newgalecampsite.co.uk
07539 906 611

A very popular site right on the beach at Newgale. Best location if you like surfing or beach walking. Pub and surf shop next door.

Newgale Campsite

SLEEP

Caerfai Farm

24 BEST FOR ITS OWN PRIVATE BEACH

Caerfai Campsite

Caerfai Farm, St Davids,
  Pembrokeshire, SA62 6QT
www.caerfaifarm.co.uk
01437 720 548

A lovely farm campsite with
views overlooking the sea
– and its own private beach.

25 BEST FOR AMAZING BEACH AND WALKS

Whitesands Camping

Whitesands, St Davids,
  Pembrokeshire, SA62 6PS
www.whitesandscamping.co.uk
info@whitesandscamping.co.uk

Great location above Whitesands
Beach near St Davids.

26 BEST FOR MALHAM

Riverside Campsite

Town Head Farm, Cove Road,
  Malham, Skipton, North
  Yorkshire, BD23 4DE
www.malhamdale.com/camping.htm
01729 830 287

This is one of those campsites
you used to stay in when you were
a Scout or with the school outward
bound group. It is a bit niggly but
the location is so good, and the
owners so friendly and easygoing,
that you forgive them their note-
writing habits.

27 BEST FOR BUDE AND BEACHES

Wooda Farm Holiday Park

Poughill, Bude, Cornwall, EX23 9HJ
www.wooda.co.uk
enquiries@wooda.co.uk
01288 352 069

Cae Gwyn

28 BEST FOR SNOWDON

Cae Gwyn Campsite

Nant Peris, Snowdonia, LL55 4UH
01286 870 718

A small, friendly site with space for camper vans, that's close to Llyn Trawsfynyd and Coed y Brenin Bike Park.

29 BEST FOR DORCHESTER AND MAIDEN CASTLE

The Manor House

Winterborne Monkton,
  Dorchester, Dorset, DT2 9PT
www.caravanclub.co.uk/
  certificated-locations/england/
  dorset/dorchester/the-
  manor-house

A delightful Certificated Location right next to Maiden Castle.

30 BEST FOR THE LLYN

Morfa Mawr Caravan and Camping Site

Morfa Mawr, Aberdaron, Pwllheli,
  Gwynedd, LL53 8BD
www.facebook.com/MorfaMawr
01758 760 264

Your reward for crawling up the mountain is a spot overlooking Aberdaron beach, just a few hundred yards from the village and in the right place to take some spectacular walks. OK, so the facilities are basic – just showers and loos and a sanitation point – but you'll have everything with you anyway so what does it matter?

31 BEST FOR INDEPENDENT SPIRIT

Henry's Campsite

The Lizard, Helston,
  Cornwall, TR12 7NX
henryscampsite.co.uk
info@henryscampsite.co.uk
01326 290 596

Brilliant site in the heart of The Lizard, with all its quirky ways.

32 BEST FOR LAKESIDE SHENANIGANS

Outdoor and Active Roadford

Roadford Lake, Lower
Goodacre, Broadwoodwidger,
  Lifton, Devon, PL16 0JL
www.swlakestrust.org.uk
roadfordwatersports
  @swlakestrust.org.uk
01409 211 507

33 BEST FOR SALISBURY AND THE DROVES

Salisbury Campsite at Bake Farm

Bake Farm, Coombe Bissett,
  Salisbury, Wiltshire, SP5 4JT
www.salisburycampsite.co.uk
vj@salisburycampsite.co.uk
07973 601 727

A site based on a farm and with only the most basic of facilities. Even so, a good location and nice people. Handy for cycling the drove roads and seeing Salisbury.

Roadford Lake

Ireland

1 BEST FOR GALWAY CITY

Salthill Caravan Park

Salthill, Galway, H91 K856
www.salthillcaravanpark.com
info@salthillcaravanpark.com
091 523 972
086 817 5551

Salthill is the seaside suburb of Galway heading west, which means it's a great place to stay if you want to explore the city. A path will take you 40 minutes to get to the city centre by foot. Oh yes, the motorhome pitches are right on the sea wall. Fab location.

2 BEST FOR PRIVATE BEACH AND VIEWS

Clifden Eco Beach Camping & Caravanning Park

Claddaghduff Road, Leagaun, Clifden, Co. Galway, H71 W024
www.clifdenecocamping.ie
0954 4036

Kriss's amazing campsite, situated right on the beach near Clifden, is a gem of a place. There are few frills and basic facilities, but friendly service, all with a heart of eco gold. Go, stay, take a fishing rod, say I told you. You will love it.

3 BEST FOR GOING TO THE PUB

Keogh's Ballyconneely

Keoghs Ballyconneely, Ballyconneely, Co. Galway, H71 PX25
www.keoghsballyconneely.com
info@keoghsballyconneely.com
095 235 22

A Britstop with a big car park out front for motorhomes. Very welcoming. Shop and fuel, too. Gave us free crab claws when we sat in the bar with a couple of pints of Guinness.

4 BEST FOR CROAGH PATRICK

Westport House Camping and Caravanning

Westport House, Westport, Co. Mayo, F28 TY45
www.westporthouse.ie/ caravan-camping-mayo
info@westporthouse.ie
098 277 66

A modern campsite in the grounds of Westport House, with lots of activities and extras on site, including a pirate adventure park. Great location!

5 BEST FOR THE SHANNON

Battlebridge Caravan & Camping Park

Leitrim Village, Carrick-on-Shannon, Co. Leitrim
www.battlebridgecaravan
  andcamping.ie/
  camp@battlebridgecaravan
  andcamping.ie
071 965 0824

A great site with a brilliant pub on site that's right next to the Shannon and canal. With its own marina, plus glamping and camping.

6 BEST FOR THE WICKLOW MOUNTAINS

Hidden Valley Holiday Park

Lower Main St, Glasnarget North, Rathdrum, Co. Wicklow, A67 XY56
www.irelandholidaypark.com
info@irelandholidaypark.com
086 727 2872

Nice, mixed use park on a bend in the River Avonmore in Rathdrum. Open all year. Very handy for the mountains as close to Glendalough.

7 BEST FOR THE SOUTH COAST

The Norman View Motorhome Park

Ramstown Farm, Fethard-on-Sea,
New Ross, Co. Wexford, Y34 VP08
www.thenormanview.com/
motorhome-park.html
087 245 3687

A new aire with seven spaces on a private farm. Very helpful and friendly.

8 BEST FOR THE VEE AND COMERAGH

Parsons Green Farm and Park

Parson's Green, Clogheen,
Co. Tipperary, E21A377
www.clogheen.com
parsonsgreeninfo@gmail.com
052 746 5290

A small, friendly site in the valley below the Vee drive on an open farm.

9 BEST FOR BEACHES AND THE SOUTH

Ardmore Seaview Motorhome Park

Duffcarrick, Ardmore
www.facebook.com/profile
  .php?id=100057644492281
086 389 5755

Dick's Field (as it's sometimes known) is a fantastic flat field with 'leccy and water, right on the beach at Ardmore.

10 BEST FOR THE BOYNE VALLEY HISTORY

Loughcrew Megalithic Centre Campervan Site

Summerbank, Oldcastle,
  Co. Meath, A82 A6N7
info@loughcrewmegalithic
  centre.com
086 736 1948

A nice quiet site next to Loughcrew cairns, part of a complex. Open all year.

11 BEST FOR BEING THE BEST

Strandcamping, Doonbeg

Killard Road, Doonbeg, Co. Clare,
  V15 W659
www.strandcampingdoonbeg.com
strandcampingdoonbeg
  @gmail.com
065 905 5345

A fantastic site, run like you'd want it run if it were yours. A lovely, friendly place with basic but good facilities. Immaculately clean and well-loved. Right next to the beach.

12 BEST FOR DINGLE

O'Connor's Guesthouse

Main Street, Drom West,
  Cloghane, Co. Kerry, V92 PV48
www.cloghane.com
oconnorscloghane@gmail.com
066 713 8113

An idyllic site overlooking the water and out the back of the traditional pub that's on the Dingle peninsula and just a short drive from Dingle town.

13 BEST FOR VALENCIA AND THE SKELLIGS

Mannix Point Camping and Caravan Park

Ring of Kerry, Garranebane,
 Cahersiveen, Co. Kerry
www.campinginkerry.com
mortimer@campinginkerry.com
066 947 2806

Best campsite in Ireland?
Possibly, probably, maybe.
The awards would tell you it is.
The site has 500m of waterfront
to pitch up on and plenty going
on. Just a short drive from
Portmagee and the jumping-
off point for the Skelligs.

14 BEST FOR WATERSIDE PITCHES

Wave Crest Caravan and Camping Park

Glanbeg, Caherdaniel, Co. Kerry,
 V93 V2YP
www.wavecrestcamping.com
info@wavecrestcaravanpark.ie
066 947 5188

A site with direct access to the
shore in a beautiful setting not
far from the world's best beach.
Need I say more?

15 BEST FOR KILLARNEY

Fleming's White Bridge Killarney Holiday Park

White Bridge, Ballycasheen Road,
 Killarney, Co. Kerry, V93 HW56
www.killarneycamping.com
info@killarneycamping.com
064 663 1590/086 363 0266

A nicely laid out holiday
park on the River Flesk. Good
facilities, just a shame it's €1
a pop for the douche.

17 BEST FOR JUMPERS AND RING OF KERRY

Goosey Island Motorhome Park

Church St, Inchinaleega East,
 Sneem, Co. Kerry, V93 F3AY
www.gooseyislandsneem.com
087 671 0106

A beautifully sited private motorhome park in the heart of Sneem. No website, just pay in Dan Murphy's Pub on the main square or ask for Sean who may be contacted on 0876 710 106.

€15 for 24 hrs. EHU €5. Located on the southern section of the Ring and very handy for jumper shopping. Lots of gift shops in the village.

16 BEST FOR THE BEARA

Eyeries Motorhome Park

Eyeries Village, Beara, Co. Cork,
 P75 WY02
www.facebook.com/eyeries
 motorhomepark
Colmanf12@gmail.com
086 220 8743

Located in the very pretty village of Eyeries, a private moho park adjacent to Cindy's Gems Café. Great location at the end of the Beara Peninsula.

18 BEST FOR THE HEALY PASS

Creveen Lodge Camping and Caravan Park

Healy Pass Road, Lauragh,
 Co. Kerry
www.creveenlodge.com
info@creveenlodge.com
064 668 3131

This family-run campsite lies on the road up to the Healy Pass, in a lovely, quiet spot.

19 BEST FOR KAYAKING AND WALKING

Hungry Hill Lodge and Campsite

Adrigole, Beara Peninsula,
  Co. Cork, P75 CY62
www.hungryhilllodgeand
  campsite.com
info@hungryhilllodgeand
  campsite.com
083 119 6659

A wonderful little site in Adrigole, not far from the walk to Hungry Hill and Mare's Tail Falls and the enclosed (and safe for kayaking) harbour. Very friendly, VERY clean, free showers.

20 BEST FOR KISSING

Blarney Caravan & Camping Park

Stoneview, Blarney, Co. Cork,
  T23 R85R
www.blarneycaravanpark.com
info@blarneycaravanpark.com
021 451 6519

A nicely laid out and tidy park just outside Blarney. Good for an overnight before a day in Cork or for special stone-kissing purposes.

21 BEST FOR VIEWS ON ARRAN

Achill Seal Caves Caravan & Camping

Seal Caves, Doogort, Co. Mayo
www.achillsealcaves.com
info@achillsealcaves.com
087 353 6379

I don't think I've met any campsite owner who was more helpful. He even printed out fishing marks for us. The site itself is set on a hill overlooking Doogort Beach, with terraces going up the hillside. The higher you go, the better the views. Pub just a 5-minute walk away. Beach 3 minutes. Perfect.

22 BEST FOR MOUNTAIN VIEWS AND THE BAR

Pier Head Hotel, Spa & Leisure Centre

Mullaghmore Harbour,
  Kilkilloge, Mullaghmore,
  Co. Sligo, F91 AP8H
www.pierheadhotel.ie
reception@pierheadhotel.ie
071 916 6171

Motorhome parking right next to the Pier Head Hotel in Mullaghmore. Spa facilities and pub with food right on the quayside.

23 BEST FOR SURF ACCESS

Keel Sandybanks Caravan & Camping Park

Keel East, Achill
  Island, Co. Mayo
www.achillcamping
  .com
info@achillcamping
  .com
098 43211

A mixed-use touring park right on the sand at Keel Beach. Great location, close to the village. Please note: ownership is currently being transferred and so details may change in near future.

24 BEST FOR COOL SURF-TOWN VIBES

Strandhill Caravan & Camping Park

Airport Road,
  Killaspugbrone,
  Strandhill, Co. Sligo,
  F91 W540
www.sligocaravan
  andcamping.ie
071 916 8111

Great location in a campsite that's been here for aeons. Mixed use, so not that pretty, but a great location right next to the surf.

25 BEST FOR PUB AND BEACH

The Beach Bar

Aughris, Templeboy,
  Co. Sligo, F91 YE98
www.thebeach
  barsligo.com
info@thebeach
  barsligo.com
071 917 6465

Could you ask for a better placed campsite? Right on the beach, in the pub garden.

26 BEST FOR DONEGAL AND IRISH MUSIC

Sleepy Hollows Campsite

Meenaleck, Crolly, Co. Donegal,
 F92 HK73
www.sleepyhollows.ie
hello@sleepyhollows.ie
074 954 8909

A small, adults only campsite
just off the N56 outside Crolly.
A site with a lovely, friendly vibe,
isolated and leafy and yet just up
the road from the famous music
pub that spawned Enya and
Clannad, Leo's Tavern.

27 BEST FOR BELFAST

Jordanstown Loughshore Park

A2 Shore Road, BT37 0PS,
 Jordanstown
www.visitantrimandnewtown
 abbey.com/places-to-stay/
 caravan-parks/jordanstown
 -loughshore-caravan-park
028 9034 0137

A fantastic facility on the
shores of Belfast Lough that's
council run. Great showers, online
booking, grey and black water and
great views. Also there's a café on
site. Security is excellent.

28 BEST FOR FOREST WALKS AND WATERFALLS

Glenariff Forest Park Touring Site

www.nidirect.gov.uk/services/
glenariff-forest-park-touring
-online-booking

There is a touring site for motorhomes at Glenariff, which is protected by a barrier. It has full facilities and hardstanding for all pitches. You can book online (recommended) or pay at the park, although a skeleton staff on some days may mean it's not possible.

29 BEST FOR CYCLING FISHING AND WALKING

Castlewellan Forest Park

www.nidirect.gov.uk/
articles/castlewellan-
forest-park

Government-owned site for camping, touring caravans and camper vans. Pay online for access to showers etc. or pay at the centre.

REPEAT

DO IT AGAIN

It's OK to admit that camper van living isn't always plain sailing. Things can, do and will go wrong. The secret to making your trips a success is doing all you can to prevent things going wrong, and if they do, you'll be able to smile through it, knowing it was *force majeure* that spelled disaster for your camper van trip.

I hope.

Sometimes there's nothing you can do to stop the wheels of fate. At some point, your tyres will wear down, your grey water tank will fill to the brim and your energy will face a low ebb. These are the times when you need to rouse the hardy camper inside and soldier on. When you need to reach down into your soul and find your inner Baden-Powell, the stoic, self-sufficient and ever chipper (but probably quite annoying) being that dwells deep inside us all.

This section is all about keeping going. It's about making one day run seamlessly into the next, taking care of the places you camp in, keeping mind, spirit and body going in difficult times.

Goodness knows we've all been there.

In the following chapter you'll find advice on everything from getting up in the morning to putting a camper away for the winter. It includes a few tips on long-stay trips, too.

GETTING UP IN THE MORNING

Find your routine – feel amazing

Driving can take its toll on your back, especially if you're hunched over the wheel for hours on end, tackling stressful roads or sitting in traffic. Equally, sleeping in an unfamiliar bed in the van can upset your routine and leave you feeling stiff and uncomfortable.

I've had my fair share of bad back days, partly due to an injury to my back from years ago. It's taken me a long time to get to the bottom of it – osteoarthritis in my spine – and to manage it. But, I am happy to say, I can.

Here are my tips for keeping yourself feeling good on your trips:

- Drink lots of water.
- Stop regularly and move about when you do.
- Keep a stash of something nearby if you skip lunch or meals because you're driving. I always travel with a stack of emergency bananas to hand.
- Breathe deeply if you feel stressed.
- Remember that you're responsible for your own health.

Stretching every morning

I do stretches every day to help combat the tightness and pain after a long drive or a difficult night's sleep. For a time, I was dealing with costochondritis, which made me feel as though I was having a heart attack every day, but now the chest pains and bad back are infrequent.

This is what works for me. You might have to find your own version, but start with this and start gently. See what a difference it makes. If necessary, go to a physio and tell them you want help so you don't have to come back. It's music to their ears. My physio set me up with the following, plus there are a couple of stretches I picked up along the way. Look them up if you aren't sure how to do them.

5 x cat and cow

5 good threading the needle alternate with 5 seconds of stretch

5 seconds of child's pose, twist to each side for 5 seconds

5 seconds of sitting stretch back, each side

Reaching x 10

Twisting x 10, each side

Twisting and dip x 10, each side

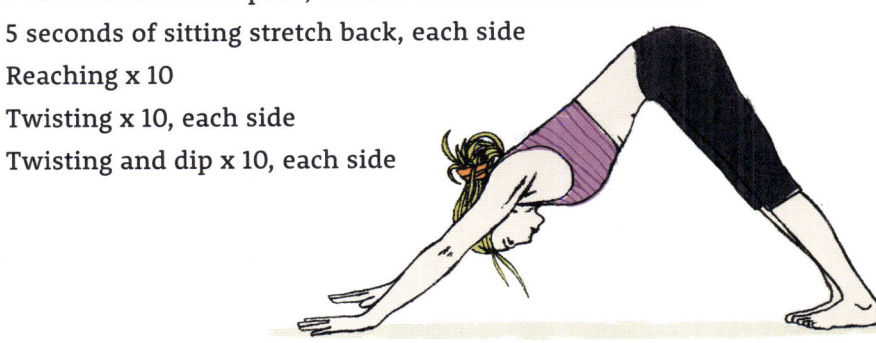

STAY WARM, STAY GREEN, STAY HAPPY

Camping in winter? Staying warm is vital. Apart from the fact that it can be dangerous to let yourself get cold, it's just not any fun to be cold on a camping trip. However, with the right gear, a cosy space to return to and the promise of a hot cuppa, it can be an awful lot of fun camping out in the cold.

Cold weather gear

When it comes to gear, buying once and buying well is the secret to a happy – and clutter-free – life. And all the more so when it comes to wet and cold weather gear. It's the same for sleeping bags, as we saw earlier in the book (see pages 250–253).

CAMPING GEAR AND THE ENVIRONMENT

Camping gear is often made from fossil fuels (nylon base layers, for example, are made from plastic) or nasty chemicals are used to make them waterproof. One particularly concerning aspect of camping gear is the use of perfluorocarbons (PFCs), which help your tent and/or jacket to repel water. Some PFCs escape into the atmosphere and into waste water during production. Small amounts may remain as residue on the clothing itself.

PFCs have been in use since the 1950s, but their effects were only discovered in the early 2000s, when scientists began to release data on the toxicity of PFAs and how they persist in the environment. Perfluorooctanoic acid, or PFOA, for example, is a suspected human carcinogen that has been linked to cancer, kidney damage and reproductive problems in rats. It accumulates in drinking water and is persistent, which means it doesn't dissolve or break down. Some PFCs have been linked to reduced immune response in children.

Whether you believe it or not is up to you. But it's worth considering if you care about yourself and the environment. How ironic that the stuff we use to access the places we love may also be killing it.

The solution? Lots of manufacturers have been working towards ridding their products of PFCs, but it isn't easy. Many have been working hard to be greener in other ways, too.

While we can't ever hope to remove all nasty chemicals and plastic from our lives, we can take measures to buy kit that is PFC-free, comes from responsible companies and isn't made from plastic.

- Merino or wool is natural and is great for layering. It wicks naturally and even gets warmer when wet. It's also very warm, but cool in summer, amazingly. Ain't nature brilliant?!
- Hemp or flax and linen are natural and cool for hot climates. Hemp, for example, requires a lot less water to grow than cotton.
- Ventile cotton uses a very tight weave to make it waterproof while being chemical-free. It was developed during the Second World War for airmen who were dying of cold while bailing out of their aeroplanes, preventing many deaths. It's a wonderful material but is very expensive.
- Stretchy fabrics contain Lycra, which is a form of plastic. It will not break down.
- Down is an extremely efficient filler for jackets and sleeping bags, but it can get wet easily and clag up. Sadly, it doesn't come without its other drawbacks, which is the animal welfare aspect. Some companies use 'ethically produced' down, but in reality this means that the down is plucked from the bird after it has died instead of before.

BUY FROM NICE PEOPLE

Lots of outdoor brands these days are doing their utmost to protect and preserve the environment. From internet giants Internet Fusion, who are removing all plastic packaging from their products, to those who use recycled content in their clothing and even those who repair and reuse

your old gear, things are changing. By supporting those brands who do good things you help to improve the world, even as a consumer.

DONATE YOUR OLD GEAR

Once you're done with your old gear, if it's still in good working order, donate it. It'll have a new lease of life and won't end up in landfill.

LOOKING FOR GOOD OUTDOOR GEAR?

Try these companies first. They make great stuff and also have a strong record of supporting environmental initiatives.

- FJALLRAVEN makes coats, tents, trousers and hats from waxed cotton fabrics and recycled nylon. Great jumpers, too. All-round Swedish wonder brand.
- SURFDOME sells all kinds of outdoor kit and has a zero-to-landfill policy, which means they recycle everything. Your gear will arrive plastic-free, too, so if you're thinking of buying from a big brand, Surfdome will supply it in plastic-free packaging.
- RAPA NUI makes T-shirts out of recycled cotton and they're the go-to people for environmental organisations selling campaign tees.
- ALPKIT, based in the Peak District, repairs old kit for you and uses PFC-free waterproofing. It also donates your old kit to people who need it, so giving it another life.

- FINISTERRE is a Cornish company that has strong ethics and makes amazing socks and merino base layers.
- HOWIES makes great jeans and outdoor gear with an eco-bent.
- PATAGONIA is the ultimate in green gear and always delivers, even on a global scale.

GET GOOD SOCKS

Decent socks are hard to come by these days. It's all nylon and cotton-blend rubbish. But if you want to stay happy in the cold, your socks are, in my humble opinion, the single most important piece of camping gear. Once cold hits your feet it's all over, so don't scrimp on the socks. Keep fibres natural and consider the extra expense of merino, alpaca or good old-fashioned wool an investment.

Merino is antibacterial, so you can wear it every day for a few days and not stink up the place), and it actually heats up when wet, so even if your feet get a dousing they won't get cold. Plus, it's soft. Merino also wicks water away from the body when you sweat, so that you won't stay wet. The same goes for alpaca and wool.

Oh, and wool is harder wearing, so it lasts longer than rubbish cheap socks – so enabling you to justify a higher initial price tag. It's also sustainable, natural and non-polluting. And if you leave one in the woods by accident it'll biodegrade down to nothing. Can your nylon socks do that? Nope.

BUY DECENT BOOTS

Again, don't scrimp on the footwear, for reasons outlined above. Decent boots pay you back many times over when compared to cheap shoes, trainers or sneakers. Gore-Tex breathes, but won't stay waterproof forever, whereas leather, when treated properly with old-fashioned protection such as dubbin, will stay waterproof and supple for years to come.

GET A GOOD WATERPROOF COAT

Staying dry is important if you're camping. It can be tough to get dry again, so invest in a good waterproof coat. When buying, look at the breathability and waterproof rating, but don't forget about PFCs; lots of modern fabrics are made waterproof without the use of PFCS, so seek them out if you can.

Waterproof ratings

Waterproof ratings are measured using a hydrostatic head test. The test fabric is pulled tight under a 2.5cm-diameter sealed tube of water. It's then observed over 24 hours to see how many millimetres of water the fabric can withstand before it soaks through. The level at which water starts to penetrate the fabric is the hydrostatic head, which is measured in millimetres (mm). The higher the mm rating, the better. Anything around 10,000 is going to be adequate for the heaviest of rain, with 20,000mm being about the upper limits of waterproofing. I recommend going for the highest rating in mm in the fabric you want.

Breathability

This is rated in grams per square metre and refers to the amount of moisture a fabric can let out. A good rating for walking is anywhere between 5,000g/m^2 with the upper limits for rigorous walking and back country skiing being 20,000g/m^2 and upwards.

COLD WEATHER GEAR

INVEST IN LONG JOHNS

Surprisingly effective, a good pair of leggings or long johns (preferably merino) can make a cool night warm. They can even be worn under a pair of shorts if you get caught out being optimistic. For cool nights, go for cotton. For cold nights, it has to be merino or silk.

LAYER UP

Layering enables you to better regulate your body temperature, as you remove layers when you get too hot and add them again as you cool off. There is a lot to be said for a super warm Arran or Fair Isle sweater, but it's either boiling hot on or freezing cold without. Lighter layers, and more of them, gives you more control.

GO LIGHTWEIGHT BUT WARM

I have a jacket that weighs practically nothing but keeps me really warm in all but the coldest weather. It's not waterproof but I have an outer shell for that. This coat also packs down really small, is super light and makes a really cosy pillow. It's the ultimate two-in-one camping coat. OK so it's yellow. I don't mind that.

FINALLY, LOOK AFTER YOUR KIT

... and it will look after you.

On-board heating

Whatever camper you own, there will come a time when your life would benefit from a little ambient warmth. It could be because you want to head north or maybe you want to camp out of the summer season. Either way, this is the time to think about on-board heating. Though it can be costly, it's one investment worth making. It extends the camping season – at the very least – and makes the whole thing a lot more civilised and fun. As I've said before, there's nothing worse than being cold on a camping trip. And there's really no need.

If you're retrofitting a heater into an existing camper van, the most popular choice would be either an LPG Propex or petrol/diesel Webasto or Eberspächer unit. Petrol or diesel-powered heaters draw fuel from the vehicle's fuel tank, so the heater's fuel supply is topped up with every visit to the filling station. Although more expensive, running costs are lower and fuel is more readily available.

These heaters can also be thermostatically controlled and typically use around 0.1l of fuel per hour, making them suitable for all-night running if needed.

DO NOT USE the burners on a gas stove to keep warm. Prolonged use of a stove inside a closed camper van gradually reduces the oxygen content of the air and then starts to produce carbon monoxide, risking suffocation and carbon monoxide poisoning. ALWAYS CARRY A CARBON MONOXIDE ALARM.

PROPEX HEATERS

These are the easiest way to heat a camper and use a similar system to many other heaters. They are gas powered and create heat by combusting the gas in a closed combustion unit. Clean outside air is then heated via heat exchangers inside the unit and blown into the cab of the van.

Propex heaters can be controlled via a basic thermostat, which regulates the temperature and then cuts in when it drops. They are extremely effective when they work properly, but can be somewhat temperamental.

Propex heaters run off both propane and butane, but it's worth remembering the following:

- If you intend to camp in weather below around 5°C then you'll need propane.
- Butane, while burning more efficiently, will not convert to a gas below −1°C, so there will be no pressure in your gas bottle and therefore no heat, as there'll be nothing to combust.
- Butane generally comes in blue bottles and is characterised by Campingaz (it's actually a mixture of the two gases).
- Propane comes in red bottles and works at temperatures as low as −45°C, which is why it's always been more popular for cooking and domestic heating.
- Most motorhomes use propane, whereas the leisure camping market tends to rely on butane.

EBERSPÄCHER/WEBASTO

This is another piece of kit that can be retrofitted to your camper van. These heaters are popular in more modern vehicles and tend to cost more than the Propex heaters. They work in the same way as Propex heaters, with closed combustion and inlet and exhaust ports outside the van. The only difference is they take fuel directly from the fuel tank (about 0.1l overnight) so you don't have to worry about extra gas bottles or the type of gas you use. One thing to remember is to use it when you're not running on fumes, or you'll not go anywhere the next day.

TRUMA BLOWN AIR

Similar in working to Propex heaters, blown air heating systems are often the first choice of motorhome manufacturers. They have more features, such as the ability to communicate with your heating system via an app, hot water, hot water boost and a timer, and are significantly more expensive. They work off gas and electricity, and also just electricity, although the heat is better when running off gas. Trauma heaters also include a hot water mode. Set the thermostat, get into your long johns and relax...

TRUMA CONVECTION HEATERS

These are gas-powered heaters and are similar to blown air heaters. They're popular with many caravanners and can even come with a gas fire effect (get you, with your home comforts!). They require a flue to be operated safely.

WET HEATING SYSTEMS

These systems are very similar to the kind of heating system you might find at home. The boiler (running off gas or electricity) heats up a liquid (water and glycol), which is then pumped around the vehicle through a series of radiators or in underfloor heating. It's very efficient and silent, which is why it's popular. Alde are the brand leaders.

WOOD BURNER

For large home conversions, a wood burner can be a good alternative. It's also got a lot more personality! But it does come with problems, such as needing to make sure everything around it is heatproof, and that you have a decent fireproof hearth and a two-part flue to keep the heat away from the roof. You'll also need adequate ventilation and a carbon monoxide alarm. But oh, those flames!

Camping in the winter

Winter is the time when a good camper van or motorhome really comes into its own. You can stretch out the camping season and stay warm and dry when all around you is chaos, snow, ice, wind and rain. Vans can make a winter adventure or a cheap skiing or snowboarding trip very possible. For kayakers, climbers, bikers, surfers, walkers and runners, the camper van becomes a cocoon for warming up, hanging up the kit to dry and enjoying a few home-from-home comforts before the next day's adventure.

EXTRA KIT TO CARRY DURING WINTER

- Anti-slip mats
- Snow chains and a mat to lie on
- Bucket for your grey waste
- Extra blankets
- Shovel or folding spade
- Soft broom for sweeping snow off the camper van

WINTERISING THE VAN

Some vans and motorhomes come ready to roll in the winter when you buy them, but the chances are, if you're buying new you'll need a 'winter pack', which of course costs extra.

Winter packs include insulation for the fresh and waste tanks and wheel arches (on some models), blinds instead of curtains and tank heaters. All these things can be sourced separately if you're retrofitting.

WINTER TIPS

Plan your overnights

Plan your overnights ahead of time. A lot of campsites are closed in winter, with only a handful offering year-round pitches. Check in advance, even if you intend to wild camp (or use aires), as they're always useful for emptying tanks and filling up with water. A visit to a warm washroom and to service the van in winter at a good club site can be a godsend. Some sites have boot- and kit-drying rooms for use in winter, which can be really useful.

Use diesel additive

Diesel fuel can gel at low temperatures (around −12°C), forming a sort of wax in the fuel lines that, ultimately, can stop the engine from working. Some garages in cold countries use gel additive in their fuel in the winter, so filling up at altitude can help. Either that or use a fuel additive in the tank, which is cheap and easy to use: just put it in the tank.

Petrol is less of a problem at low temperatures, except when it comes to real extremes.

Call the heating

Truma's iNet heating system allows you to text the van before you get back to it to fire up the heating. It's a real luxury, but why not? Waiting for the van to heat up after a day on the slopes can be torture.

Cooking with gas

Propane does not vaporise (turn to gas) at −42°C (the boiling temperature), whereas butane will not vaporise at −2°C. Below this temperature, butane is useless, which means that any cooking, refrigeration (keeping the beer cold) or heating has to be done with propane instead.

Fresh water tanks

Fresh water tanks that are inside the van will stand a much better chance of staying liquid than those that are underslung. Underslung tanks can be insulated and some have elements installed to prevent freezing. However, note that heating elements can drain a battery quickly. Some exterior taps may crack in cold weather, so it may be a good idea to wrap your fresh drain tap if you know it's going to get cold overnight.

Waste tanks

Waste tanks can also freeze. A good way to avoid this (other than insulating the tank and heating it) is to open the drain and place a bucket beneath it. Any waste will freeze in the bucket and not in your tank or pipes.

Keep the battery well topped up

This can be an issue in colder temperatures. If your leisure battery falls below a certain voltage (around 10V) most types of heating won't work. Fridges can drain batteries, as can elements in waste tanks and lots of lights left on. Additional temporary solar panels (they can be integrated into insulated window screens) can increase top-up during the day.

Keep an eye on the battery's voltage and run the engine or go for a drive if it's starting to get low. Better still, plug into electric to charge up, if possible.

Lithium Ion batteries keep a constant voltage until they are completely empty, which means they be a more efficient choice of a leisure battery if you intend to camp in the winter.

Condensation

This can be a big problem. Making sure you have at least a little ventilation will help to stop condensation forming on the inside, even if it's freezing outside.

Take extra blankets

Pack extra blankets as a precaution because, while heating is generally reliable, you may find it cuts out or you run out of gas unexpectedly, especially if your leisure battery dies.

Exterior window covers

These can be useful when it's icy or snowing. They remove the need for scraping off ice and can also provide extra insulation.

Drying room

Set up a drying room in the bathroom. In lots of vans, the bathroom can become the warmest space (because it's enclosed) and therefore the best place to hang up wet kit. Also, it doesn't matter if it drips!

Retrofit heating

In smaller vans, it is possible to retrofit heaters that run either off the petrol or the diesel tank (Eberspächer heating) or that run off a gas bottle (Propex Heatsource). They'll need to be fitted by an expert as they have intake and outlet pipes, and can also be set up to work as you drive (if your van's heating is rubbish).

Pop tops

It is possible to insulate pop tops with custom-made wraps made by the likes of Campervan Couture (**www.facebook.com/campervan couture**), Rainbow Screens (**www.rainbowthermalscreens.com**) and others.

Carry a broom

A broom will help to sweep snow off the roof or windscreen after heavy dumps. Snow build-up can turn to ice on the roof, which can cause damage, affect the efficacy of your solar panels and may even prove a danger to other road users when you drive away. If your van is tall, take a telescopic ladder.

Take pegs

If you don't use an exterior screen, pop pegs under your wipers to stop them from freezing to the windscreen.

Snow chains

Chains are really fiddly to put on. Have a test run in good weather before you leave. In snowy conditions, you'll get wet and cold lying on the ground while attaching them: hence take a mat along, too! Knee pads may also be useful.

Don't drive too fast with chains on – 30mph max is usually recommended – and keep your driving style very relaxed, with no fast slowing or speeding up.

BEFORE YOU GO

Organise your space

Whatever it is you drive, it's a unique space. Your needs are unique, too, which means every van is different. How you use that space is entirely up to you.

- Pack the van as a family unit and make sure that everyone knows what goes where.
- Zone your storage. This will enable everyone to find anything at any time and you'll know where to look for certain items, even if they're not in order.
- Make sure that everyone makes the effort to put things back in the right place.
- Organise the van into a 'day mode' and 'night mode' before you go. Everyone should understand where everything needs to go and so will be able to help with getting into the right mode.
- Get a system going when it comes to making beds and settling down. Make it as easy as possible – no one wants to make a bed when they're falling asleep.

- Make sure the stuff you use most regularly, like levelling wedges, hoses and table legs, are easy to get to. Same with kitchen stuff. Spices that hardly get used but that are still useful to take, for example, go at the back.
- Plastic storage boxes are useful for all kinds of things, especially for stacking, where soft holdalls and bags can be a pain.
- If you cram the van full of stuff you'll have to move it every time you need to reconfigure the van (put the bed out, for example).

- If you fill cupboards to the brim you'll have to take out all the stuff to find the thing, because, inevitably, it will be at the back.
- Less is definitely more when it comes to van living.

Service your waste and fresh tanks

If you have on-board tanks for fresh and waste water, it's important to keep them in good condition so you don't get ill from drinking water that isn't fresh, or find the van gets stinked out by unpleasant smells.

HOW TO SERVICE YOUR FRESH TANK

Cleaning your on-board tank is important because of the dangers of bacteria and biofilm building up in the tank when it's not in use. Hot days can make it worse, even when you're away and using the tank regularly, so servicing your tank is important.

- If you can get access to the tank, drain it and clean it physically with a cloth or brush. Clean the pipes too if you can.
- Add a few litres of weak solution of lemon juice or vinegar* to your tank when it is almost empty. Run the taps and shower to ensure that the solution is in all the pipes.

*Alternatively, you can use an approved motorhome tank cleaner, like Puriclean.

- Drive around for a bit to slosh the solution around the tank. Leave it for a few hours.
- Run the taps and flush the waste tank through with fresh water, while at the same time filling the fresh tank. This will help to flush out both tanks.

HOW TO SERVICE YOUR WASTE TANK

The waste tank isn't quite so important to your health but it can smell if you leave it. Adding an environmentally safe chemical to the tank can help to stop it stinking.

- Open the waste tank's drain.
- Run the taps and flush the waste tank through with fresh water, while at the same time filling the fresh tank. This will help to flush out both tanks.
- Add tank-cleaning chemicals if necessary when the tank begins to smell.

WARNING!

Do not use Milton's fluid or any other chlorine-based sterilising chemical in your fresh tank if you have an on-board water heater or Trauma heating system. The chemicals will attack the inner workings of the heater, quickly shortening its life.

Gather your resources

I have found, over the many years I've been travelling, that it's massively useful to gather a camper van library to take along. It can change for every trip and always remains fluid, depending on the nature of the trip, but the aim is always the same: to have vital information to hand. I include in this a list of campsites, addresses of friends to visit, maps, books (like this one), apps to help you along and snippets of information that may or may not be useful.

Of course, since I started travelling, the internet, Google and social media have taken over the world, which can often render 'old-school' items useless, but they can come into their own, particularly when you have no signal and the information highway breaks down.

BE RESOURCEFUL

Pack the following to ensure you have everything you need, even when there's no access to wifi or you run out of battery.

- Download apps to your phone or tablet that can be used offline
- Reference books (like this one)
- Directories of campsites/aires/ stopovers
- Maps
- Guide books
- Field guides
- Address book, including contact details for campsites, friends and family
- Notebook of useful things, clues and snippets
- Membership cards for organisations, for discounts/ access

SAFETY AND SECURITY

In order to keep repeating those wonderful adventures you're going to go on, it's important to keep yourself together in such a way that you can enjoy your life while you have it. So this is the small print, the 'nanny state' part, the overbearing-but-well-meaning words of wisdom to help you on your way.

Seat belt law

The following information refers to UK law, with guidance from the Department for Transport. Seat belt law differs across the world so what applies in the UK may not apply where you are. However, the advice given in this book concerns the safety of you and your passengers. In that respect, it can be followed wherever you go. Just because there may be no law about seat belt safety in the country in which you travel, it doesn't mean you shouldn't take safety advice. The consequences of ignoring advice are the same, whatever the law.

If you crash and you're not wearing seat belts then you are likely to suffer much more serious injuries than if you had worn them. You may also injure others.

ADULTS

When travelling in the front and rear, seat belts must be used if available. If they're not available, you are not obliged to used them. But safety says, don't travel if seat belts aren't available. It's not cool or clever to be dead. (See below for more information.)

CHILDREN

In the front, all those up to 135cm in height (or 12 years or over, whichever comes first) must use the correct child seat/booster for their weight, with no exceptions. If over 135cm or 12 years and above, treat as adults.

In the rear, where seat belts are fitted, the same rules as for front seats apply but there are a few exceptions. If belts are not fitted in the rear, then those three years and above may travel unrestrained. Those under three must always use the correct baby/child seat.

SIDEWAYS FACING SEATS

There is no legal requirement for seat belts to be fitted in sideways facing seats. However, in an impact, those in such seats have an increased risk of serious injury. If seat belts are installed then they must be used by adults.

Children may not travel on booster seats or child seats facing sideways, as their use prohibits it. Also, they may not use adult belts in sideways facing seats as they must be in the appropriate seats for their weight and age.

SEATS WITHOUT BELTS

As mentioned above, adults may travel in seats without belts. However, my advice is don't. Besides, the police can take action against you if you carry passengers so that 'the manner in which they are carried is such that the use of the motor vehicle or trailer involves a danger of injury to any person.' (UK Department for Transport)

INSURANCE AND NO BELTS

What view does your insurance company have on passengers in your vehicle not using belts? If you have a crash and are sued by a non-belt-wearing passenger for damages, will they support you? Think about it.

Likewise, if you're away from home and need medical treatment following a crash, will your travel insurance pay your medical bills if they find out you were travelling without a seat belt? Read the small print.

REAR TRAVEL

Although it is not specifically illegal to travel in the accommodation area of a camper van, you should bear in mind that this area is not designed for use when travelling. You may be liable for prosecution (in the UK) if your manner of carrying passengers is deemed to be of risk to their safety or the safety of other road users.

Basically, just belt up. That is all.

DRIVING IN EUROPE

Under EU law, drivers and passengers must wear a seat belt in any seat fitted with one.

Children under 1.35m tall or travelling in cars/lorries fitted with safety devices must use an approved device for their size. Taller children may use an adult seat belt.

Rear-facing child restraints are no longer allowed on front passenger seats unless the airbag has been deactivated.

SEAT BELT LAW IN THE USA

The laws in the USA differ from state to state, with some states demanding only that those in the front buckle up. In one, New Hampshire, there are no rules at all. If in doubt, buckle up.

Insurance: get proper cover

No book on camping and travel would be complete without mentioning travel cover. Whether you are accident-prone or not, it is an essential piece of kit whenever you hit the road, especially when going overseas.

FOLLOWING FCDO ADVICE

In recent years, we have been witness (and sometimes victim) to the government's advice on foreign travel. The rule to remember is that, when the government advises against all but essential travel to a country, it means your travel insurance will, most likely, not cover

you for travel in that country. This means your possessions and, more worryingly, your health is not covered. It is possible to get cover, but traditionally this has been the reserve of war correspondents and business people carrying out work in war zones and unsafe areas.

Following the Covid-19 pandemic, all that changed, and countries with an unusually high infection rate became targets for the FCDO. As well as meaning your insurance wasn't valid, it also meant you had to quarantine when you got home. See the **www.gov.uk** website or **www.who.int/europe/emergencies/situations/covid-19** for the latest information on Covid travel restrictions.

VEHICLE COVER

What if you break down while towing in Turin? Or clap out in Clacton? Would you know how to get yourself home? Or would you rather leave it to chance and hope for the best? The sensible camper makes sure the vehicle is roadworthy when they set off (obviously), but also has a plan B tucked away somewhere safe (usually in the back of their wallet) that enables them to summon their roadside assistance provider at the touch of a few buttons. Some services will get you home, put you up, talk to local garages and even send drivers out to meet you if things go wrong.

And don't forget that if you break a windscreen or lose a wheel, you'll be losing your transport AND your house all in one fell swoop. So, best get cover that will understand.

The Caravan Club's Red Pennant service does all that for their members – with the added benefit of the fact that they know what you're like. **www.caravanclub.co.uk**

PERSONAL INSURANCE

OK, so the unit is covered. Who is covering you?

Personal travel insurance is another vital part of your camping kit, especially if you plan on travelling abroad. Medical care isn't cheap; bills can soar into the thousands for those who suffer injuries or illness abroad, with bills for more serious conditions spiralling out of control – into the hundreds of thousands – in many places.

Travel insurance covers all the other replaceable bits – like luggage, paperwork and gadgets – but also provides you with the peace of mind you only get from knowing that you'll be well taken care of if something happens to your health. Even in Europe, where the EHIC card gives EU citizens access to basic care, it is vital.

THE EHIC MYTH

EU citizens are entitled to carry an EHIC card while travelling in Europe. What this entitles them to is the same free healthcare that citizens of that country would automatically receive. While this is OK for people visiting the UK, where healthcare is largely free at the point of care (for now), it is a different matter travelling to other countries where healthcare isn't free at the point of care.

If you live in the EU then carrying an EHIC card is vital, but so is having decent travel insurance. ALWAYS make sure you have personal cover for anything that doesn't come free, such as an airlift home, a doctor's appointment or even just a ride in an ambulance.

Post-Brexit for Brits

If you are a British subject you can continue to use your EHIC card until it expires. Thereafter, you will need to apply for a UK EHIC or a UK GHIC (Global Health Insurance Card), which will give you the same cover as the old EHIC in EU countries and Switzerland, Norway, Lichenstein or Iceland (with the GHIC). The UK government have plans to extend the GHIC offering to more countries, but watch this space.

Applying for GHIC or UK EHIC is free and can be done online at: **www.services.nhsbsa.nhs.uk/cra/start**

TRAVEL INSURANCE TIPS

- If you take medication, always carry a copy of your prescription so you can explain the presence of drugs in your luggage without any fuss. Make sure you take enough medication with you to last the trip, as drugs can be expensive abroad compared to at home.
- Always declare your medical conditions, as insurers won't pay out if you neglect to mention something and it leads to a claim.
- Be aware that being under the influence of drink or drugs can invalidate claims.
- Remember that your vehicle is also your home, so make sure your cover includes hotel stays or alternative accommodation if your van becomes unusable. This is essential for older vans, as parts can sometimes take time to arrive – a broken windscreen could put you out of action for days.

General safety

It's not always safe, but sometimes you have to take risks to enjoy life's best stuff. It's inevitable. That, to me, is camping. Camping makes us challenge ourselves. It makes us get out from under the 'cotton wool duvet', away from the comforts of home and into the 'wild', even if it's nothing more than a campsite with all mod cons. The wild, however tame, as we all know, can still be a dangerous place.

Even so, campsite safety is of utmost importance. Follow these tips to stay safe on your travels.

MIND YOUR HEAD!

If there were an injury typical of the camper van owner it's banging your head on the door frame (getting into the van), on a cupboard (when standing up too quickly) and on a worktop when bending down to pick something up. Also at risk are those who forget where they are in the morning and get out of bed too quickly.

If you've hit your head hard and are knocked unconscious, make sure that you seek medical help.

Concussion

Concussion can occur if the head is shaken at any point. After a period of unconsciousness (usually less than 3 minutes), perhaps with vomiting after, signs of response improve and you should recover.

Compression

Compression is very dangerous and occurs when the brain is placed under extreme pressure, caused by bleeding or swelling. Response worsens over time, even though recovery, at first, may seem to be normal. Seek help.

TRIP, SLIPS AND FALLS

The one thing I guarantee you will do on your next camping trip is to fall over a guy rope. Annoying though it is, it's your fault. Keep your eyes open. Better still, use hi-vis guy ropes that you can actually see, even in the semi-darkness of twilight when your guard is down.

CARBON MONOXIDE

Carbon monoxide is the silent killer. And it is a killer that visits some campsite or other every year. The reason is that people burn barbecues in their tents or awnings or keep the gas on in the van (to keep warm) without any ventilation.

There are rules about this: DO NOT EVER, UNDER ANY CIRCUMSTANCES, light a barbecue in a tent. This includes awnings or tent porches. It also includes BBQs that have been used and are still smouldering. They still give off carbon monoxide. Absolutely no excuses.

If you cook in your van, make sure there is always plenty of ventilation.

WARNING!

Install a carbon monoxide alarm in your van TODAY. Service all your equipment (fridge, cooker) regularly.

FIRE WHILE COOKING

Fire is a genuine risk in camp, as we tend to be a little freer about it than at other times. So, here are a few pointers for fire safety:

- Have you got a fire extinguisher in your camper? Get one.
- Also consider a fire blanket, which can be useful for smothering cooking fires.
- If cooking over open fires or BBQs, do it where there is no risk of grass or scrub catching light. Only light a fire or BBQ with permission from the campsite owner.
- Cook well away from any awnings or tents.
- If you want to use candles, consider tea lights inside jam jars. If they fall over, there is much less risk of fire spreading. Don't light candles inside tents or vans. Better still, use fairy lights.
- Avoid cooking with lots of hot fats.
- Extinguish any fire before you go to sleep. Never, ever leave a fire smouldering.
- If you must have a fire, do it where it can be contained, for example in a fire pit surrounded by stones, an old wheel or washing machine drum that is off the ground or on sand.
- Have a fire bucket full of water handy whenever you light a fire or BBQ.
- Don't use disposable BBQs as they are wasteful and encourage littering, as well as being dangerous.
- Don't leave your fire unattended at any time.
- All campsites should have fire points. Find out where they are.
- Don't pitch your tent or awning closer than 6m from your nearest neighbour.

REPEAT

BITES AND STINGS

Carry insect repellent, Anthisan cream and antihistamine tablets in your first aid kit. If you are allergic to bites and stings, DO NOT FORGET YOUR ADRENALINE PEN.

CAMPING ON OR NEAR WATER

Water of all types – pools, lakes, rivers and the sea – are potentially lethal to all of us.

WARNING!

If you or anyone has a near drowning incident and has taken in water or has been resuscitated, seek medical attention, even though they may seem OK. Secondary drowning – when a person has water on the lungs – can occur hours later.

On the river or lake

- Only swim if you know it is safe.
- Don't swim in or near fast-flowing water or near overhanging trees or branches.
- Don't jump into water unless you know how deep it is.
- When you enter the water, breathe out. In cold water shock, the reflex is to breathe in sharply – this is what causes drowning.
- Enter cold water slowly to acclimatise – and breathe out!

At the beach

- Only swim on lifeguarded beaches.
- Only swim between the red and yellow flags where the lifeguards can see you.
- Don't swim when the beach is red flagged as it means it's unsafe.
- If you get caught in a current, swim away at 90 degrees to it, and THEN swim into shore. Don't try to swim against it.

Daytime security

Leaving your van at the side of the road, in a car park or at a beauty spot while you go off on your bike or to do your favourite sport is a risk. I've had my clothes stolen from a vehicle while surfing, for example. I also hear of others being broken into and robbed while out. Not nice. How can you avoid it?

- Don't leave anything visible and tempting for thieves. Keep all valuables out of the way.
- Don't park in isolated spots.
- Have a secret (lockable) cubby hole for all your valuables, like passports, documents, cash and cards.
- Get an approved alarm and steering lock, and lock bikes to the bike rack. Make it really difficult.
- Lock surfboards, kayaks and roof-based toys, if you can.
- Don't leave windows open. Open roof vents if it's hot.
- Don't allow access to ladders.

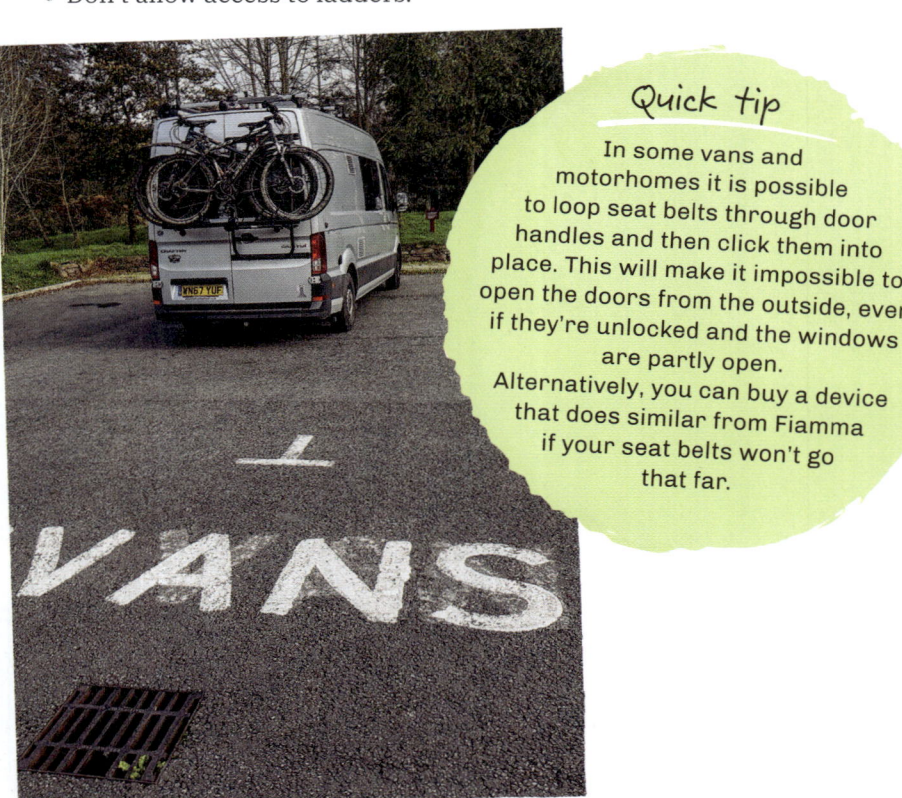

Quick tip

In some vans and motorhomes it is possible to loop seat belts through door handles and then click them into place. This will make it impossible to open the doors from the outside, even if they're unlocked and the windows are partly open. Alternatively, you can buy a device that does similar from Fiamma if your seat belts won't go that far.

Overnight security

I occasionally hear horror stories of people being robbed while they sleep in motorhomes, particularly in Europe. It's horrible to think that someone might have the audacity to do this, but it does happen.

- Leave roof vents open, with a fly screen across.
- Don't open cab windows, unless safe. Secure all other windows.
- Use the cab alarm.
- If you need to leave the tailgate open for ventilation, get a tailgate vent lock.
- Consider motion-sensitive security lights.

Keeping your spot

What happens if you're on a campsite (or an aire) and you decide to go out for the day? On sites where you have an allocated pitch it's obviously no problem as that pitch is yours for the duration. On other sites, where you can choose your own pitch, this can be an issue.

This is where awnings and pup tents come in handy. They provide a secondary purpose for marking territory – and hanging on to it. Some campers also use windbreaks or a chair and table for the task, while others carry signs that politely point out the pitch is taken, and may also include the number plate of the vehicle.

Of course, on aires you have absolutely no right to a pitch unless you are on it, and it is unreasonable to expect anyone to leave it clear for you, even if you leave a sign or polite note.

REMEMBER: It is perfectly reasonable to expect others to pitch 6m away from you, and you should also do the same.

Quick tip

Get a duplicate of your number plate, affix it to a metal spike or tent peg and bash it into the ground where you park. Then, when you go out for the day, other motorhomers and campers will know it's your spot.

PJ07 TIU

DRIVING

Driving safety

THE TWO-SECOND RULE

The two-second rule is a great one to teach the kids if you're one of those rear-enders and tailgaters who spends too much time too close to the car in front. It's pretty easy. All you have to do is find a mark at the side of the road and start counting as the car in front goes past it. Count in seconds – 'one-and-two-and' – the time it takes for you to reach the same mark. If you get there before the two seconds are up, you're too close to the car in front. If the weather or visibility is bad, double it for extra caution. Simple.

The two-second rule provides a distance of one car length per 5mph, no matter what speed you drive. The faster you go, the bigger the distance, so allowing you enough time and space to be able to stop if something happens to the car in front. The chevrons on the road work in much the same way when you see them on the motorway.

Using the two-second rule can help to reduce accidents or reduce damage if a collision happens. It can also help to save fuel and will reduce brake wear.

DEFENSIVE DRIVING

Following the two-second rule can also help to ease congestion in busy traffic, particularly those infuriating stop-start motorway journeys. By keeping a safe distance between you and the car in front you can have a significant knock-on effect on traffic and keep moving. How so?

When motorways are busy and slow, it's the little things that can bring traffic to a standstill:

someone braking, someone changing lanes, a lorry going slowly. People react naturally to brake lights by braking themselves, so starting off a chain reaction behind them. In really slow traffic, this can bring a line of cars to a standstill.

By keeping a safe distance between your van and the car in front you can slow down gradually and keep moving, albeit slowly. If you can crawl rather than braking and stopping then the traffic behind you should be able to keep moving, too. If you time it right, you will reach the queue after they have started up again, so you can continue slowly without braking, and therefore without starting up that chain reaction of panic braking behind you.

Try it. You'll be surprised by what kind of an effect your driving can have on the rest of the traffic behind you. Even if it does nothing for the traffic itself, it's better to keep moving than not move at all.

374
REPEAT

DRIVING SAFETY TIPS

- Adjust your mirrors and seat before you set off.
- Keep hydrated and make sure you eat on long drives.
- Take regular breaks and get out, walk around and stretch well.
- Break down your journey into segments.
- Stop as soon as you feel tired.
- Be extra aware at dusk or dawn.
- Wear the correct glasses.
- Keep your windscreen clear.
- Don't tailgate.
- Don't get distracted by your mobile phone.
- Don't drive on cruise control for long periods. Vary it a bit.

Can you drive it?

YOUR DRIVING LICENCE AND MOTORHOMES

Driving licences, and the categories of vehicles they allow you to drive, have changed over the years. This is relevant to camper van and motorhome drivers because it means you may need to take an additional test if you got your licence after 1 January 1997. Anyone who got their licence before then has automatic permission to drive what is now known as C1 or C1 + E categories. This allows you to drive up to 7.5 tonnes, or up to 12 tonnes with a trailer (handy if you want to tow a car, for example). Some people call it the 'Grandparent Privilege'.

For those of you who passed your test after 1 January 1997, you'll have to take an additional test to gain your C1 certification and may only drive vehicles up to and including 3.5 tonnes (in total). This includes lots of vehicles, so don't despair! A VW T6 weighs around 2,800kg while a Type 2 (Bay Window) weighs in at just over 1,100kg. A long wheel-based van, like the Ducato, weighs in at about 3,000kg.

At age 70, you'll need to renew your licence every three years. This can be done online.

How fast can you go?

On UK roads, motorhomes and motorcaravans are allowed to travel at the same speeds as cars. Obviously, it doesn't mean your vehicle is capable of going at that speed, or that you should. But, if it were possible, this would be it.

Note that in many urban and residential areas, 20mph has now been adopted as the maximum speed limit.

Janet Banks

'We love the nomadic lifestyle and all the different people we meet along the way.'

Ours is definitely not a 9-to-5 lifestyle! A fairly standard love of taking to the open roads at all opportunities in our fifties has become a way of life in our sixties. Continuing as wage slaves to put money into a pension pot just didn't satisfy our wanderlust any more, so we now use the motorhome as a means to earn a living. We freelance to provide on-site security, working wherever the job takes us, tagging on camping days when we can. We cover our bills, have a cosy home to go back to and love the nomadic lifestyle and all the different people we meet along the way. Every day is a school day!

READERS' DRIVES

Maximum speeds on UK roads (allowing for driving conditions, special circumstances etc.)

	Built-up areas mph (km/h)	Single carriageways mph (km/h)	Dual carriageways mph (km/h)	Motorways mph (km/h)
Cars, motorcycles, car-derived vans and dual-purpose vehicles	30 (48)	60 (96)	70 (112)	70 (112)
Cars, motorcycles, car-derived vans and dual-purpose vehicles when towing caravans or trailers	30 (48)	50 (80)	60 (96)	60 (96)
Motorhomes or motor caravans (not more than 3.05 tonnes maximum unladen weight)	30 (48)	60 (96)	70 (112)	70 (112)
Motorhomes or motor caravans (more than 3.05 tonnes maximum unladen weight)	30 (48)	50 (80)	60 (96)	70 (112)
Goods vehicles (not more than 7.5 tonnes maximum laden weight)	30 (48)	50 (80)	60 (96)	70 (112) 60 (96) if articulated or towing a trailer

Source: adapted from www.gov.uk/speed-limits

TIPS

- There is a difference between the speeds allowed by motorhomes under and over 3 tonnes unladen. It is therefore essential to know your vehicle's unladen weight!
- Towing or not towing makes a difference to your speed, too.
- Motorhomes are considered to be commercial vehicles if they carry goods or are used for storage and therefore are limited to the same restrictions as goods vehicles of similar weight.

SPEED LIMITS IN EUROPE

Speed limits across Europe are similar to the UK and are mostly restricted to 50km/h in built-up areas, 80 or 90km/h outside built-up areas and between 100 and 139km/h on motorways. However, the law in some places demands lower speeds in times of bad weather. Not knowing is not an excuse, so it's best to check with the country you are travelling to BEFORE you go.

WARNING FOR SELF-CONVERTERS!

If you have a van that you've converted yourself and have not changed its classification with the DVLA to 'motor caravan' (see page 143), then you'll be judged on the restrictions for that vehicle. At the time of writing the maximum speed allowed on dual carriageways for vans is 60mph, not 70mph as for cars. Motorcaravans are allowed to travel at 70mph on dual carriageways.

Beware — you may get a ticket if you speed, particularly if you go over the assumed maximum speed (70mph), as your ticketed speed will be marked a number over 60mph, not 70mph, potentially making penalties more severe.

Weights, payloads and other dimensions

The licence you hold has a bearing on the type of van or motorhome you can drive, governed by weight. And this is defined by the MAXIMUM AUTHORISED MASS (MAM), which is the total of the KERB WEIGHT plus the PAYLOAD.

The UNLADEN WEIGHT is the weight of the vehicle when it's not carrying anything, including passengers, fuel and, in the case of a van, the weight of any water or supplies.

The PAYLOAD is the amount of weight that the vehicle is allowed to carry (including passengers, fuel and supplies) before it reaches

the MAM. Anything over that means the vehicle is travelling illegally and, more importantly perhaps, unsafely. The MAM should be listed in your owner's manual or shown on the vehicle (on a plate or sticker). The MAM and WEIGHT IN SERVICE (or KERB WEIGHT – the weight of the car without people or luggage) should also be noted on your V5C registration document.

THE WEIGHT OF YOUR CONVERSION

When driving a van or motorhome, it's important also to consider the weight of the conversion, including the bed, furniture and everything that's permanently included in the can. This, of course, affects the payload, meaning you may not be able to carry all that extra stuff! If you're home-converting or have bought a conversion and the converter didn't give you the weight measurements, the only way of checking is to take your vehicle to a weighbridge.

Check the payload

When you are buying a van or motorhome, check the payload with the manufacturer. Some motorhomes have a payload of as little as 300kg, which, when you consider the average Joe weighs 60kg, isn't that much!

Check what the payload needs to include. Manufacturers may well not include the weight of gas canisters and leisure batteries in their total.

Consider the axle weight

Your vehicle has an axle weight, too, which is the maximum weight either of your axles can carry. The payload must be distributed evenly between the axles, which is a danger in motorhomes with a rear garage.

REDUCING TRAVEL WEIGHT

- First, check your licence allows you to drive the vehicle (especially if you're renting).
- Always travel with your water tank empty, or with enough for a cuppa at least.
- Shop when you get there (it helps to save on fuel and you also contribute to the local economy). It's quite surprising how much food weighs!
- Pack lightly and make a rough calculation of your payload before you go.

KNOW YOUR DIMENSIONS

How high is your van? How high is it with the kayaks on the roof? How wide is it? How long is it?

These are important questions. And if you end up asking them of yourself as you hurtle towards that low bridge, the narrow one-way street or that teeny tiny parking space, it may be too late.

It does happen. A friend of mine took off the high-top roof of her van going under a low bridge with five kids in the back. Luckily, no one was hurt, but it serves as a reminder to us all.

Knowing your dimensions will also be very useful when it comes to booking ferries and travel.

> ### Quick tip
>
> Write the dimensions of your vehicle, both laden and unladen, on a piece of paper and pop it behind your sun visor. Remind yourself of it when you need it – instead of ducking and hoping for the best.

Clean air schemes

CAN YOU GO THERE?

Air pollution is a major problem in many cities across the UK and Europe. Tackling it, and making life easier for the residents by reducing congestion, has been a major area of focus across many European cities since the EU Ambient Air Quality Directive 2008/50/EU was issued, limiting dangerous emissions.

The result is low emission zones (LEZs), congestion zones, pedestrian areas and super blocks. It might not help us as drivers, but it certainly helps cities cope with overpopulation, pollution from vehicles and congestion, so I'm all for it.

But how do you know what's in place where? And what will happen if you fail to comply?

Some cities implement controls at certain times of the day, at weekends or for certain types of vehicle. Non-compliance can result in fines. And, thanks to the EU, these fines can now follow you home.

A number of websites list all low emission zones and let you know what you need to do to comply:

- **www.urbanaccessregulations.eu** is run by the EU and has links to the relevant cities and countries. Search by map, country or city.
- **www.green-zones.eu/en** up-to-date information on current LEZ legislation. You can order stickers for your vehicle via the site.

Towing

OK, so there's no chance you're going to fit it all in. Better get a trailer.

Trailers come in all shapes and sizes, weights and legal limits, so it's important to get it right (see below for towing weights). They can tow motorbikes or even small cars if you intend to stay put on a site for a while and potter about in the car or on the bike. Some people like to tow caravans and/or teardrops, or they just need extra carrying capacity. For some, the look is all important, but for others it's the space that matters. Whatever the case, having more space separate from the van gives you much more flexibility, a greater carrying capacity and leaves your mode of transport free for getting you around. Never mind reversing in the supermarket car park.

MAXIMUM TOWING WEIGHTS

Most vehicles have a maximum weight that they can tow safely and legally. Here's how you check:

- The exact towing capacity for your vehicle is stamped on your vehicle identification number plate (VIN plate). It will usually display three or four sets of weights. Line one is the maximum authorised mass (MAM) and line two is the maximum train mass, or maximum technically permissible laden mass (MTLM). Deduct line one from line two and you have the vehicle towing limit.
- As a rule, it is inadvisable to tow more than 85 per cent of the vehicle's mass for safety.
- Make sure that the trailer doesn't exceed the trailer's own MAM or the car's maximum towing capacity. You should be able to find these in your manuals, both of the car and trailer.
- Specified maximum weights refer to unbraked or braked trailers. If the trailer weighs more than 750kg or over half the car's kerb weight (the weight of the car without people or luggage), the trailer must be fitted with brakes.
- The maximum capacity also includes the weight of the trailer, so you'll need to allow for the weight of the vehicle and the fully loaded trailer.

WHAT CAN YOU TOW?

If you have a driving licence that was issued after 19 January 2013 and have passed a category B test (car and small vehicle) then you can tow a small trailer weighing no more than 750kg or a trailer over 750kg, as long as the combined weight of the trailer and vehicle is less than the MAM. For towing heavier weights, you need a further entitlement on your licence.

If you have a driving licence that was issued after 1 January 1997 and have passed a category B (car) licence then you can drive a vehicle up to 3.5 tonnes towing a trailer up to 750kg MAM.

You can also tow a trailer over 750kg as long as the combined weight of the trailer and vehicle is no more than 3,500kg. For towing heavier weights, you need a further entitlement on your licence.

If you passed your test before 1 January 1997 you are entitled to drive a vehicle and trailer combination up to 8.25 tonnes MAM.

TOWING EQUIPMENT

Tow bars

Tow bars must be type approved for your vehicle, designed for the can and meet EU regulations. There is no need for type approval for cars first used before 1 August 1998. You must have an adequate view of the road behind you, therefore you may require towing mirrors. If you tow without them, you could be prosecuted.

Braking on trailers

Any trailer weighing over 750kg, including its load, must have a working brake system.

Number plates

You must display the number plate of the towing vehicle on the trailer. This should also include lights and indicators.

Towing cars on A-frames and dollies

If you tow a car on an A-frame (a rig that attaches to the car keeping the four wheels on the ground) then it counts as a trailer, as does a dolly (a 'half trailer' that takes the front wheels of the tow car off the ground).

In the UK, the Department for Transport has strict rules regarding towing vehicles. They regard A-frames and dollies as trailers, which means they must comply with trailer rules as highlighted above. These rules also state that if a trailer is fitted with a braking system then it must be operational. So, your tow car's brakes must work in conjunction with your towing vehicle's.

Dollies are mostly used for recovery, but UK law states that if a dolly is to be used for a functioning vehicle then it must have a braking system working on the wheels on the ground. Additional rules state that the upper limits for speed using a dolly are 40mph on a motorway and 20mph on other roads.

For more detailed information on towing in Europe, we recommend seeking further information. However, certain towing rules mean towing cars on A-frames may be interpreted by some police forces as against the law, for which you may be liable for a fine.

Conor McCarthy

'Our camper van affords us priceless family time, time to talk and be together, time to travel and explore our island of Ireland, time to be ourselves and, most of all, time to be present and in the moment.'

I couldn't ever imagine life without our camper van 'Saol'. Since I can remember, I have always been a classic camper van enthusiast. This passion became a reality when I bought my first camper van, a 1978 VW, for my 21st birthday! From then on, Tanya (my now wife) and I were bitten by the classic camper van bug. Fast-forward 27 years and two boys later! When our first boy, Fionn, was born, we needed a camper van large enough for our expanding family. Saol has always been part of our boys' adventures and any time we were away on our travels, our youngest boy, Rian, would say 'this is the life!' So that is how we named her – *saol* is the Irish for life!

Saol is an integral part of our family. We love the spontaneity and the freedom she brings to our lives. These days, life can be stressful and fast-paced, but the minute the four of us sit in her and start that engine, all our worries fade away and we just look forward to the open road and adventures that lie ahead. Our camper van affords us priceless family time, time to talk and be together, time to travel and explore our island of Ireland, time to be ourselves and, most of all, time to be present and in the moment.

Photography, food, walking and dipping in the ocean are passions we all enjoy. Camper van life certainly gives us this in abundance. Be it crab claws by a pier, cheese in a local cheese-mongers, buying the local catch of the day to grill on our BBQ under the warm glow of an Irish sunset, these are experiences we feel we cannot live without.

ON THE ROAD

Keep the motor running

This isn't a book about motor vehicle maintenance. Don't worry. However, we are concerned with keeping the motor running, whatever vehicle it is you drive. And that means doing a few checks and top-ups to keep it going.

Sometimes you're not going to be able to do anything about breakdowns and blips because things happen that you have no control over. But you can do a few things to minimise the chances. The more you keep up your maintenance routine, the more chance you've got of keeping that motor running, even on an old banger.

Choose your van for the mechanic you are

The most sensible advice I can give you, after more than 20 years of owning classic campers, funny vehicles and quirky rides, is to choose your ride according to the mechanic you are, or the budget you think you'll need to keep it on the road.

Over the years, I have spent thousands on repairs and services because I loved the feeling that driving a classic brought me. However, that comes at a price. If you don't know how to look after a classic then it may well cost you a small fortune to keep it on the road. Find a good mechanic and stick with them. Otherwise, learn how to do the basics yourself.

If you don't want to, think hard about what you're going for: if you can't check your points, change the oil and set your tappets (I can't), owning a classic camper may not be for you, no matter how cool it may make you appear. Old campers have shorter service intervals (typically around 3,000 miles) and need more coaxing than modern campers. And that means big bills or lots of oil on your hands.

Essential vehicle checks

AAA (ANOTHER ANNOYING ACRONYM)

Everyone loves an acronym, don't they? The acronym, as far as I am concerned, is the realm of the middle manager and should be avoided at all costs. However, from time to time I come across one that I actually

think might be useful. I call these BUMS (brilliantly useful mnemonics) and one of them is the POWER, or POWDER or even POWDERY, which is used to describe checks that you should make each time you get into your vehicle.

So, in the name of safety, here it is. Consult your vehicle manual for more detail.

P IS FOR PETROL

Is there enough in it to get you where you are going? Is it the right type? Are you running diesel, petrol, bioethanol or LPG? Start off on the right foot and get this spot on because if you don't, you won't get very far.

Add AdBlue or a diesel additive if you're running a diesel in the mountains in winter.

Swims Cycles Runs

READERS' DRIVES

'It's like a temperamental nest on wheels.'

Van life. We happened to get our T4 pop top just as our middle son threw in his job at the local shop and announced he wanted to resit his A-levels and go to university. Luckily, he managed to get a place on a foundation year instead, based on his existing qualifications, but in Aberystwyth, 240 miles and five hours away. Did I mention we had just got a camper?

The van has been instrumental in our son's university life, filled with all the essentials from freezers to 3D printers, up and down through the Brecons and Ceredigion Mountains. But it's not just a van – it has meant I can drive up there, spend a few days and nights parked up in glorious scenery or by the beach with walks and wild swims galore, before or after loading up and driving there and back.

Of course, if you buy a 20-year-old van that has evolved over that time, expect a few problems. The very first time we went to see my son, the main battery simply gave up and we had to get a new one delivered to the roadside. It turned out the electrics had been truly botched! And last summer I ripped out the cupboards and rebuilt it with a fridge. It is a challenge but also a matter of great love and pride, bundling up through the hills or along the coast and, of course, we have been elsewhere but it is a lifeline to our son. Perhaps my favourite moment was going off to collect him a few days before Christmas and ending up parked at the end of a dead-end lane with a bit of Christmas tree that had been left by the forestry, with wind and rain shaking the van while decorating it with a handful of bits I had got from a filling station, all nice and comfortable. It's like a temperamental nest on wheels.

O IS FOR OIL

Check it. Check it again. And keep checking it, especially if you run an old machine that is more likely to spring leaks or burn it up fast. Find out what the difference is between the marks on your dip stick (around a litre) so you know how much you need to top up.

Oil also stands for your reservoirs, which may or may not include brake and clutch fluid, gearbox oil and power steering. Find out where they are and check them regularly.

W IS FOR WATER

Simple enough, this. Check your reservoirs of water if you are water cooled. These include your radiator/coolant, windscreen washers and battery levels.

D IS FOR DAMAGE

Check the vehicle for damage to mirrors, lights and tyres. This isn't just cosmetic damage that doesn't affect the way your vehicle drives, but damage that will affect your safety.

E IS FOR ELECTRICS

Again, this is important. Check your lights are working, that indicators are functioning properly and that your horn toots properly.

R IS FOR RUBBER

This means checking your tyres are legal and have enough tread to be safe. You should also check the wear pattern: if your tyres are wearing on one side and not the other then this may be an indication of damage to your tracking or suspension.

ESSENTIAL VEHICLE CHECKS

Y IS FOR YOURSELF

This is the final check and it's one you shouldn't really have to make. You should know if you are fit to drive but it's worth remembering anyway. Do you need glasses to read maps or drive at night? Are you healthy enough to drive? If you were out the night before, have you left enough time to be within the legal limit for driving? Are you taking any medication that may affect your ability to drive?

Finally, if there's anything you should take from this section, it's this: CHECK IT. CHECK IT AGAIN. THEN CHECK IT AGAIN.

Drive safe. We need you for the next chapter.

Extra protection for your van

Whatever kind of camper you drive, you'll want to keep it on the road for as long as possible. So, in addition to the checks and regular servicing, there are a couple of extra bits of love and attention that you should be thinking of lavishing on your van, especially when winter comes around.

- Avoid road salt. It is extremely damaging to old vehicles that don't have the kind of rust protection most modern cars enjoy, so don't drive when it's been put down. If you have to, wash off the underside of the van with fresh water when you get home.
- Apply Waxoyl to the underside of the van, a layer that protects the van from water ingress and therefore corrosion. Clean off the underneath of the van with a wire brush and then apply.

- Get mudguards fitted. They'll prevent mud, stones and road salt from damaging paintwork, therefore limiting corrosion.
- Keep the van clean by washing off any dirt, bird droppings, tar or salt. Waxing will help to protect the paintwork even further.

BUS BOOT CAMP

What if you could find someone to show you how to avoid breaking down? What if there were a course that could tell you the five most common problems affecting old campers and how you can get them fixed without calling for back-up? What if you could be more than just a tyre kicker?

The good news is there are various organisations that run specialist courses on old vehicles, with a particular emphasis on Volkswagens. And if you don't own a Volkswagen then there's still no excuse for spending a fortune on garage bills. Most local colleges run evening courses on basic car and vehicle maintenance so that you can diagnose and repair minor problems, and perhaps even undertake basic servicing. And if you want to learn how to tune your engine, how to set your points and even – God forbid – you wanted to learn how to drop the engine, they will show you how. No bother.

Type 2 Detectives (**www.busbootcamp.com**) provides VW maintenance training courses.

Find Courses (**www.findcourses.co.uk**) is an online directory of evening courses of all types, including car maintenance.

Keeping it clean: toilets and tanks

TOILETS

There are lots of good reasons for travelling with your own on-board toilet. For one thing, it's very useful to be able to go whenever you need it. It's not always possible to find a public loo when you are out and about, and it's a pain to have to trudge across a campsite in the middle of the night.

If you're wild camping or staying on *aires de camping car* in Europe, you'll have to have one, as most of those places don't have loos.

Most large vans and motorhomes have a toilet, but many smaller van conversions do not. The solution is to carry a Porta Potti or a chemiloo, or trust that you'll always be able to find somewhere. And perhaps make sure you have a spade.

In 2020, many campsites were unable to open to anyone who wasn't self-contained, as they didn't open their washrooms. Suddenly, your on-board bathroom or Porta Potti became a golden ticket to camping in the post-Covid world. It's worth investing in case, God forbid, it ever happens again.

Porta Potties and chemiloos

Porta Potties are self-contained camping toilets that have their own mini water and chemical reservoir for flushing and a container for the waste. They come apart and can be separated for ease of handling and cleaning. Chemicals are

Quick tip

Thetford, Dometic and Campingaz make portable toilets.

added to the flushing reservoir (often known as pink chemicals) as well as the waste container (blue or green chemicals) to aid cleaning and waste breakdown.

When buying chemicals for your Porta Potti you can choose eco-friendly products or non-eco-friendly, which are products that may be more effective but that can be harmful outside the contained usage of the loo. Some campsites specify the use of eco-friendly chemicals only.

The advantage of Porta Potties is that they can travel, even when used, so you don't have to worry about emptying them immediately after use. But don't leave them any longer than a day or two.

Cassette toilets

These are the type of toilets you find in motorhomes. Some may have electric flushes and all kinds of luxuries. These combine with an integral loo inside the vehicle. The cassette is usually removed from the vehicle for emptying from a hatch outside the motorhome.

The flush tank and waste tank take chemicals like the Porta Potti. Some of these contain formaldehyde to break down the waste and reduce smells. These chemicals must only ever be emptied where there are proper facilities.

Quick tip

Make sure you have soap and water handy to wash hands after handling or emptying your loo.

CARING FOR YOUR CASSETTE TOILET

Cassette toilets have a seal between the bowl and the cassette and a sliding plate above the seal, which slides to allow you to flush your doings into the container before you seal it off again to eliminate whiffs. If the integrity of this seal is compromised, it could mean having to clear up a mess. This can happen when you don't flush paper (or other matter) properly. It can get caught in the seal and cause leaks. This then leads to fluid leaking either inside the space that holds the cassette or into your van, if it's a lot. A small reservoir at the bottom of this space holds a certain amount of liquid, but it will overflow. You can lift the lid of this reservoir when you're emptying your cassette to check it hasn't got any liquid in it. Ensure it is empty and clean and dry before you replace the cassette.

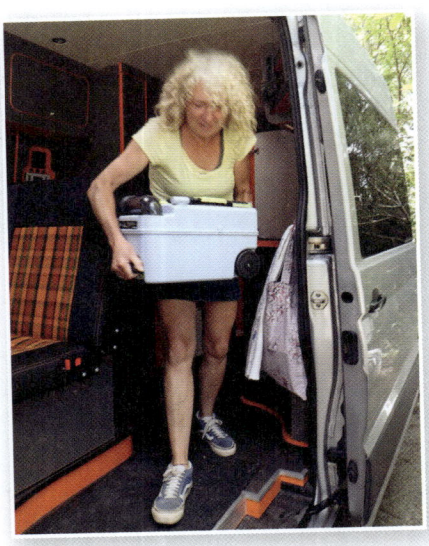

- Ensure the cassette is locked into place when you replace it after emptying.
- Do not let toilet paper get caught in the slider or compromise the seal.
- Check the inside of the void that holds the cassette and the reservoir at the bottom.
- Flushing the loo well before removing the cassette helps to stop fluid dripping as you remove the cassette.

Quick tip

Use green liquid for your loo as traditional blue chemical toilet liquids should not be disposed of in a lot of places, especially places with septic tanks and public toilets.

The SOG toilet

Some motorhomes have SOG units attached to their cassette toilets. These units use a fan to draw smells away from the toilet and cassette and vent them to the outside, via a carbon filter. They are said to remove the need for using nasty (formaldehyde) chemicals to break down waste and remove odours. Opinion is split and the jury remains out, but it's worth considering if you want to avoid using chemicals and may need to dispose of your waste in a normal loo from time to time, as it makes it possible. In that respect it's greener, but some people claim they're not effective and can result in smells on the campsite, especially if the carbon filter isn't changed regularly.

Bucket and chuck it toilets

Really? Yes. There are very simple products available that are nothing more than a bucket with a seat. You go, then you pour it away, but you wouldn't really want to be too far from an emptying point as it's not going to travel well. And you can't just empty it anywhere (see below).

Spade and straddle

If you must dig a hole (and you must dig a hole rather than not dig a hole), do it at least 200m from any water courses, rivers, streams, paths or the sea, cover it up properly and restore the ground to how it was before you got there.

Quick tip

Carry a folding spade or trowel if you camp wild and need to go in nature. Be responsible.

Toilet powders

There are some products available that use powders to gelify waste in a biodegradable plastic bag. These are then put into a standard bin or compost. The advantage of such a system is that all the components pack neatly down and contain no water. It's all dry.

EMPTYING YOUR TANKS

This is where it gets fun. On campsites all over Europe, at around 8 a.m. you'll find a steady stream of grim-faced men between the ages of 35 and 85 strolling over to the 'slophopper'. Once there, they'll make weak jokes about the day only getting better from here on in while they

slop out their tank with a stoical smile. There's a knack to it to avoid unpleasant splashback, with some tanks having an air release valve to make for a better flow, but it's still unpleasant.

Anyway, the rules are that you do not empty your tanks anywhere there is fresh water because the toxic melange must go into the sewage system and be treated properly. It must not be emptied into drains, overflows or rivers. Some campsites have special areas for out-swilling. Use them.

LOO PAPER

It's recommended that you use special 'quick dissolve' toilet paper in chemical loos. This is because it breaks down quicker and leads to less clogging. It's not the cheapest option but it does work.

Alternatively, use thin, cheap paper as this breaks down fairly easily too.

WARNING!

Do not use wet wipes in chemical toilets! They don't dissolve and will cause blockages that YOU'LL have to sort out.

Personal hygiene

WASH KIT

You might think that you can just lob your usual wash kit into the van and everything will be dandy. It will, of course, but you can do better to make your life a lot easier, both on the road and on site.

So, if it's OK with you, I'd like to share some tips with you.

- Take only what you need, otherwise all you're doing is carrying a lot of useless wash stuff and, ultimately, paying for it in fuel.
- Decant big bottles of shampoo and conditioner into little reusable bottles, which take up less space.
- Better still, use solid soaps and shampoos to cut down on waste and make things tidier. Put them in tins to stop them from messing up your wash bag.
- Soap on a rope comes into its own in a camper van. No more dropping the soap. No more mess. No more hassle...
- Men should use shaving soap bars and a shaving brush to save waste and space that might be taken up by aerosol shaving foam.
- Reusable safety razors cut down on space and waste (and save you oodles of cash).
- Take kit in a wash bag you can hang from a hook in the cubicle. Easier access and stays dry.

LAKE OR RIVER WASHING

Sometimes, keeping clean can present a challenge when you're out and about in a camper van or motorhome. If you have on-board facilities it's easier of course, but if you haven't, washing needn't be a real issue.

For those who dare, washing in rivers and lakes is OK as long as you don't use detergents that will kill fish and damage the natural environment you've worked so hard to enjoy. And that, perhaps surprisingly, means not using any at all. Or at least using, and disposing of it, well away from the river or lake. Why? Because soaps, even biodegradable soaps, break water tension and can cause algal blooms.

- Fill a washing up bowl with water.
- Dip yourself in the lake or river.
- Use soap and detergent away from the watercourse (at least 200m).
- Wash with a flannel. Rinse off using the water from the bowl.
- Dispose of the water where it won't enter the watercourse directly (see below).

HANDWASHING

This is especially important these days, for all the usual reasons and more. Before preparing food, after going to the loo, after being out in shops or where there are other people, it's wise to use soap and water.

If you can't use soap, use an alcohol liquid. Don't use hand sanitiser gel – it's made with plastic.

FOR CAMPERS AND MOTORHOMES WITH ON-BOARD WASHING FACILITIES

Washing in on-board bathrooms can present challenges, mainly due to the space but also water usage. Some on-board bathrooms are bona fide wet rooms and can handle a shower, others not so much.

Showering in wet rooms

- Be organised and quick.
- Expect everything to get wet.
- Make sure you have enough space in your waste tank.
- Use eco-friendly soaps.
- Soap on a rope keeps the soap in place!

If you're trying to conserve water, flannels are your friend!

- Use flannels to wash in a basin. Wash them regularly with laundry (or hand wash).
- Use different flannels for face, bums and pits. (Do not use wet wipes. They do not break down and often contain plastic.)
- Hang flannels from pegs on a coat hanger to keep them separate and dry.

Emptying your grey water tank

Grey water tanks contain food particles and the residue of your washing up, washing and showering. Unless you use 100 per cent environmentally friendly detergents, soaps and toothpastes (which are otherwise particularly bad), your grey water can be harmful to the environment, water courses and wildlife.

Food particles in grey water can help to attract rodents and scavengers if it is dumped at the side of the road, on a pitch or over someone's hedge. Dumping your grey water tank on your pitch, everyone agrees, is unsociable and leads to bad smells and unhealthy patches. So, don't do it.

Dumping grey water while driving along is also considered bad practice and unsociable. It may also lead to prosecution for polluting. At the very least, it gives all us campers a bad name. Dumping grey water down a drain at the side of the road isn't good practice. Unless you can guarantee that a roadside drain flows into the mains sewerage plant or into the mains drainage it could pollute and cause harm to wildlife. Therefore it's not good practice.

Best practice is to:

- use a motorhome service point if there is one available
- if there isn't one available, consider emptying your grey water into a container and disposing of it in approved drains or sinks.

FOR CAMPERS AND MOTORHOMES WITHOUT ON-BOARD WASHING FACILITIES

Keeping clean in a van without a shower can be a challenge sometimes. But it is possible.

Using a bowl and a flannel works well anywhere and ensures, at least, that you keep the vital bits sweet (see page 401).

Solar showers

Showering in the wild using a solar shower – great in Europe or on hot days – can be a laugh (I would recommend taking a bit of rope to hang your shower from an appropriate tree branch). However, avoid using soaps or shampoos, even if they are 100 per cent biodegradable. When you consider what some of the chemicals we put on our bodies can do to watercourses or plants, it's a wonder we use them in the first place.

Use a dry wash
These products are useful if you can't get to water. They cleanse and then evaporate, so can be a useful stopgap until you get to a decent bathroom. Available as body washes and shampoos.

Take a dip in the pool
If you want to avoid campsite showers, consider showering at a swimming pool, gym or leisure centre. Some leisure centres even allow you to pay for just a shower, which is perfect. The same can be said of some hot springs facilities, spas and beach showers.

Service stations
In the UK, service stations signposted from the motorway are required to provide showering and washing facilities for HGV drivers. You may have to ask for the key. I've used those at Tebay and Gloucester services and they are clean and well looked after.

> **WARNING!**
>
> -
>
> Tempting though it might be, don't freshen up with baby wipes.
> Unless they're made from biodegradable materials, they contain
> plastics that will not disintegrate like toilet paper. If you flush
> them, they cause blockages in the sewer system. And when you
> leave them in a hedge, they won't rot down.
>   Be suspicious of 'flushable' wipes, too. Some campsite waste
> systems cannot cope with them.

WASH AND BRUSH-UP STOPS

Part of the romance of travelling by camper van is that you have
everything on board, enabling you to live off-grid: water, cooker, fridge,
food, heating and a loo. Lots of vans are capable of keeping you moving
for protracted periods, especially the larger motorhomes that have
150l or 200l fresh water tanks and huge fridges!

However, aside from the issues of camping wild, including the
legality and practicality of finding places to stay, there are times when
you'll need a proper wash, in a proper shower, with space and hot
water and all the comforts.

Even in Europe, where you can refill water and remove waste, you
might struggle to wash clothes or get a proper shower. This is where
campsites are worth their weight in gold. Checking in to a campsite
every few days – or even once a week – will allow you to spend a day
servicing yourselves and the van. Empty and fill waste tanks. Wash
and dry clothes. Shower and wash hair. Charge up the batteries
ready for the next adventure.

Some people think it's cheating, but really, it isn't – it's being
practical! And it's likely to cost anything between £20 and £40 per
24 hours, which, in the grand scheme of things, isn't much for a
'full service'.

WASHROOM TIPS AND ETIQUETTE

Heading to the campsite washroom? Have you brushed up on your
etiquette yet? Take a moment to ponder the finer points of life on a
campsite. And remember, it's all about other people. That and
keeping your clothes dry.

- Use a wash bag with a hanging hook so you can get access to your
  stuff in a shower cubicle and keep it out of the way of the shower.

- Take a clothes bag with you into the shower to store your clean clothes while you shower. A waterproof bag is good but not vital.
- Carry your soap in a tin or soap dish to keep it from messing up your washbag.
- Leave your shoes outside the cubicle to stop them from getting wet and to let others know you're in there. Don't take your best ones.
- Don't put your clothes in a cubicle to nab it and then go off and do something else. If you're going, go.
- Squeegee out the shower cubicle after you have finished to leave it nice for the next person.
- If your campsite charges for showers (I hate this with a passion) then make sure you have more than enough coinage or tokens to last you.
- If showering in the outdoors, don't use soaps. Shower to get wet, wash with a flannel and bucket to avoid soap getting into rivers or streams. Dispose of it in a hole in the ground at least 200m from a river.
- Leave sinks clean and tidy after shaving or washing.
- Don't slop out Porta Potties or toilet cassettes in a toilet. Use the slophopper/elsan point.

GETTING YOUR SMALLS DONE

If you intend to stay away for more than a few days, you'll need to do washing at some point. You might just need a knicker and sock wash. If you've been away longer, you may need to bring out the big guns and wash sheets, towels and jeans. It all depends on how much you packed and how grubby you get. But, at some point, it must get done.

Most large campsites have washing machines and tumble dryers that you can use and most cities have launderettes that will do a service wash for you. In Ireland, many service stations have launderettes, as do some supermarkets in the UK.

Find your nearest launderette at **www.yell.com/l/launderettes.html**.

Tips for getting washing done on the road

- Decant washing liquid or powder into a smaller container to avoid extra weight.
- If you're camping away from sites, plan to do your washing as part of your wash and brush-up days.
- Find a launderette and get a service wash while you have a day out.
- Take a washing-up bowl for hand washing.
- Take a laundry bag to fill with dirty clothes.
- Have plenty of change standing by for washing machines or to exchange for tokens.
- Take a few pegs and a length of washing line. Bungee cords are quite useful if you're drying washing yourself.
- Bike racks and wing mirrors can be useful for hanging out clothes and gear to dry!

LPG and gas filling

LPG FILLING/CHANGING BOTTLES

Unless you're using an induction hob, whatever fuel you're using to cook and keep warm, you'll need to refill at some point. Bottles are generally available all over Europe but LPG stored in underslung tanks can be an issue. Refilling LPG tanks is relatively straightforward, although the procedure can be different depending on where you are. You may have to pay in advance, ask the cashier to zero the counter or even ask the garage to do it for you.

Quick tip

When filling LPG in service stations, talk to the cashier first before attempting to fill up.

- Make sure you have the correct adaptor for the country you are travelling to. Find out what you need at **www.mylpg.eu/adapters**.
- Refillable bottles for LPG are available from Gaslow, Gas It and Safefill, which replace the returnable bottles. There is even a handy Gaslow bottle for smaller vans.
- Beware that it is illegal to refill some types of gas canisters in France. Only cylinders that are EN1949 European Standard compliant may be refilled.
- Campingaz is widely available in Europe.

FINDING LPG STATIONS

It's not always easy to find stations to fill up with LPG. I use **www.mylpg.eu**, which has a map and an app that help you locate your nearest LPG station.

It's not a bad plan to keep an eye on your levels before you head off somewhere and make sure you can get gas if necessary. In some places, you may have to drive a fair way to get to your nearest station. In winter, if you're running heating from your tank, it can get used up quickly, so be prepared and vigilant.

Quick tip

Buy a set of LPG nozzles if you intend to camp in Europe or even in the Republic of Ireland. Europe uses different filling nozzles to the UK, with some countries using different ones again. Try **www.lpgshop.co.uk** for all types of adaptors.

Stay connected

I know you can't live without the internet, even though you try.
I know your kids can't live without the internet. The great news is that
you don't have to. And especially on the road. Your phone, of course,
will give you access to the internet with 4G or 5G, but there are ways
you can set up your van as a mini-hotspot (without using your phone).
When it comes to tech, the sky's the limit!

LOGGING ON

I'm sure I don't need to point it out, but wifi is very useful in a van.
When it comes to planning routes, paying for tolls or congestion
charges (in Ireland, for example, you can only pay the M50 charge
online), searching for campsites, using apps and generally looking for
information to improve your trip, it's really useful to be able to log on
with a laptop or tablet, instead of a phone. Doing a bit of basic research
at a campsite or over lunch can really make the difference between
a good trip and a mediocre trip.

Wifi dongles

The simplest way of getting internet in the van is to get yourself a
wifi dongle and buy a SIM card with a data package. You can simply
walk into a phone shop and pick one up. Dongles/SIMs allow you to
connect a laptop or phone as easily as if it were your home wifi. They're
also relatively cheap. The downside is that they're affected by the walls
of the van, so they often work best when placed on the dashboard or
balanced precariously on a skylight.

On-board wifi

Dongles have one disadvantage in that they rely on a good signal to
get good speeds. Often, you may find that your phone may get a better
signal. The way to get around this is to fit a wifi booster or antenna and
router. A booster will boost a wifi signal into the motorhome if there is
one. This is useful when you're staying on campsites, especially if the
walls and roof of your van serve to block the signal. They can also be
deployed only when needed and removed when driving.

A 4G or 5G antenna and router will pick up and amplify any 4G or 5G
signal and boost it (as well as boosting wifi signal), which is very handy
for off-grid camping, although a lot costlier than a dongle (typical costs
are around £300–£400). The aerial mounts on the roof of the van,
which connects to a router inside and is powered by your 12V or 240V

when plugged into an electric hook-up. This then amplifies the 4G or 5G signal, creating a wifi hotspot inside the van.

They're fixed permanently to the van and are massively useful for anyone thinking about going off-grid. All you need to power it is a data-only SIM. Some makes will also boost a wifi signal on a campsite automatically.

Check out **www.motorhomewifi.com** for more information.

USEFUL APPS AND WEBSITES

Your phone is your lifeline when it comes to motorhoming today. You can get access to so much information at the touch of a touchscreen. Aside from all the usual apps, such as Spotify, Twitter and on-demand TV platforms, there are a bunch of specialist apps that will help you to navigate, save yourself and find a place to stay.

CARAVAN AND MOTORHOME CLUB lists all club sites and certificated locations. UK only. Club membership required.

FACEBOOK is ubiquitous, of course, and has just about every kind of group on it, camper van and motorhome-related groups included. There are a few that share overnights (whether legal or not). Camper van Overnight Parking has over 110k members.

MAGICSEAWEED is a great app for surfers but also very useful when it comes to tide times and heights, daylight hours and weather. It's very accurate.

MOTORHOME PARKING IRELAND is useful for the Emerald Isle, and pretty much useless everywhere else.

MYLPG.EU is essential for finding LPG stations in both the UK and in Europe.

ORDNANCE SURVEY is the UK's mapping agency. This great app gives you access to all OS maps online (and offline) for just £28.99 per year. Maps are downloadable and include aerial maps as well as standard maps at all scales.

PARK4NIGHT is similar to SEARCHFORSITES (below) but without as many locations.

PETROL PRICES compares prices at thousands of petrol stations across the UK if you're looking for a cheaper fill-up.

SEARCHFORSITES is one of the most popular campervanning apps. It lists 60,000 car parks, cafés, aires, campsites and wild spots across Europe. There's an online version for use when you're at home and planning your next trip.

WHAT3WORDS could save your life. It divides the globe into segments, each with a unique set of just three words. Get in trouble and those three words will help the emergency services find you quickly and easily, even in remote locations.

SMART VANS — TECHING UP YOUR MOHO

I've already talked about calling the van to put the heating on. Well, you can go so much further than that if you want to. You can set up your wifi to work with a voice command system like Alexa, Siri or Google Voice to perform commands in the van, such as turning your security lights on, setting CCTV to record, setting the alarm, changing the music or, upping the ante, altering the mood lighting.

Don't forget that every bit of kit uses up your payload so do keep an eye on it.

In time, you may well be able to do all the same kind of things that you can do with 'the internet of things' already in your home. Wouldn't it be great if your shopping, which your fridge ordered for you because you were getting a bit low, turned up on the campsite, all paid for and sorted?

Or would it?

Laura Walker

'More than anything it's given us great memories with hopefully many more to come.'

First, I'm not sure I've ever been this attached to a vehicle! We all love it, and with children aged two and five, we thought it was the perfect time to get one. We have so much to see in the UK alone and what better way to see it?

We use the van as a daily driver – even that's fun as people just smile when they see campers. It's so handy as a day-trip van, to instant picnic spots and changing places for soaking wet/muddy kids. More than anything it's given us great memories with hopefully many more to come. It comes with an urge for us to take the kids to see, explore and do things away from screens and to keep the sense of adventure alive in them.

POWER

Camping electrics: batteries

LEISURE BATTERIES

Most campers have some kind of camping electrics, running off a separate leisure battery.

They are 'deep cycle' batteries and are different from your average car battery because they're designed to be regularly deeply discharged, using most of its capacity. They have to cope with a lifetime of being drained and then topped up, instead of a burst (to start the engine) followed by constant topping up (from the alternator) in the case of a car battery.

Leisure batteries are generally topped up via the split relay charger that delivers a topping up current when the engine is running and by mains charging when plugged in to a 240V hook-up, although not all campers have 240v chargers for their leisure electrics.

Different batteries have different ratings that are measured in AMP HOURS. This is the time the battery will run when drawing power, measured in amps. If you have a 100Ah battery and you run a lamp on it that draws 10 amps, the battery will last for 10 hours before it is fully discharged.

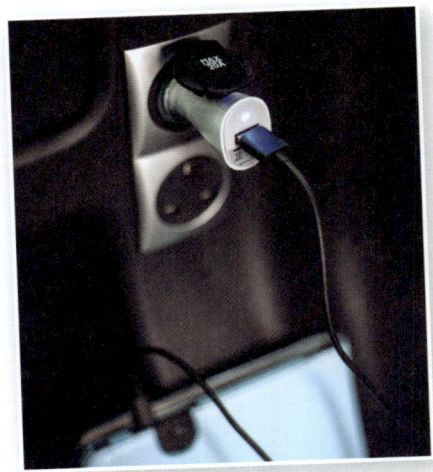

However, it is never recommended to discharge a leisure battery more than 50 per cent as they may not recover fully. So, it's important to get one that will be able to cope with the demands you place on it.

LITHIUM-ION BATTERIES

The advantages of lithium-ion batteries are that they are lighter than normal leisure batteries and can discharge and be fully charged many more times before becoming defunct. They also discharge

16 amp C-form hook-up   TV aerial

at 100 per cent power all through their cycle. Normal leisure batteries lose their voltage over time and this may affect the operation of some electrics as the voltage reduces.

Lithium-ion batteries also keep their charge over time, so they don't need topping up if you decide to store the van for a few months. Normal batteries discharge over time and may become unusable if they are left for long periods.

HOW TO WORK OUT HOW MUCH POWER YOUR CAMPER DEMANDS

Every piece of electrical equipment in your camper draws a certain amount of power, in amps. Times that by the number of hours you use it for on average each day and add it all up together to get your power usage (say a TV draws 2 amps and you use it for five hours a day, it will draw 10Ah). Add up all the appliances and the time you use them for and you'll get some idea of the size of battery you need.

However, since it is inadvisable to drain leisure batteries by more than 50 per cent, double your average usage to get an approximation of your power needs. Leisure batteries start at around 75Ah to a whopping 170Ah for more demanding motorhomes.

It's also important to choose a leisure battery that will fit your battery compartment. And bear in mind that all batteries must now be properly secured for your UK MOT. Standard batteries must also be vented.

Topping up with solar

Solar panels enable you to keep your leisure battery topped up when camping away from a campsite or if you are parked up and not running the engine for a few days.

In general, you'll need to choose a solar panel that produces the same amount of power you use each day on an average trip. That way, it will be powerful enough to top up your battery as you use up power the way you normally do. Of course, this depends on what kind of devices you have connected to your camping electrics. If you run an absorption fridge, it will require more power than a compressor fridge (for example), so you'll need more topping up power from your solar.

Similarly, if all you ever do is charge your phone and use a few lights, something smaller – and much cheaper – will do.

Calculate your solar power needs

You may already have worked out how much power you consume on a typical camping trip (see page 413), and therefore what size battery you need. So, all you need to do next is choose a solar panel that can produce as much energy as you use.

The power generation rating of a solar panel is given in watts (W). To calculate the energy it can supply to the battery, multiply W by the hours exposed to sunshine, then multiply the result by 0.85 (this factor allows for natural system losses). So, in four hours, a 10W panel will produce 34 watt-hours (WH) of energy to the battery.

Size your system

The idea with a solar system is to balance the power going in with the power going out over a period of days or weeks. Here's a simple way to calculate the size of a system based on your power usage.

- **Find out the wattage of your appliances:** if you can only find the figure in amps, times this by 12 to get the W figure.
- **Work out your daily WH needs:** work out how many hours you use an appliance for per week, then divide by seven. Multiply each appliance's wattage by the hours you'll use it for in a day. Add the totals together for your daily WH usage.
- **Work out your panel size:** divide the daily total WH by the hours of useable light in an average day. In the UK, you can expect one hour in winter, rising to four in summer.
- **What do you need?** Most motorhomes have panels from 80W and above due to the typical gadgets in use (fridges, phone chargers,

Ready reckoner for solar panels

VEHICLE	Camper van, caravan and small motorhome, 110Ah battery	Camper van, caravan and small motorhome, 110Ah battery	Large motorhome, 200Ah battery	Large motorhome, 200Ah battery
WHEN	Spring–autumn	All year round	Spring–autumn	All year round
60W	Lights, water pump, radio and TV for 2hrs/day	Lights, water pump, radio and CD	Lights, water pump, radio and CD	Lights, water pump, radio and CD
85W	Lights, water pump, radio, TV for 3hrs/day and 240v appliances	Lights, water pump, radio and TV for 2hrs/day	Lights, water pump, radio and TV for 2hrs/day	Lights, water pump, radio and CD
130W	Lights, water pump, radio, TV for 5hrs/day and 240V appliances	Lights, water pump, radio, TV for 3hrs/day and 240v appliances	Lights, water pump, radio, TV for 3hrs/day and 240v appliances	Lights, water pump, radio and TV for 2hrs/day

radio, lighting etc.). Bear in mind that laptops require at least 25W for a useful trickle charge.

* **Work out what space you have:** panels come in various sizes, shapes and ratings, so it may be possible to fit two instead of one if the size were right.

Charge controllers

The charge controller (or regulator) connects between the panel and the battery and protects the batteries from overcharging and the panel from power going back into it from the batteries at night. It also helps to maintain battery condition by keeping the battery voltage high.

For more in-depth information about requirements, panels, fitting and a useful glossary of the terms used in solar power generation, please see **www.selectsolar.co.uk**.

Cold weather battery performance

In cold weather, the performance of a battery is reduced considerably (when you need it most), so it can help to have the leisure battery inside the van if you camp into winter. However, all lead acid and sealed-for-life gel batteries vent hydrogen as part of their normal working life, so should always be kept in a separate compartment from the living space and with a vent to allow hydrogen to escape.

Using a power inverter

Power inverters change direct current (DC) power from a battery into conventional mains alternating current (AC) power at 230V. This means that you can use one to operate all kinds of devices such as your laptop, power tools or kitchen appliances.

The inverter draws its power from a 12V battery (preferably your deep-cycle camping battery). However, the battery will need to be recharged as the power is drawn out of it by the inverter. You can do this by running the engine, with 10 minutes of running time per hour of inverter use being recommended. Most leisure batteries provide an ample power supply for 30 to 60 minutes even when the engine is off, although actual time may vary depending on the age and condition of the battery, and the power demand being placed on it by the equipment being operated by the inverter.

Again, see **www.selectsolar.co.uk** for more information.

Coiling cables

If you're using an electric hook-up on a campsite, you'll have to deal with the cable sooner or later. Uncoiling and coiling it away neatly are skills that make life a lot easier, keep your cupboards tidier and ensure your patience goes untested.

CABLE COILING: SOME TIPS

- Cables are harder to coil up when it's been cold overnight. Leave them in the sun, or until it warms up a little before coiling, if possible. If it continues to be cold, let the stiffened coils of the cable guide you when you coil it up. Don't fight them.
- Don't leave excess length from cables in tight coils when you're using them. This effectively creates an electromagnet and may cause heating of the coil.

- Some people use the thumb to elbow method (pictures A and B, below), which involves winding a cable around the thumb of one hand and then around the elbow of that arm. This can get you a uniform coil, but doesn't iron out kinks and can end in a cable that's twisted in places.
- When winding the cable into a coil, hold it in your left hand and then gather the cable with your right, making the loops as you go (pictures C and D, below). If the cable has a natural twist in it, use it, otherwise, turn the cable a half turn with your right hand before putting it on to the coil.
- Your cable will have a memory of how it's been coiled before. Use it to recoil it and make a neat coil.
- If your cable gets into a mess, wait for a warm day and then twist all the kinks out of it as if it were a long skipping rope.

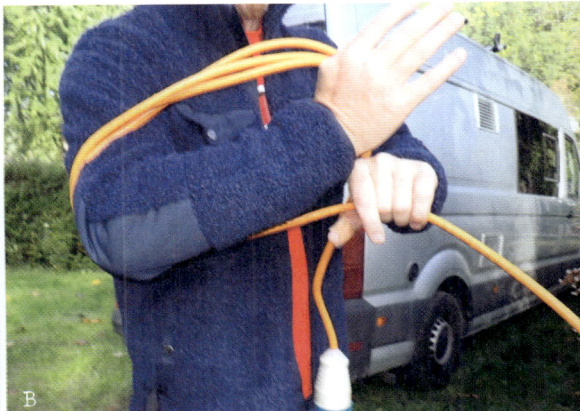

TAKING YOUR VAN ABROAD

While exploring close to home can be massively rewarding, driving your camper or motorhome further afield will take you to places that are completely different from what you're used to. Whatever it is you go in search of – whether that's weather, sports, culture, art or just a change of scene – going in a camper makes it easier. You'll have all you need with you, which is especially useful if you need medicines or specialist equipment to live comfortably, and you won't have to rely on hotels, public transport or accommodation once you get there.

As long as you are confident driving abroad, then the world – or at least Europe – is your oyster. If you live in Europe, you'll have open borders to sail across if you choose to stay in the EU or Schengen Area. If you live in the UK, it's not as simple as it used to be but not insurmountable to get away to Europe – and beyond.

This section is all about taking your motorhome or camper van abroad and includes all the things you should be thinking about before you go, along with a few useful lists and pointers. While this information is far from comprehensive, it's based on over 35 years of experience of taking vans from the UK to Ireland and Europe.

But first:

- Always travel with your driving licence, passport, vehicle documents, travel insurance details and any other insurances to hand.
- Make sure you're permitted to drive in that country.
- Check local rules before leaving. The RAC (**www.rac.co.uk**) and AA (**www.aa.com**) are useful here.
- Make sure you have good insurance.
- Make sure the vehicle is fit to go long distances.
- ALWAYS carry prescriptions of any medicines you need to take – they may be illegal in the country you are travelling to.
- If necessary, check your Covid or vaccination status against local requirements.

Travelling to Europe post–Brexit

SCHENGEN AREA

Brexit has made travel and long stays in the EU more difficult for UK citizens. As members of a 'third country' we no longer have the right to travel, live, work and stay for long periods in Europe like we used to. I am still very sad about this.

You can travel on tourist visas for up to 90 days in the Schengen Area as a UK citizen. After that, you may only return after a further 90 days. Basically, you may stay for 90 days out of any given 180, which rather puts a stop to the idea of taking six months out over the winter to hang out in the sun. Sunbirds can fly no more!!!

- Overstaying may result in fines and you being refused entry in the future.
- Working out how many days you are permitted to stay is easier with the Schengen Calculator: **www.schengenvisainfo.com/ visa-calculator**

EU VISAS

It is possible to get visas for extended stays in the Schengen Area, but it's not easy (I have been through it myself). You require a valid reason (mine was work), a lot of time and patience. You may need to travel to a visa centre in London, Manchester or Glasgow, and will require all kinds of paperwork, such as police reports, details of your financial situation, accommodation, sponsors and work or family situation. It's a right pain.

Why did we vote to leave? Why?

Travel and vehicle insurance

- Make sure your travel insurance covers you for the places you're going. If the Foreign, Commonwealth & Development Office (FCDO) advises against travel to a country, your insurance will be invalid, unless you get specialist cover from the likes of **www.battleface.com**.
- Make sure you declare any activities you'll be doing, like surfing, winter sports or cycling. They may be excluded from your policy.
- Make sure your vehicle insurance covers you for travelling abroad!
- Don't just go with 'the policy you got free with your bank', as it may not be enough for you. Check before you go.
- Travel insurance should also cover your possessions and clothes if you get mugged or the van gets broken into.

Medical and vehicle cover

MEDICAL COVER

Not all countries offer medical services like the UK and a lot of them rely on private healthcare. That means you will have to pay to see a doctor, break a leg or need emergency care. ALWAYS travel with adequate medical insurance. Breaking a leg in Spain, for example, may cost as much as £15,000. Getting airlifted home may well cost you your home.

It's just not worth the risk.

- Multi-trip policies enable you to travel regularly without the hassle of taking out new policies each time you go.
- Specialist travel insurers like **www.world-first.co.uk** can cover you for medical conditions that other companies might not.
- Don't count on your 'free with' travel cover. It may not be enough.
- Your cover may be invalid if you go to destinations declared as unsafe by the FCDO.

VEHICLE COVER

Your vehicle insurance will cover you if you have a smash, but not if you break down.

Getting breakdown cover enables you to get a tow, have your vehicle fixed, repatriate your vehicle and also repatriate yourself if your trip gets cut short.

Specialist insurance policies, like the Caravan and Motorhome Club's Red Pennant, are designed for people who live and travel in their vehicles, so making it very easy to explain to an insurer why you need a hotel after a breakdown!

- Breakdown cover isn't cheap but it could save you a fortune if something goes wrong.
- Multi-trip cover lasts for a year and allows you to take multiple trips without having to reorganise cover.
- Some vehicle cover also covers you for medical and possessions.
- Some insurers may not cover older vehicles.
- Check local rules for motorhomes and towing/carrying gear.

Crossing the Channel

FERRIES

There are a vast choice of ferry routes from the UK to the Continent to choose from. You can head to Ireland, France, Spain and the Netherlands. From there, you can go anywhere the road takes you, as long as the border crossings allow.

Ferries in the UK leave from ports all the over the UK, including Newcastle, Liverpool, Plymouth and Aberdeen.

- When booking, always give an accurate description of your vehicle's length and height.
- Remember to switch off your gas – at the tank – before you board.

- Be prepared for customs officers to come aboard your motorhome.
- Always have your documents handy.
- Some ferry companies will require you to book accommodation if it's a long crossing.
- Long crossings to Spain or the Netherlands may cost more, but will save on driving and fuel costs.

EUROTUNNEL

The Eurotunnel runs a shuttle service that takes vehicles through the Channel Tunnel. It's a really efficient service that takes around 30 minutes to get from Folkestone to Calais and allows motorhomes of all sizes to travel. Booking online is easy and trains run every few minutes throughout the day and night.

- You drive on to the train and remain in your vehicle, then drive off again at the other side. Simple!
- There are toilets on the train, but you are advised to remain in your vehicle at all times.
- When you arrive to check in, ensure you follow signs for the large vehicles embarkation (unless you're in a small van – it helps to know your height here – with bikes, kayaks and extra stuff on the roof).
- Make sure you have all your paperwork ready.

Martin Bellamy

'We've visited parts of the UK and Europe that we'd never have seen without her, met friends for life and have learned to live a chilled life after 40 years of chasing the corporate dream.'

We'd thought about buying a classic sixties or seventies camper van, but I don't have the mechanical skills to keep one on the road. The thought of being stranded by the roadside with my limited skill-set fills me with dread. What we wanted was something reliable that we could use at weekends and for summer holidays.

So, it had to be a Brazilian T2.

Our first sight of Absinthe was fantastic and we couldn't wait to drive her home. Paperwork done, Mrs B took the wheel and we set off. What was immediately obvious after years of driving modern automatic cars was that this one was going to need to be *driven*. The gearbox and gear stick seemed to have minds of their own and the steering was eccentric to say the least. That didn't stop us from grinning from ear to ear, though (what we now recognise as the permagrin of the VW enthusiast), and being thrilled by the waves from other VW owners.

The VW world is a small one with lots of interconnections, and in the main we've been welcomed wherever we've gone. Sure, there are one or two die-hards who consider anything without an air-cooled engine as less than authentic but, in the main, Absinthe brings a smile to most people's faces.

We use Absinthe almost every weekend from spring until late autumn and the pleasure we've had from her has been immense. We've visited parts of the UK and Europe that we'd never have seen without her, met friends for life and have learned to live a chilled life after 40 years of chasing the corporate dream. We've had three-week runs through France and Spain and weekends away throughout the UK. We've done our first festivals and have used her as overspill family accommodation at our static caravan in the Dales. She's shifted furniture and been to the tip. We've had afternoon teas overlooking the coast and icy mornings in the Cotswolds. She's even part of our Xmas decorations over the holiday break. Why's she called Absinthe? Like the drink, she's green and takes us to places we've never been before!

Would we swap her? No!

Low emission zones in Europe

Cities all over Europe have low emission zones (LEZs), congestion charges, tolls and all kinds of complications. If you know where you're going you can apply for permission to drive in those areas with your vehicle. Paris, for example, has an LEZ that requires you to display a sticker in the windscreen that states your emissions and ability to enter the city (you can buy permits online in the UK). Barcelona, however, has a slightly different system that requires you to register with the city beforehand, so you don't get caught by the cameras when you enter. It too can be done online.

You can get more information on all of Europe's LEZs at **www.urbanaccessregulations.eu**.

- Don't forget that fines can now follow you home, including unpaid electronic tolls.
- Fines for breaching emission zones are hefty and may be as much as €3,500.

Finding places to stay

Not everyone wants to book accommodation in advance. And the beauty of travelling by motorhome or camper van is that you don't have to. But it may be a good plan to book a first night if you arrive late or have a heavy day of travelling. Thereafter, much of Europe is easy.

- Europe caters very well for motorhomes, with thousands of *aires de camping car* in lots of countries. Directories are available from Vicarious Books: **www.vicarious-shop.com**.
- Europe is also very well catered for in terms of campsites, with thousands of them in every country. Find them on Search for Sites (**www.searchforsites.co.uk**) or Alan Rogers (**www.alanrogers.com**) lists a selection.
- Use schemes that allow members to stay on private land, such as vineyards or farms, throughout Europe (for example, France Passion in France and Britstops in the UK). To gain entry, all you need is the book, which costs around £32, for a year's membership.
- Wild camping rules vary throughout Europe so please check before parking up. In some countries, it is permitted, while in others it is banned. Please be respectful and kind when parking on someone's land.

TRAVELLING WITH PETS

Motorhomes make perfect homes for travelling pets and there are plenty of you who travel with your furry friends. It makes a lot of sense because it's familiar, it's relatively easy and means companionship on the road. For people on their own, it also means an extra level of security if you're travelling with a dog (although ferrets are, apparently, the ones to watch when it comes to security).

Please remember:

- Dogs die in hot vans. Unless you have air con and can guarantee your pet will be OK, don't leave them alone in a vehicle on a hot day.
- Dogs and ferrets aren't always welcome in restaurants, museums, art galleries and tourist attractions. Cats even less so. Your trip will have to revolve around your pet/s to a certain extent if you are to avoid abandoning them.
- Some countries require a dog to wear a muzzle on public transport and some breeds may require them more often. Check with the country you are travelling to.
- You might need to take your fussy pet's favourite food with you if it's not available in the country you're visiting.

Pet passports post-Brexit

The Pet Passport allowed UK-based owners to take their dogs, cats and ferrets to Europe until January 2021. However, since the UK voted to leave the European Union, it's become a little more complicated and will, more than likely, involve the following:

Your pet must be microchipped and vaccinated against rabies.

Your pet must have a blood sample taken at least 30 days after its primary rabies vaccination, which will be sent to an EU-approved blood testing laboratory.

After three months, you may travel, as long as the test is positive, with a copy of the test results in an animal health certificate (AHC).

As long as you keep your pet's rabies vaccinations up to date, you will not need to get repeat blood tests for repeat trips to the EU.

You must also take your pet to a vet not more than 10 days before travel to update your AHC. You'll need your pet's microchipping date, vaccination history and a successful rabies antibody blood test result.

Your pet's AHC will be valid for:

- 10 days after the date of issue for entry into the EU
- onward travel within the EU for four months after the date of issue
- re-entry to Great Britain for four months after the date of issue.

Your pet will need a new health certificate for each trip to the EU. (Source: gov.uk)

Safe travels with pets

The Highway Code states that dogs must be suitably restrained so they cannot distract you or cause injury to you or themselves if you have to stop quickly. This means having a harness or a dog cage (that's properly secured) in the van.

In addition, if you have an accident with an unrestrained dog in the car your insurance may be invalid. You may also face huge fines and points for driving without due care.

CHECKING IN ON YOUR PET

Thanks to technology, it is now possible to check in on your pet while you're away from your motorhome using wifi, apps and CCTV cameras. Some technology also allows you to offer treats and start two-way conversations with your pet while you're away. That said, leaving an animal in a vehicle when it's too hot or too cold can end tragically. Make the right call.

Ian Huws

'My van brought me life from a troubled past with fresh thoughts and sensations and feelings.'

From the best seat in the world, the waft of van-made coffee fills my nostrils as a warm wind blows over me and I feel the presence of my camper van muttmutt as he gently settles in next to me on the side step of my van. I close my eyes for a moment and pictures dance across my mind of scenes past, places visited, panoramas taken in, all neatly filed in the top drawer of my mind. What does my van mean to me? Life itself, kind of like water and food, only better. You can't live without either but my van brought me life from a troubled past with fresh thoughts and sensations and feelings, with a touch or a smell, a thousand pictures from a mind's eye, a smile, a sense of peace, a connection to your soul, a connection to the land, a connection to your Creator. Freedom of spirit that my van gives is friendship beyond words.

THE THINGS WE LEARN ALONG THE WAY: A FINAL WORD

It's been eight years since I wrote the first edition of *The Camper Van Bible*, in 2015. A lot has changed since then. We've had a global pandemic that has served to prove our way of life is perfect for self-contained trips away. For a while there in 2020, the motorhome was the only way to holiday in the UK. It showed a lot of people that travelling by van or motorhome means you can travel

and take your home comforts with you. I resist saying 'I told you so'.

In that time, #vanlife has become a global movement devoted to living in camper vans, RVs and motorhomes, and more and more people are buying or converting vans and taking off. This is because, as always, camper vans offer another way. I'm not surprised. But it's maybe a little sad that people turn to vans because they can't afford to pay rent or can't get mortgages because of house prices being so high. Still, you could also argue that a van is a very neat answer to the housing crisis. At least the internet – and the radical shift in working culture – has enabled us to work remotely much more easily today. Why would you work in a big city when you can work from the beach?

The phrase 'digital nomad' didn't exist in the mainstream in 2015 even though it had been around for a while. I'm not sure influencers held such sway then either, and certainly not as a way of advertising to masses of social media users. Today, though, the #vanlife digital nomad influencer is a powerful force for going places and taking your 'favourite brands' with you. I think this is fine, and welcome the side hustle as much as anyone, as long as you don't have to sell out along the way.

Since 2015, I have owned a few different vans and have upsized to a van conversion with a bathroom, solar, an induction hob and all the knobs and whistles. It allows me to travel further and for longer, with even more freedom to go wild and do it properly and responsibly. Water and battery management have become a part of life. Apps have made finding campsites easier and Google has made getting there a whole lot faster and more peaceful. I guess that's what happens when you get older – you yearn for more immediate comforts and space, and less hassle. It's a natural progression.

The optimism and fire haven't gone away, though. I still hope that the next campsite will be the best one yet and I still get as angry as I used to about other people's litter. I am pleased that there are more facilities for motorhomes and camper vans, thanks to local councils, private individuals and groups like CAMpRA, who campaign for aires in the UK. But I am less pleased when I hear rumours about overcrowding and antisocial behaviour.

I realise that we are at a moment when what we do has a bearing on what will come. There are more of us than ever. And that ends

up putting more pressure on the places we go from an environmental and cultural perspective. So it's all the more vital that we learn from what we've seen along the way and act accordingly if we are to have a great future on the road.

Given what we now know, I see it as vitally important to head into the future full of optimism but with great caution and an even greater sense of responsibility. Travel is a privilege, not a right, and we should try to remember that we go places because they are nice, so it makes sense to work hard to ensure they remain nice. I want to be welcomed back!

What does this mean? I think it means immersing ourselves more in the places we go by slowing down. We could easily ease off the gas and be more respectful. We could stop long enough to find out which way the wind is blowing. That could mean getting involved in local community actions like clean-ups or just going along to local events. It could mean shopping in local shops or from local producers, or helping your fellow campervanners and motorhomers to be more responsible and to think about the communities in which they travel. Being in a camper van makes you a constant visitor and, if we are to continue to be welcomed, we need to be perfect house guests. Hurtling around the NC500 in two days eating food you bought in your local Tesco does nothing for the locals.

On another level, we can use our money to support people who are doing the right thing. We can choose to stay at campsites with a good sustainability policy and we can choose to support green initiatives within the industry. We can also spend our money on products that don't have a huge environmental cost. If we choose to, we can make the good guys rich. At the very least, we can put our recycling in the correct bin at the campsite!

I, for one, am more than happy to adapt my way of travelling to be more responsible, sustainable and immersive because I think that's how we'll have more authentic experiences.

The sunsets will be just as good, I promise.

RESOURCES TO GET YOU STARTED

Use the following pages to make notes of your favourite sites, accessories shops, books or blogs. For starters, here are a few of my personal suggestions:

PLACES TO STAY

BRITSTOPS
www.britstops.com
The UK version of France Passion. Lots of free overnights at private locations. They now have an app for both Android and Apple.

CAMPING AND CARAVANNING CLUB
www.campingand caravanningclub.co.uk
Club sites plus a network of small sites. Some open all year.

CARAVAN AND MOTORHOME CLUB
www.caravanclub.co.uk
Club sites plus a network of small sites. Some open all year.

PARK4NIGHT
www.park4night.com
An app (also available online) that includes service points, aires, club sites and certified locations (CLs) as well as Britstops and free 'wild' spots. The 'navigate' option makes it invaluable when it comes to navigating to aires and campsites.

PITCHUP
www.pitchup.com
Useful for booking on your phone when you are out and about. Easy, handy.

SEARCH4SITES
www.searchforsites.co.uk
Like Park4Night but with fewer places, especially in Europe. Best for using in the UK.

BOOKS AND REFERENCES

MARTIN DOREY BOOKSHOP
www.martindorey.com
Camper van guides for England and Wales, Scotland, Ireland, France and Spain and Portugal.

STANFORD'S
www.stanfords.co.uk
The very best travel bookshop in the world! Maps, maps, maps and travel books, too.

VICARIOUS MEDIA
www.vicarious-shop.com
Lots of moho and camper van reference books, including aires, stopovers, accessories and maps.

WILD GUIDES
www.wildthingspublishing.com
Wild Things Publishing are putting out some wonderful books. Full of adventure and love.

GEAR AND ACCESSORIES

JUST KAMPERS
www.justkampers.com
Lots of bits and bobs, plus parts and accessories for all things VW.

ROADPRO
www.roadpro.co.uk
Moho accessories from the people who know a lot about moho accessories. Make them your first call.

ROSE AWNINGS
www.roseawnings.co.uk
Friendly service and stockists of Thule bike racks and equipment, among other things.

THAT LEISURE SHOP
www.thatleisureshop.com
All the bits and pieces for vans and mohos.

RENTALS AND RENTING

GOBOONY
www.goboony.co.uk
Sort of like Airbnb for camper vans. Rent a camper or rent yours out.

QUIRKY CAMPERS
www.quirkycampers.com
Information about converting your own camper, hiring a camper and also hiring out your own camper.

GLOSSARY

Jargon, to many, is a dirty word. It exists because it describes things that cannot be described in any other way. Jargon should never be used as a weapon against the uninitiated to make them feel inferior or unknowledgeable. So, time for a quick brush-up before the rest of the campers get here...

3-way fridge fridge that can run off battery power, mains electrics and also gas. Not what you might have thought.

A-Class type of motorhome that's built entirely by the manufacturer on to a chassis. Does not include a manufacture supplied cab like a coachbuilt. Typified by 1980s Hymer motorhomes.

aire designated parking for motorhomes and camper vans. From the French *aires de camping car*. A missed opportunity by many local councils in the UK (do you hear me?).

Alde type of heating that uses a wet system.

awning additional tent that attaches to the side of a camper van or motorhome to add another room or extra space to your van. Useful if you want to take the van away for the day and leave stuff behind. Don't drive away and forget to detach it.

Bay/Bay Window later edition of the VW Type 2 Transporter, with a curved bay window. Made from 1969 to 1979.

black waste the waste from a chemical toilet. Must be disposed of properly. Goes down the **slophopper** (see page 443).

blue (or green) chemicals chemicals added to the waste reservoir of a chemical toilet.

buddy box/seat small box that sits behind the passenger seat and is used for sitting on. Typically a box without a backrest. Don't look inside; it's the most likely place you'll find the Porta Potti.

Bulli one of the original names for the VW transporter that wasn't used but is now used by fans. Also the concept car by Volkswagen.

Brazibay Brazilian Bay Window VW Type 2 Camper.

Brick affectionate name for the Type 3 or Type 25 Transporter because of its brick-like shape. Insults are the sincerest form of flattery...

Britstop not a type of music for campers, but the UK version of the French Passion network that allows free overnight parking at pubs, farm shops, farms and producers.

Camping Box removable piece of furniture made by Westfalia that fits into a camper for camping. The earliest type of camping interior.

captain seats seats with bases that swivel to enlarge a living area.

cassette toilet waste cassette of a toilet that is in-built into a motorhome and can be removed from the motorhome. Eeeew.

C-form type of waterproof 16-amp plug and socket used on campsites.

chocks triangular pieces of wood or plastic to keep a vehicle from rolling away. Most often used in conjunction with levelling wedges.

CO chemical symbol for carbon monoxide, the deadly gas that is created when fossil fuels are burned. Extremely dangerous, especially from disposable BBQs.

coachbuilt motorhome that's built on to the chassis of an existing vehicle rather than inside a van.

Combi name for VW Type 2 campers in the USA and Mexico.

crash testing action of testing vehicles (most often rock and roll beds in camper vans) to ensure they can withhold the force of a crash. Tested as crashed, as opposed to a **pull test** (see page 442), which is pulled using the same forces you would experience in a crash.

Danbury UK brand of camper van converter. Importer of VW Type 2s from Brazil.

designated seats seats with approved and crash tested seat belts to allow passengers to travel in the back of a motorhome. The only seats allowed for children.

Devon UK make of camper van.

Dormobile UK-based camper converter. One of the earliest converters.

dubber someone who loves V-Dubs (VWs).

EHU electric hook-up, an electric power point provided at some camping pitches.

Fiamma popular brand of bike rack and accessories for camper vans and motorhomes.

fire pit off-the-ground container for lighting fires in places where they might otherwise be prohibited.

fly sheet outer layer of a tent, generally the waterproof outer skin but often the outside skin of a tent that isn't waterproof.

gin palace on wheels super swish motorhome with all knobs, whistles and luxuries.

glamping glamorous camping. A form of camping that involves as much luxury as possible. As far from bushcraft camping as camping gets.

grey waste waste water from your shower, sink and basin run-off. Must be disposed of in the appropriate place.

hardstanding area of a campsite or pitch where motorhomes and campers can be parked without fear of becoming bogged in mud.

high top not a pair of shoes but a high roof on a camper van.

J bars accessories for roof bars that can be used for carrying kayaks or adapted for surfboards.

Karmann German coachbuilder responsible for the Karmann Ghia as well as lots of other VW special editions.

Kombi common name for VW campers in Australia and Brazil.

leisure battery additional battery used to run camping electrics so they don't run down the main battery.

levelling wedges triangular pieces of wood or plastic that allow camper drivers to ensure their vans are level.

MAM maximum authorised mass. The maximum allowable weight of your van including any payload.

Microbus early incarnation of the Type 2 Splitty in Germany, a passenger vehicle. Also common term for VW buses in the USA.

micro camper camper van that's made from a small vehicle like a Bedford Rascal or similar. Small. Very, very small.

moho shorthand for motorhome.

motor caravan term used by the UK Driver and Vehicle Licensing Agency (DVLA) for a vehicle with sleeping and cooking facilities, a side window, table and water tank.

outfit not something you put on for a club meet, but actually a generic term for your 'rig', 'unit' or van.

Passion site not what you think. Overnight parking for self-contained motorhomes and camper vans in Europe. See also **Britstop**.

payload useful allowable weight in a van. Includes petrol, water, you, and your kit and caboodle.

pink chemicals term for the chemicals added to the water reservoir of a camping toilet.

pitch area where you pitch your tent or park your van.

pop top extendable camper van roof to allow for more space.

pull test type of test for rock and roll beds in which the bed is pulled using the same forces you would experience in a crash.

pup tent little tent to chuck stuff in away from the camper van. Useful for storing children on camping trips when parents are frisky.

rag top convertible or cloth sunroof.

rat look/ratty camper that is purposefully made to look old and tatty.

rock and roll bed seat that converts into a bed.

RV recreational vehicle. Generally larger than your average motorhome and therefore not suitable for trips around Cornwall. More likely to be found Stateside.

shaka hand sign often used by VW drivers or by people being passed by VW drivers.

side elevating roof camper van roof that opens up from the side. Characterised by the Viking and Devon Moonraker roofs.

slide out section of a motorhome or camper that slides out from the main body to create more living space.

slider side-opening sliding door on most camper vans.

slophopper brilliant German name for the place where you empty your elsan, slop tank or Porta Potti. Literally the place to slop out.

split charge relay switching system that diverts power from the alternator to the leisure battery to top up the charge when the main battery is fully charged during driving.

Splitty Split Screen VW camper. Also known as the Type 2 Split-Screen. Revered by many, owned by few. Often appears printed on cushions and curtains, and used by clothing brands to appear cooler than they are.

stealth camping camping in a van that appears to be no more than a standard panel van on the outside. Inside though, it's a palace.

Syncro 4 x 4 version of the T25 water cooled Transporter, production of which began in 1985.

thunderbox do we have to spell it out? Like a Porta Potti but more dangerous.

tin top camper van with the original factory roof rather than a pop top or a high top.

top box ugly additions to car roof racks for extra storage. For use on people carriers and family saloons.

touring park large campsite often frequented by caravans and motorhomes. Usually with lots of facilities.

Truma make of heating that can run off gas or electric and uses hot blown air.

twin slider camper with a sliding door on either side.

unit colloquialism for motorhome or large camper.

Westfalia German company that converted the first VW campers. Much sought-after.

wild camping camping away from designated camping areas or out of reach of standard facilities. Illegal in much of England and Wales.

Winnebago generic term for big motorhomes from Winnebago Industries, a US company that makes motorhomes. Favoured by pop stars and the film industry for their luxury and space on location.

zig unit basic control panel showing the state of charging of a leisure battery.

441

INDEX

442

445

446

ACKNOWLEDGEMENTS AND CREDITS

With grateful thanks to the following people for their wit and wisdom and for helping me to make this book happen, in whatever small way it was.

All the camper van owners who opened their hearts to tell me what their campers mean to them. Thank you!

The Team at Bloomsbury: Jenny, Lucy B, Lucy D and Austin.

Tim and the team at PFD.

Danbury Motor Caravans.

Nikki Nichols at The Caravan and Motorhome Club.

Marquis Motorhomes.

Slidepods.

Paul and Sarah Greenings.

Terry Exell.

Paul Potgeiter.

Al Hesselbart, RV expert.

David and Cee Eccles.

The Camper Coffee Company.

Louisa and EVERYONE on the Eireball.

Steve and Mandy at Britstops

O'Brien's Camping www.obrienscamping.co.uk

The Classic Camper Club.

Andrew Blake.

Select Solar.

Credits

All photographs are © Martin Dorey with the exception of the following:

P126, P359 © Georgia Glynn Smith

P4, P16, P31, P61, P65, P338, P398, P420 © Dr Elizabeth Kay

P48, P49, P69, P72, P99, P100, P267, P270, P271, P360, P401 © The Caravan and Motorhome Club

P75, P163, P 165, P167, P168, P170, P181, P186 © Andrew Price

P123, P130 © Sheltapod

P148, P150 © Karla and Stephen Baker

All studio shots lit by Bob Williams c/o www.thescottidog.com